Winston-Salem

Winston-Salem

A Twin City History

Michael Bricker

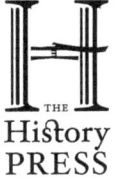

Published by The History Press
Charleston, SC 29403
www.historypress.net

Copyright © 2008 by Michael Bricker
All rights reserved

Cover design by Marshall Hudson.

All images courtesy of the Michael Bricker collection unless otherwise noted.

First published 2008

ISBN 978-1-5402-1788-2

Library of Congress Cataloging-in-Publication Data
Bricker, Michael L.
Winston-Salem : a twin city history / Michael Bricker.
p. cm.
Includes bibliographical references.
ISBN 978-1-59629-304-5
1. Winston-Salem (N.C.)--History. 2. Moravians--North Carolina--Winston-Salem--History. I. Title.
F264.W8B755 2008
975.6'67--dc22
2008004622

Notice: The information in this book is true and complete to the best of our knowledge. It is offered without guarantee on the part of the author or The History Press. The author and The History Press disclaim all liability in connection with the use of this book.

All rights reserved. No part of this book may be reproduced or transmitted in any form whatsoever without prior written permission from the publisher except in the case of brief quotations embodied in critical articles and reviews.

Contents

Acknowledgements		7
Introduction		9
Chapter 1.	In the Beginning	11
Chapter 2.	God and Country	29
Chapter 3.	The Jobs We Do	53
Chapter 4.	The People	79
Chapter 5.	How Does Our Garden Grow?	99
Chapter 6.	The Three Rs	113
Chapter 7.	The Neighborhoods	131
Chapter 8.	What Have We Learned?	143
Bibliography		157

Acknowledgements

To recognize all who have helped in this 250-year history search of the Twin City could fill a book in itself. The highlights of those souls and entities who have passed through Salem and Winston are presented in a timeline of my life. History has been important to me from day one. As a child of three toddling the sidewalk on South Main in the newly created Old Salem of the 1950s, I remember being awed by the huge metal coffeepot across the street from my residence at the corner of Main and Belews. Equally as memorable was the building of Interstate 40 through Salem. The coffeepot and Interstate 40 both survived, but much of the history associated with them would not.

My first history journey occurred in 1960, at the dividing line between Winston and Salem. The mom and pop Green Front Cash Store at North Broad and First Street resided here and was run by Mr. and Mrs. Robert Turner. This store was our food market, but was also much, much more. Mr. Turner had been in the grocery business since the 1910s. His stories were priceless. His patrons to the establishment were priceless as well. The "old-timers," what we kids knew them by, were older, retired gentlemen who "hung around and reminisced of old times in the store." The past came alive in their stories and I began to want to know more about it. Two individuals who often kept the old-timers on their toes, so their history lessons did not become "whoppers" or "fish stories," were journal men. Frank Jones and Roy Thompson worked for the *Winston-Salem Journal and Sentinel* as a photographer and reporter, respectively. The old-timers said these two were just as full of hot air as they were. Heated debates in history were slung back and forth between these patrons. For entertainment purposes to the "youngens," it was better than the movies on Saturday afternoon, and also louder. This book is dedicated to them all.

My grandmother, Mary, was a lady who had stories of the roaring 1920s, the Great Depression and both World Wars. Her ninety years of life experiences made me realize history should not be relegated only to the rich and powerful. This prize she bestowed on me was as priceless as any fortune could be.

The bicentennial period of the founding of our country in 1976 opened up a new chapter in my fascination with history. Winston-Salem was abuzz with the past. Everyone in the city seemed to have "history fever." Fambrough Brownlee authored his book, *Winston-Salem: A*

Acknowledgements

Pictorial History, in 1977. The past became alive once more with his extensive pictorial of the Twin City's history. "Historic Winston," the counterpart of the Moravian archives of Salem, brought together a series on Winston-Salem history as well. Adelaide Fries's groundbreaking book of Forsyth County, which had been authored just prior to her passing in 1949, was rereleased in 1977, due to the history fever. All the folks who were associated with these accomplishments during the bicentennial period are saluted for taking my local history interest to new heights.

If I could have generated my local history interest into monetary backing, a Winston-Salem museum surely would have existed these past thirty years. Unfortunately, this did not happen. It seemed, for reasons beyond my years of research, I was told Winston-Salem could not monetarily support two history museums, Old Salem and Historic Winston. Historic Winston was eventually absorbed into Old Salem Incorporated with the thought that the new center of Old Salem was large enough to present all the history.

Introduction

American history is one of the youngest histories of the world. Many towns and hamlets have experienced the American landscape for no longer than two hundred years. Winston-Salem is one such town. Winston-Salem is unique and the town has also played an important part in our country's rise to superpower status. Wars, famine and sacrifice helped to make our country strong; Winston-Salem has experienced these hardships as well. Throughout the challenges and triumphs, Winston-Salem residents arose to the occasion to mold a history that is colorful and enduring.

This book will take the reader behind the scenes of our local history to present the players, places and things that built the town. Spanning the development of the town of Salem to the beginning of Winston and forward to the Twin City we know today, all avenues of the city's past will be explored. Positive and negative, twists and turns abound in the roads of Winston's past. Many histories will be revealed, from the establishment of the early neighborhoods to the evolvement from a small isolated Moravian town. Over the years many fine books, text and pictorials have been written on the city's history; however, the majority of these publications have contained only the histories of the wealthy leaders and business barons. Digging deeper beneath the façade of the prominent movers and shakers, the other heroes of our great city will be discovered. These heroes were the workers who encompassed the heart, soul and backbone of our early businesses and industries. The tobacco and textile millworkers helped to build two giants in the industry: Reynolds Tobacco and P.H. Hanes Company. With the economic and political power generated by these two companies, in 1916 Winston-Salem established itself as a port of entry to outside trade. No city this far inland had ever been thought to be strong enough to be a port town; Winston-Salem was the first.

Winston-Salem is a unique mix of two cultures. Our search will explain the "string saver" Moravians of Salem and the boldness of its upstart child, Winston. In Salem, nothing went unnoticed or unrecorded. The city and the nation were offered a day-to-day look into the Moravians' meticulous lives. Through their music, the Moravians, whom some have called the most musical group in all America, exposed classical and religious musicians and composers to the rural and wild North Carolina backcountry. The Moravian craftsmen and

Introduction

artists created silver, pottery, cabinetry and gunsmith techniques only found in Old World culture. All of these could be found in the "Oasis in the Wilderness," as coined by President Washington during his eighteenth-century visit to Salem.

Winston was founded as a necessity by the Moravians, so as not to invite the many outsiders who had migrated to the area after Salem was designated the seat of government of the new county of Forsyth in 1849. Winston's growth and prestige in the state after the Civil War were fueled by textiles and tobacco. Education, medicine and the arts all arose out of Salem's ingenuity and Winston's purse to create a Twin City known throughout the nation, boasting such institutions as Salem College, Wake Forest University, Winston-Salem State, North Carolina Baptist Medical Center and Forsyth Medical Center and the North Carolina School of the Arts.

The preservation interest of our leader families, such as Fries, Gray, Hanes and Reynolds, allowed one of the most authentic and historical eighteenth- and nineteenth-century villages in America to be created. Old Salem has been known throughout the United States and abroad for more than fifty years. Until recently most of what is known of the Twin City's successes and accomplishments has been presented to the public in the streets of Old Salem or Reynolda Village, with a few select families being trumpeted. Our search attempts to uncover the individuals behind the scenes, with the hope to present a more complete picture. I hope readers will grasp the opportunity to identify with these diverse individuals, rich and poor, thereby beginning their own search into their own family's history. When a nation understands, identifies and appreciates all of its citizens' pasts, a better country can be had for ourselves and our children. Please join me in this Twin City journey.

CHAPTER 1.

In the Beginning

Winston-Salem would not exist if not for one individual who, ironically, never made a trip to North Carolina. His name was Count Nicholas Ludwig Von Zinzendorf, and his influence can be felt across our Piedmont area. He is credited as the architect of the renewed Moravian Church. His belief in his God laid the foundation for all future Moravians to follow. With the assistance of his wealth and philanthropy, he had made a commitment to his Lord at an early age. He interpreted God's message to all mankind to mean salvation through faith and actions. Zinzendorf's practice led to his belief that heaven awaited him and all else he could bring to the Lord.

As Jesus Christ embraced all men, so did Count Zinzendorf. Despite the advice of the aristocrats of his time, he chose to worship with the commoners. Putting on buckskins, as Moravians did in the settlement of Bethlehem, Pennsylvania, he ventured out to evangelize the American Indians. This impressed even the locals, since many Christians of the time considered Indians to be godless savages. He broke more new ground in his evangelizing of slaves brought from Africa. Count Zinzendorf is responsible for setting the standard for a strong humanitarian base through faith in Winston-Salem. He joined his Lord in 1760, and is memorialized in Winston-Salem with two very prominent hotels bearing his name.

In researching the long history of Winston-Salem, one discovers several beginnings to the story. The most well-known and meticulously documented version begins with the arrival of the Moravians in 1753. The Moravians' eye for detail in their documentation of daily events is unmatched. Fruits of their labor appear throughout American history in music, crafts, art and religious practices. For more than fifty years, historic Old Salem has been unmatched in its authentic presentation of colonial life in America.

Before Moravians arrived, other settlements existed. Several Indian tribes established many trails and passes throughout the Piedmont. Many of the early British and continental roads were built over these Indian trails. King's Road was one such road passing through the future Forsyth County borders. This key road in western Salem connected to the town of Salisbury. An extension of this road is presently known as Old Salisbury Road. With the roads and the richness of the Piedmont, many early colonial settlements preceded the Moravians in and around the land we know today as Forsyth County. One such settlement existed in

Winston-Salem

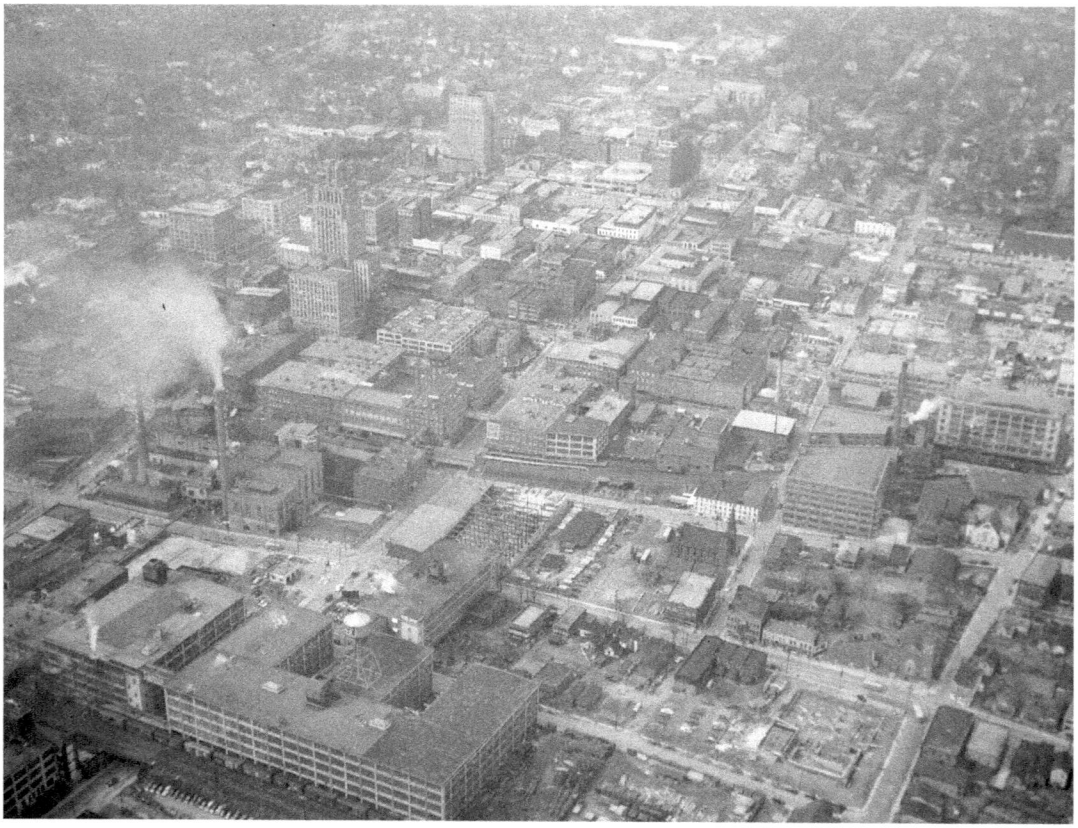

The 1940s and 1950s saw a City of Industry and a City of Churches and Neighborhoods existing as one.

the western side of the original town lot of Salem. The Lagenauer settlement consisted of a small German clan that arrived sometime between the 1720s and the 1740s. Records are somewhat sketchy on the exact time of arrival. What is known is that the small clan concentrated around the mill that was identified as the Lagenauer mill. In today's landscape, the mill would have been set on Salem Creek near the present Silas Creek Parkway. Several of the older homesteads that may have been part of the Lagenauer settlement existed until the 1960s, when the Peters Creek Parkway highway system was developed between the older neighborhoods of West Salem, West End and Ardmore. According to family records, two of these homes were constructed in the middle 1700s next to Petersbach (Peters Creek), near the present intersection of Peters Creek Parkway and Link Road. One house was a rock house similar to those found in other old German settlements. The other home was a German-style structure similar to those found in Old Salem today. The Old Salem–style home was taken down and the materials were later used to reconstruct several houses in the Old Salem Village.

Early settlements did not stand in the way of the Moravians establishing their official town, Salem. Moravians believed deeply that God had destined the Salem tract of land for

In the Beginning

them, since the land was unoccupied on their arrival to the Piedmont. In their words, the tract had the best location of water sources and quality of rich farmland to be found in all of North Carolina.

During the colonial period, the Piedmont section of central North Carolina was rugged and wild. Moravians, a Protestant sect, had come to America from the European region of Moravia by way of the Pennsylvania colony. Moravians were seeking a home where they could practice their religion in isolation and harmony. The North Carolina Piedmont was chosen and a 100,000-acre tract was purchased from Lord Granville. The landscape and climate suited the Moravians nicely, as the tract reminded them of their home country's geography. After a long journey, the first Moravians arrived and named their settlement Bethabara in 1753. This was the temporary headquarters until the true town was built. Moravians had planned their central town before leaving Pennsylvania. The town was to be called Salem, which means peace. Salem was no ordinary town, but was the seat of the religious hierarchy of North Carolina and a trade and craftsman village. Salem was not a farming community; farms and industry were laid to the west of town, and with that West Salem was born.

Moravians brought much to the area of the Piedmont. One important feature of their culture was order. Combining this social order with a meticulous eye for detail, Moravians were always prepared for what lay ahead. The Moravian town lot of Salem was created with this foresight. The Moravian surveyor who helped design and lay out the town was Brother Gottlieb Rueter. His early maps are still researched and studied today. In mapping the central town of Salem, Brother Rueter made one important distinction: the center of town was divided with an imaginary border into two sections. East Salem was the location of the congregational town leadership, as well as the center of commerce. The church and the hierarchy, along with the tradesmen and craftsmen, lived, worked and worshiped here. Much of this history is documented and presented in the interpretative history of Old Salem Incorporated. The western area, or "the other side of Salem," as it is called today, was home to early Salem's farms and industry. West Salem is less documented, and much of its history would have been lost to time if not for its rescue by a few local historians, who established the West Salem Historic District in 1782 through the National Register of Historic Places and its parent overseer, the National Park Service. As a result, the twenty-first century holds much promise for the presentation of the history of the western section of the town lot. The Moravian hierarchy had proclaimed from the very beginning that the congregational town was not to be a farming community. With Rueter's border drawn between the two Salem worlds, the proclamation was assured.

Once the eastern congregational part of the town lot and the corresponding western farm and industrial section were established, the planning and building of Salem, the town of peace, could commence. Expanding upon earlier plans from Herrnhurt, Germany, the church council hoped to build a utopia where the best vision of European and North American ideals could be manifested in a harmonious land, a place where all people could adopt the religious principles of the residence by serving God and each other. Citizens of the congregational town worked and lived as a family. This eastern section of the town lot was ruled by the church, which oversaw the spiritual and secular lives of all men, women and children. Trade and commerce of the Wachovia tract of the Moravians was also controlled by the congregational church leaders.

Winston-Salem

Ideals of the church leaders served the early town well; however, as time passed, outsiders began to arrive in the Piedmont and the rest of North Carolina, and brought with them more open-minded views. These newcomers respected the views of the Moravians, but were hesitant to adopt them as their own. Trade and commerce by non-Moravians continued, but the town's outsiders took on the mindset that Salem was a monopoly-oriented town with cult-like beliefs. Church leaders had anticipated that these views could arise, so to avoid alienating or inhibiting trade and commerce with non-Moravians, they allowed the western side of Salem, consisting of the farms and industry, to be a more open-minded part of town.

The church elders controlled the complete Wachovia tract, which included the Salem town lot. Unlike in East Salem, West Salem's non-Moravian residents (or *aussenseiter*, as they were called) could lease land and housing from the church. Rules were less strict to the west of the boundary line separating the two parts of the town. As the farms and industry grew in Salem, groups of residents of different religions and ethnic beliefs grew also. Methodists, Baptist, Quakers and non-Moravian German clans could be found working and worshiping here. Even though no organized church structure was erected in West Salem until the Moravian Elm Street Chapel was erected in 1862, tent meetings and wagon revivals could be found as early as the late eighteenth century. One of the earliest of these religious meetings was established around the Paper Mill Settlement in 1791. In today's landscape, the Salem mill sat on the Academy Street edge of Peters Creek. The expanse of the current Peters Creek Parkway was home to several industrial sites and farms of the Paper Mill Settlement, which played a key role throughout the eighteenth and nineteenth centuries in providing much of Salem's prosperity. The paper mill was erected by Gottlieb Schober, an early Moravian town leader, the same year Salem hosted an important visitor.

After the Revolutionary War ended and our independence was secured, President George Washington made his promised visit to all the newly formed states. In 1791, he arrived with his entourage in Salem. Well-documented accounts of his visit and overnight stay in Salem's congregational town are presented through the interpretive expression of Old Salem Incorporated. Due to President Washington's interest in industry and surveying, he and the governor of North Carolina inspected West Salem's first modern paper mill. In recording his memoirs after his journey to the states, President Washington dubbed Salem an "oasis in the wilderness." East Salem warranted this title for its religious and business accomplishments, and West Salem for its inventive farming and industrial ventures.

Christian Gottlieb Rueter, who surveyed the land and drew up the maps for Wachovia, was one of the nation's most skilled surveyors, foresters, mapmakers, naturalists and botanists. His Salem town lot choice was confirmed with another Moravian belief, the Lot, which was a practice based on the Biblical references contained in Numbers 33:54 and Acts 1:26. Three pieces of paper were used in the Lot to decide an issue. The first page contained the German word *ja*, meaning "yes"; the second *nein*, meaning "no"; and the third was left blank. The blank piece was used if more study and deliberation was needed before making a decision. The Lot was used until 1818 for most important decisions of the church. Between 1818 and 1889, it was phased out. Fortunately for Brother Rueter and Salem, the ridge of land between Petersbach (now Peters Creek) to the west and the Wach (Salem Creek) to the east was approved.

The landscape to the north of the town lot was bordered by the Annaberg, which became the future site of Winston. Annaberg, or Anna's mountain (hill) in English, was named for an

In the Beginning

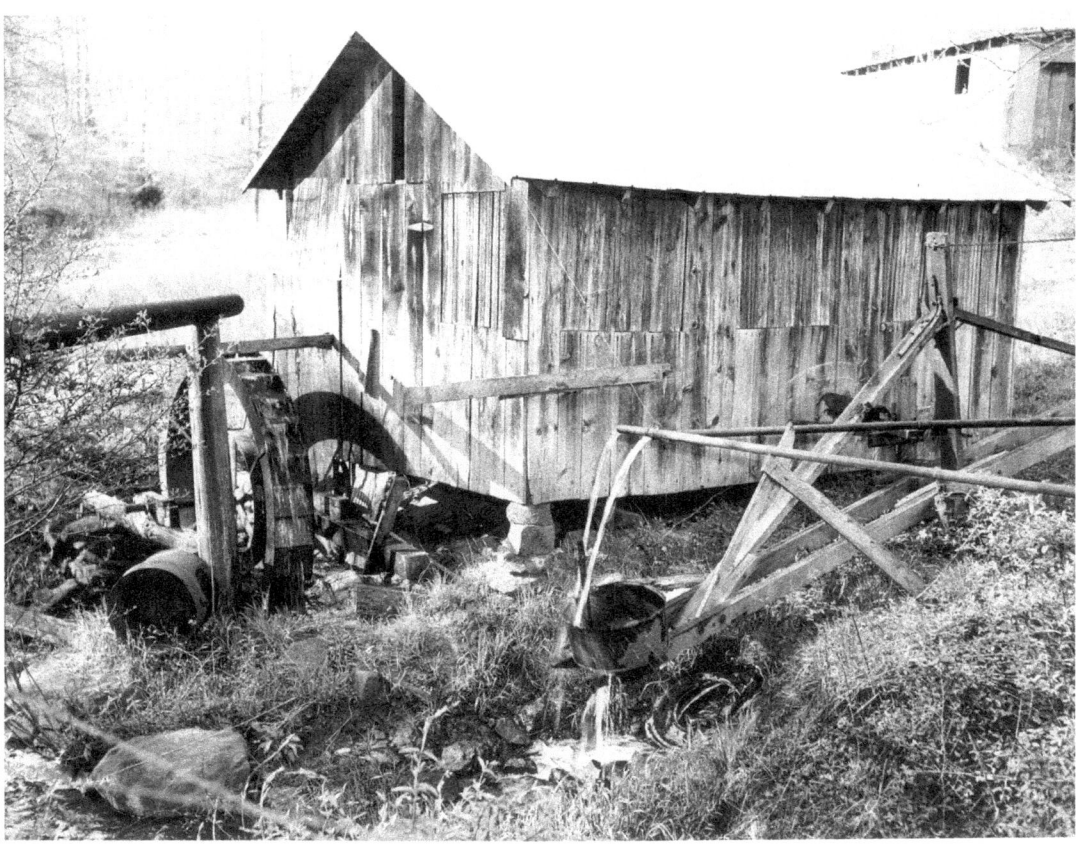

Waiting to be restored, mills and other industries are arriving from the past.

early Moravian, Anna Katherina, wife of Brother Rueter, the Salem surveyor. The terrain was familiar to the Moravians, as it resembled their former home in the European Moravia. From the Annaberg to the Wach the ground sloped in both directions, east and west, with many good springs to supply the necessary water sources for drinking and industry. Indians of earlier years had dubbed the Wachovia tract with the English title "Land of a Thousand Streams." Many streams flowed underground to reveal themselves as clear freshwater branches. One branch on the western side of the town lot, the Tar Branch, supplied the needs of the town until wells could be dug. Ridges were also abundant and the central streets were cut along the tops of these ridges for the congregational town. A quote from the original Moravian archives dated January 6, 1766, best depicts the beginning of the building of Salem:

> *Monday, a dozen brethren partly from Bethania, partly from Bethabara, took a wagon and went to the new town site where in the afternoon they cut down the trees on the place where the first house was to stand, singing several stanzas as they worked. Our text for the day was beautifully appropriate for this little beginning in building: I will defend this city.*

Winston-Salem

Main Street was the first cut and the building of the first and second houses commenced. Mrs. Adelaide Fries, the first Moravian historian of the twentieth century, described in her own words the erection of the first and second houses:

> *Within a matter of months the first house was built on the Main Street. It was a frame construction. Available material was not well-suited for the building of a log house and so another method was used. Heavy timbers were erected for the framing, then rude laths, wrapped in a mixture of clay and straw were inserted horizontally from one groove upright to another. When pressed down, they made a thick wall, as warm as brick. If the clay began to wash out after years of service, the wall could be weather boarded and made good as new. When the first room was finished, Gottfried Praezel moved in and set up his loom, a forecast of Forsyth's textile industry of the future. The second house on the Main Street was known for years as the two-story house. The first house and other's of that period were generally of one story, with a high-pitched roof and a cellar. On the first floor of the two-story house was the first meeting hall of Salem. Until it was built, worship services had been held in one of the rooms in the small first house. Immediate preparation of a place of worship indicates the*

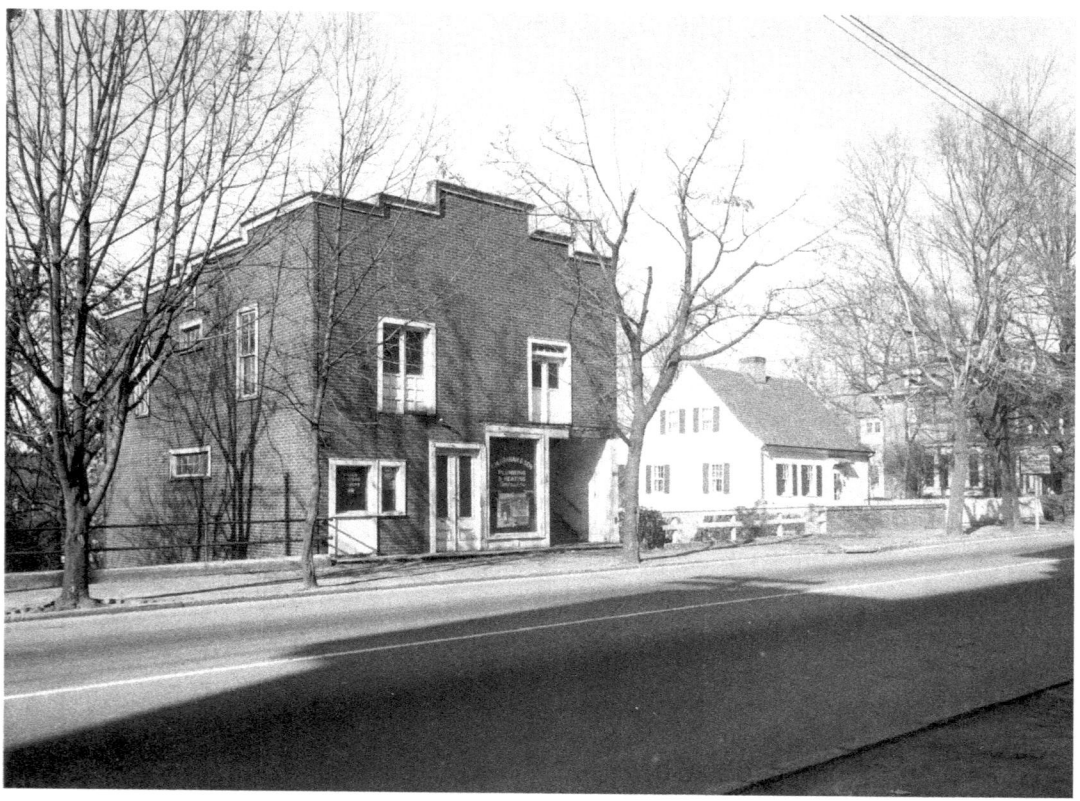

The Graham Plumbing Company on South Main was replaced by one of the reconstructed first houses of Salem.

In the Beginning

primary purpose for which the Moravians had come to North Carolina—freedom to worship God in their devout, practical way. They had an inherited belief that religion was a personal matter between a man and his God, but they believed also in a religion to be lived every day, seven days a week.

By the close of 1766, two more houses had been built to the north on Main, followed by a potter's shop and a blacksmith shop. Today, the first houses have been reconstructed, with hopes of reconstructing the blacksmith shop and potter's shop in the near future. These houses are part of the Moravian village and are located at Main and Bank Streets directly across from the majestic Belo House, an antebellum home from the mid-nineteenth century. Building continued in the original village, with each project becoming more of a challenge. Brick and tile work were used with professional craftsmanship. Potters had discovered a good source of clay in a meadow by Salem Creek, near the present-day Salem College athletic field. Brick makers, not the potters, were responsible for the handmade bricks. This practice of brick making exhibited another unique trait of the Moravians. Salem did not import brick from Europe, as most of the major seaport towns of the east did. This town was able to be self-sufficient because the Moravian foresight led to importing settlers who were trained craftsmen, as opposed to just importing goods. Furniture making was carried out this way as well.

More elaborate building took place in 1768, with the erection of the Single Brothers' house. This operation became the central workshop of the Moravian journeymen and their young apprentices. These Moravian craftsmen arrived in 1769 from Bethabara, where they had lived and studied until the new building was completed in Salem. The Single Brothers organization had begun in Bethabara with the intention and planning by the church to be transplanted to its permanent home in Salem. The organization was independent and kept to itself, with its own finances, kitchen and farm, which extended into West Salem. For many years the Single Brothers' house was the center of the community. Brothers oversaw the tannery, brewery and farm outlets of West Salem, while the church builders controlled the congregational village in East Salem.

After the Brothers' establishment moved to Salem, Bethabara became a Moravian farming community for the remainder of its existence. The Brothers' house was different than the other frame structures in Salem. In other structures the bricks that were used for the chimney were often too soft and weathered badly if exposed to the elements. In the construction of the Brothers' house, a second type of framing was created and more inside braces were added; the softer brick filled the intervening spaces. Adding mortar completed the task. Salem ingenuity, applied to a vexing situation that otherwise could have been rather costly and even devastating to the Brothers' complex, added to the list of pioneering accomplishments of the Salem Moravians. The Single Brothers' establishment continues today, teaching craftsmen arts of long ago to tourists and locals alike.

The next type of major structure that stood for many years as the largest house in Salem was the Gemeinhaus, which rose to three stories. Its foundation consisted of uncut stone laid up with clay; both granite and clay were prevalent in the landscape of Salem. A granite quarry was established in West Salem in the late eighteenth century. The walls of the Gemeinhaus were made very thick to compensate for the lack of lyme in its binding, as lyme was scarce and hard to get in the early years of the colonies. The second story of the house brought a new feature to Salem construction: a high pitched roof permitting several rooms on a third story.

Gemeinhaus was central to the Salem congregation, much like the Single Brothers' house was central to the industrial interest of the community. The second floor of the Gemeinhaus was consecrated in November 1771 as the meeting hall for the Salem congregation. The northern ends of the first and second floors were allotted as apartments for the congregational ministers. The southern halves of the first and third floors were used by the single sisters for workrooms and living rooms. Gemeinhaus unfortunately was razed in the mid-1800s to make way for Salem College's new structures. The bustling Gemeinhaus tradition lives on with the restoration of the Single Sisters' house of 1771, which was located next door to Gemeinhaus for nearly one hundred years. The Single Sisters' house may one day in the near future present the history that was found in the early Gemeinhaus. Salem College and Old Salem Incorporated hope to make this so.

Construction and progress continued for the Moravians in 1772, with the community store moving into the first floor of the second (two-story) house of Salem. The second story was reserved for another prominent family moving from Bethabara, Traugott Bagge and family. Brother Bagge was to become a major mover and shaker in Salem. While managing the Salem Community Store, he and Brother Gottlieb Schober, the paper mill owner, used their experience in diplomacy to weather the Revolutionary War and bring the Salem town community through the troubled times nearly unscathed. Brother Bagge founded Baggetown to the south of Salem in 1800. Baggetown later became known as Waughtown, and is today one of the oldest neighborhoods in Winston-Salem. Brother Matthew Miksch built a small house on Main Street and, like Brother Praezel of textile fame, Brother Miksch was the forerunner to the future Winston-Salem's other industry and powerhouse: tobacco manufacturing. He sold both snuff and smoking tobacco. His house has been dubbed the "Tobacco House" and is an important tour stop in Old Salem.

The Tanyard in West Salem, which was part of the Single Brothers' complex, was run by Brother Heinrich Herbst, and Brother Jacob Meyer ran the Salem Tavern on Main Street. By the end of 1772, several more houses had been built and most of the residents of Bethabara were now calling Salem their permanent home. The congregational side of East Salem continued to serve the community well until the founding of Winston in 1849. By 1850, East Salem was much like the other central cities of North Carolina. West Salem, beginning in 1769, took another road that was important to the town and future state. Much of West Salem's history was lost until the pursuit of the National Register Historical status of the area in the year 2000. While East Salem and its congregational town has been well documented and expanded on for more than fifty years, with investments from the 1950s to the present day, West Salem's investments were confined to the church and individual ownership. The historical beginning of West Salem is accurately presented here.

The following timeline of the "Other Side of Salem" is an overview from the 1770s to the 1870s. After Reconstruction, the 1880s ushered in the beginning of the modern-day neighborhoods of our United States cities. Winston-Salem was no exception.

In the Beginning

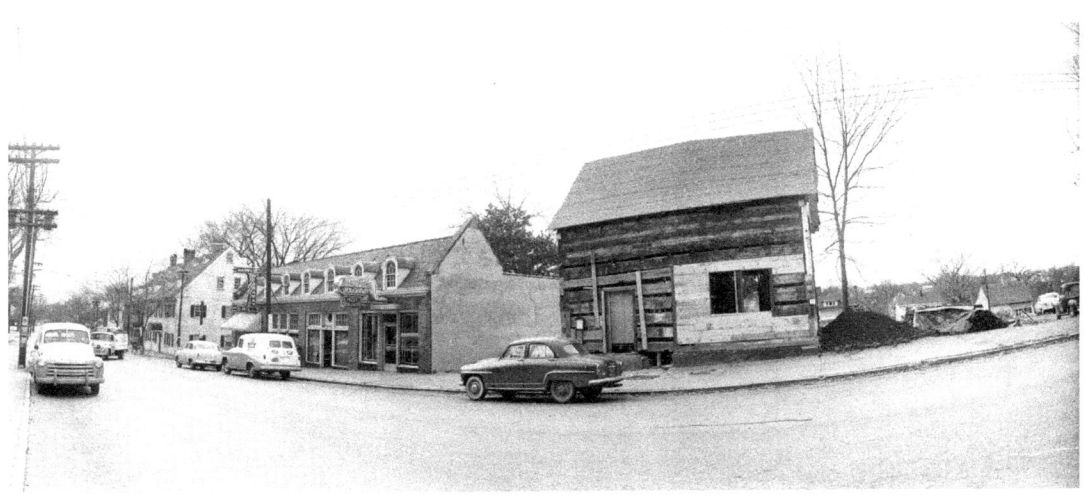

The ending of the new and the beginning of the old is contrasted on Main Street during the reconstruction of Old Salem, circa 1950. The Miksch Tobacco House rises as a phoenix from the past.

The landscape of West Salem from the 1770s to the years of the Civil War was confined to farms and industry. The industrial complex of the Brothers' tanyard, slaughterhouse and brewery can be found documented in the Old Salem experience. However, an important industry that helped Winston-Salem to become the largest city in North Carolina in the 1920s was a lesser-known one: textiles.

The first textile mill venture in Salem came about in 1836. Originally the Moravians were hesitant to allow such an establishment in the town, because they believed their way of life could have been compromised with such a business. But the Moravian hierarchy ultimately agreed to the venture, and Salem's first textile mill, the Salem Manufacturing Company, was created. This industry brought a new livelihood to West Salem, which began as the farm and industry sector of the Salem congregation and evolved over time to become the backbone and home to mills and industry workers. Much of the fortunes of Winston and Salem elite—Reynolds, Gray, Hanes and Fries—were built on the backs of West Salem workers. In addition to its success, however, the Salem Manufacturing Company also brought to Salem a large problem—more outsiders. In the 1830s, farms in the Piedmont of North Carolina were devastated by drought, depression and failing crops. Many people from Stokes, Guilford and Davidson Counties came to the mill looking for steady pay and work. Unfortunately, the Moravians tried to assert control over the workers, as if they were Moravians. This contributed to the failure of the venture. The Salem Manufacturing Company closed in 1849, after several declining years. The next textile venture was more successful.

No one could speak of North Carolina's mill owners without noting one of the most successful—Francis L. Fries, Salem's first industrialist. In their time, the Fries family wielded more power than the Reynoldses, Haneses and Grays, who in their own right later became Winston industrialists. Francis Fries grew up on his father's farm, which was

Winston-Salem

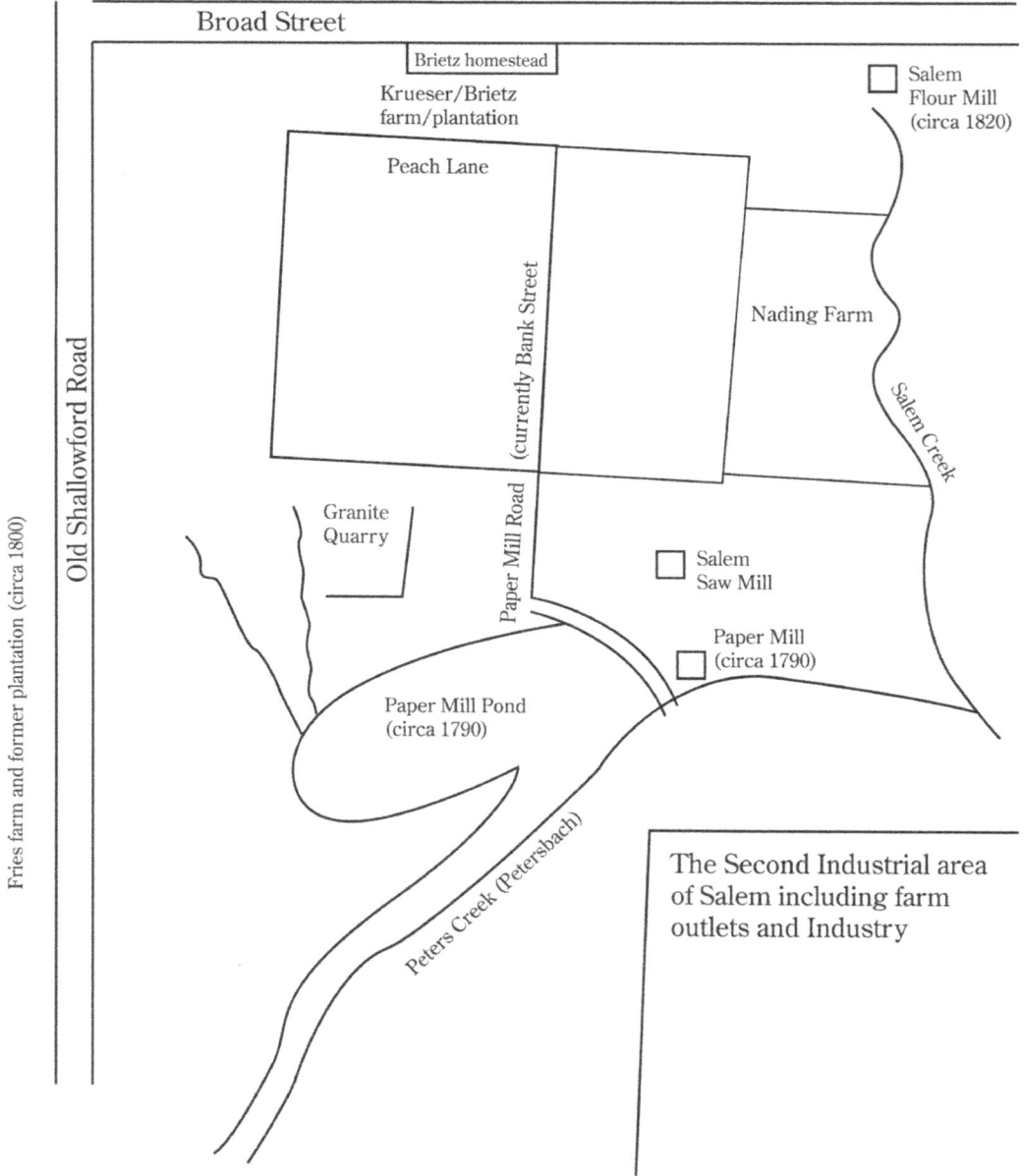

Between 1790 and 1877, the Paper Mill Settlement of Winston was alive with industry and diversity.

one of, if not the largest in Salem. His farmland was located in the northern part of West Salem. The West End Historic District rests in a part of that landscape today. Francis was groomed by his family in the Boys School of Salem to become a Moravian minister, but he chose law instead. In 1836, at the age of twenty-four, he became an agent for the Salem Manufacturing Company. His mill education took him to New England to study machinery and its functions. After four years in the mill, he was ready to try his hand at his own mill. Fries Woolen Mill was born in 1840 and was located at New Shallowford Road and Salt Street (today's Brookstown Avenue and Liberty Street). The new Winston-Salem Children's Museum occupies a large part of that lot. The building of the mill was unique in one way: Francis Fries and his brother literally built the factory with their own hands, brick by brick. Henry Fries joined his brother as a partner in 1846. The name of the mill was changed to the F&H Company. During the Civil War, the mill supplied uniforms for the Confederate soldiers. The mill survived Reconstruction at a time when most mills and businesses of the South were destroyed by the advancing Union army or later by the Northern carpetbaggers. The success of the Fries Mill Complex in the 1840s signaled the end of the old ways of Salem business. The F&H mill was enlarged and the new mills were built by the family in the twentieth century. Beginning in the 1880s and continuing through 1910, several other local mills were begun and joined the F&H Company in the West Salem landscape.

The farm outlot, or portion of land that is not intended for building development, was another feature of the West Salem landscape. An example of a farm outlot is best documented by the Krueser-Brietz farm lot of 1816. In 1837, the farm lot was purchased by the Brietz family and became known before and after the Civil War period as the Brietz plantation. Jim Jurney, a direct descendant of the Brietz family who served on the Manhattan Project in the 1940s, used his research and archivist skills to present the family's homestead's history. His studies of the Moravian archives, covering the time period from 1816 to 1837, enabled us to share a glimpse into plantation life. The following description contains excerpts from these records.

The Krueser-Brietz farm and plantation in historic West Salem lasted from 1816 to 1960. Spanning nearly 150 years of history in this manner creates a great impact on any neighborhood across America. Over 200 years ago the new United States of America had a population of less than four million people. More than ninety out of one hundred of these people lived and worked on farms. Salem outlots and farms were the lifeblood of the congregational town and the Krueser-Brietz farm provided many essential food products. Krueser had planned the thirty-plus acres of farmland to be his retirement homestead from the Salem store that he ran, located in the heart of the town. Krueser handled the farm for nine years. The Levering family of Salem took over the farm in 1825, exchanging their house on Main Street to Krueser and family for the farm and outlot. The Levering-Krueser house was rebuilt by Old Salem Incorporated on Main Street.

In the mid- to late nineteenth century, Levin Brietz, who was then owner of the Krueser-Brietz farm, began a large commercial hog trade on his farm. He sold his wares throughout the town and beyond. His farm's success was due to another ingenious industrial invention involving a refrigeration process. In the eighteenth and nineteenth centuries, the winter climate of the area was much colder than it is today. Jurney, Levin Brietz's grandson, related an interesting story concerning his ancestor's ingenious invention:

> *Mr. Brietz would venture down to Peters Creek to paper mill pond. There he would cut the newly frozen ice from the pond by hand. He would haul the ice by wagon up Paper Mill Road (Bank Street today) to his farm. He would have a pit dug close to his barn and fill the pit with ice and straw. Then his wares would be stored safely in the ice. The ice process would keep the product until the summer.*

Brietz was by all accounts one of our state's first commercial meatpackers.

The stories of the Brietzes and other families of early Salem were documented in the Moravian archives on a day-to-day basis. In excerpts from volumes seven and eight of the Moravian archives dated between 1816 and 1837, the property's transition from farm into Brietz plantation is presented. On October 7, 1816, it was recorded that the place Conrad Krueser would take west of town did not interfere with the supply of water for the paper mill. According to records, he would take thirty acres. The paper mill was located on Peters Creek, just north of where Academy Street presently crosses the creek. Krueser conducted the congregational store with diligence and faithfulness.

At the end of April 1816, Krueser turned the store over to his former assistant, Brother Jacob Blum. In March 1817, it was evident that Blum's clerk, Brother Byhan, and his barkeeper, Brother Levering, did not get along well together. Levering seemed to have been better suited to be a clerk in the store, and when the retirement of Krueser opened the way, Brother Levering could be transferred into the store as he and Jacob Blum had wished.

In May 1822, Brother Steiner held a meeting at Krueser's farm, and on September 1 of that year he preached and married Brother John Emanuel to Sarah, who belonged to Brother Zevely. In May 1825, Krueser, who had been living outside the town, exchanged houses with Brother Levering, who had been living in Salem. In June 1825, the former Krueser land had been surveyed for Charles Levering. According to the surveyor's plat it contained twenty-eight acres, for which he should have paid an annual rent of fifty cents per acre. Levering's land was on a ridge west of Salem. The sky over the Krueser-Levering-Brietz farm reflected deep clouds of bright reds and yellows similar to early paintings depicting the environment of hell. This represents a common weather condition of brilliant sunsets in the western neighborhood; however, this weather type was unknown to the early superstitious Moravians of the nineteenth century, leading to the amusing German saying that goes, "When skies were clear in the west the weather wise would predict good weather for the next because it was, Hell over Levering."

On December 13, 1830, Charles Levering wanted to arrange an exchange with Brother Fries, whereby the former was to move into the Fries house. Levering thought he could support himself with his tailor work without continuing to operate the known Fries corner business. Fries was busy with his building work and was willing to sign the lease prepared according to the congregation ordinances. On April 5, 1831, the request of Charles Levering for a town lease was so far granted in that the collegium would give him a lease drawn up according to congregation regulations, as was minded to give Brother Fries. On

In the Beginning

ALMANACS.

THE Farmers' and Planters' Almanac for 1851, for sale—wholesale and retail—by BLUM & SON.

SALEM PAPER MILL.

THE subscriber has taken charge of this old and well known Establishment, and is prepared to attend to all orders for

PRINTING PAPER,

Merchant's and Factory

WRAPPING, &C.

The Mill has recently been thoroughly refitted with new machinery, and the subscriber believes he can furnish paper of as good quality and at as cheap prices as can be purchased any where—North or South.

CHARLES E. SHOBER

Salem, June 7, 1851.   19

The paper mill on Peters Creek has been remodeled in this 1851 advertisement. People's Press, *circa 1851.*

April 17, 1831, it is recorded that Levering wished to have the promise of the diacony put into his lease that if it came to the worst, for example his demise, at least $1,000 were to be paid his estate for his house and improvements. Also, he wanted to have two acres added to his fields. On May 16, 1831, since Levering felt entitled to have a lease different from that offered by the Aufseher Collegium on April 5, 1831, this matter was brought up again. He insisted that in the last change made in the lease to Krueser, the diacony received an equivalent in the exchange of Krueser's house for his own outside of town and, therefore, it was fair to give him the advantage of this in the town lease. After much discussion, a motion was made in order to avoid all appearances of an unfair transfer to include in the lease equity of $800, or the probable worth of the former Levering (now Krueser) house. This would have to be decided shortly, along with the second proposal to put both leases of the former Krueser and Levering houses in force as they were before the exchange.

On July 25, 1831, the proposal made to Levering was found to be acceptable to him, but he added a petition that in the future, the land on which he lived should be sold by the congregation diacony. Since the congregation diacony probably would never sell this land and the collegium did not wish to insert this new clause in the lease, the collegium stood by the original proposal, without further conditions or clauses. On April 30, 1832, Levering asked for several more acres of land in addition to the twenty-eight acres rented to him and designated a little tract located between the southwest corner of the middle lane and the southeast corner of the newest clearing. This little piece had been almost denuded of wood by Krueser. Levering promised to use the remaining wood for firewood and to make fence rails for his plantation and to sell none. He gave as a reason for his petition that he wished to raise grass on his uplands, having no meadow, and thus he lacked several acres for raising corn. The collegium believed that Levering profited by reducing his acreage, and his petition was granted in the following manner: he was to use half of the piece of land at first, and when he had used up the wood he could use up the other half. The rent would be fifty cents per acre, as determined by the contents of the new field. Regarding cutting of trees, the terms of the lease were to be followed. On May 18, 1836, Levering and his wife set out for Nazareth, Pennsylvania, with their seven children and Andreas Kern, a boy from Nazareth who had been visiting Salem. The family never returned to Salem. On October 23, 1837, Brother Christian Brietz had moved to the Levering farm outside the community. The Brietz farm continued into the mid-twentieth century before the homestead was razed by Piedmont Bible College on Broad Street. The college hopes to use the homestead lot as the site of its new library project. The library will be built to resemble the architecture of the 1880 homestead.

David Blum was another early resident of Salem who called West Salem home. His story is different from the Levering and Brietz stories, since his family chose to sell his farm lot and move to East Salem, the congregational side of town. Blum was born in 1787 in Pennsylvania. In 1808, Blum married Sarah Hege at the home of her parents, Brother and Sister Lazarus Hege of Friedburg, near Salem. Brother Blum took charge of a farm near Salem in Bethabara.

The Blum story continues in the Moravian records from 1811. The Wachovia branch of the Society of the Brethren for Propagating the Gospel Among the Heathen met on

In the Beginning

August 21, 1811. Brother David Blum, Matthaeus Reuz and Johann Christian Lehmann were received as new members. On February 4, 1812, Brother Blum had applied to Brother Hulthin for the still house of the single brethren. The collegium had no objection, but it was required that Brother Blum give a written guarantee that he would observe the rules of a congregational town. On March 2, 1812, Brother David and Sister Sarah Blum and their daughter, Catharina, moved to Salem from the neighborhood of Bethabara. David would take charge of the brewery and distillery. On October 27, 1813, Brother and Sister Bagge and their five-year-old daughter, Rebecca Matilda, moved from Friedland to Salem, into Eberhard's house on the west side of Main Street (the second house south of West Street), which they had bought. Brother Eberhard and his children moved temporarily into the house vacated by Brother and Sister Blum and their family, who had moved to their own farm in the neighborhood.

By March 9, 1825, Brother Blum and another of his aussenseiter (outsider) brethren and neighbors had applied for a place on Unity land near the northeast corner of the Salem tract. They wished to build a schoolhouse there for the instruction of their children. Neither the collegium nor the Aeltesten Conferenz had any serious objection to offer, so Brother Schultz gave the desired permission. The town of Liberty was located in the area of the Salem tract in the early nineteenth century. A schoolhouse was built there and served Moravians and non-Moravians, including Methodists. The name of Liberty Street in Winston-Salem was also coined from this early township.

At one o'clock on the afternoon of September 9, 1830, the funeral was held for the departed married Sister Sarah Blum, maiden name Hege, who died on September 7, 1830. Sister Blum was born in Friedburg on April 25, 1789. She married Brother Joann David Blum on November 24, 1808, and they moved into the neighborhood of Salem and joined the congregation there. Since her dear husband had been building a new house on another part of their plantation, she wished soon to move into the new dwelling in hopes that the change would contribute to her recovery. Her wish for moving was granted on September 3, 1830, to her joy, but it was destined that she should soon move into the home prepared in heaven, for which she prepared herself in all silence. Brother Blum continued as a widower until marrying Sister Louisa Herman on January 19, 1842. Blum, a non-resident member of the church, wished to move from West Salem into East Salem after selling his plantation and slaves so that his children could be educated in the schools there and the family would be near the church. The elders' conference had no objection and the matter was referred to the Aufseher Collegium. The rules of the Moravians of Salem stipulated that in order for the children to attend the Salem schools, they had to live within the boundaries of the congregational town. Brother Blum was widowed for the second time and sold his house in Salem to Augustus Zevely in June 1845. The Zevely house is located in today's landscape opposite the Salem Tavern and is used as an inn. Moravians of the nineteenth century were often widowed, with both males and females remarrying several times.

The following is the final will and testament of Brother David Blum:

> *I give & bequeath to my beloved wife Amelia Blum one silver watch, one bureau and bookcase, one wardrobe, two beds and furniture, one rocking chair, six other chairs, two tables, and such*

other household and kitchen furniture as my said wife may select, and as may be proper and suitable for her housekeeping establishment. I also give to my wife my house clock and desk until my son Samuel J arrives at the age of twenty one when they shall be his. I will and direct that all the money I may happen to have on hand at the time of my death shall be equally divided between my said wife Amelia Blum and my children Catharine Everhard, Henrietta Murchison, George A. Blum, Charlotte P. Smith, Ernestine E. Reed, David H. Blum, Eliza L. Lash and Samuel J. Blum—to be equally divided & share and share alike provided however such sums may be needed for the wants of the family for the year or part thereof that may elapse before closing the crop and breaking up the household establishment. With the exceptions of the foregoing special bequests, I will and direct my Executors to make public sale of all my personal property and effects, and the proceeds arising from such sale, with all and singular the debts and demands due and in any way whatever and also the entire amount arising from the above directed sale of my lands and slaves I give and bequeath to my said wife Amelia Blum and my before-mentioned children to be equally divided among them share and share alike. I further will and direct that whenever money amounting to the sum of one hundred dollars or more shall be in the possession of my Executors as a part of my estate that they hand over the sum to those entitled under my will, without waiting for the lapse of two years or any other period, so that from time to time as money may be perceived, my legatees shall be put in possession thereof.

Should any of my children die in my lifetime, I will and direct that my Executors pay to the children or the children of the one dying the share of my estate to which the parent of surviving one was to have entitled. In order to provide a home for my wife in case she should outlive me—more desirable to her than which we now occupy.

I give and devise unto my said wife Amelia Blum the house and lot owned by me in the town of Salem, N. Carolina with all the other slips of land and life or widowhood, and upon her death or future marriage, I will that my Executors and the survivors or survivor of them shall sell said possessions under the regulations herein before presented for the sale of my other lands—and the proceeds of said sale I will and bequeath to all my children to be divided equally.

I appoint my wife Amelia Blum guardian to my infant son Samuel Blum, with a hope for the due execution of the provisions of this my will and testament. I do hereby appoint my wife Amelia Blum, my son David H. Blum and my son-in-law Henry M. Lash Executrix and Executors thereof without intending to control the authority of the above named—to lives, but with a view to their convenience, I desire that the papers which are kept by me in my desk may for their safety be continued there during the process of settling my Estate.

Revoking all other wills for me made or directed to be made, I do hereby declare and publish this to be truly and alone my last will and testament. In testimony of which I have signed the same and made due publication thereof this 19th day of September 1860.

David Blum [seal]

*Signed and published in
Presence of
C.L. Boner*

In the Beginning

As one studies the Moravian records, the day-to-day lives of many Salem citizens come to light. The lives of Brother Fries, Brother Brietz and Brother Blum are examples of early history in both East and West Salem. The overlapping histories of these two sections of town created many movers and shakers who set the framework for the creation of the greatest nation of the modern world, America. Salem and Winston reaped the rewards from these early industrious workers who led the way for what was to come—the city's national dominance in textiles and tobacco.

CHAPTER 2.

God and Country

The connection between God's laws and the laws of America is unbreakable, and has been since the founding of our nation, despite the calls of modern people for separation. Winston-Salem has battled with this question for more than two hundred years. The old saying "joined at the hip" aptly describes the relationship between Winston-Salem's churches and its local government. One needs to look no further than the Moravian archives to find the proof. Volume six of Larry Tise's *Winston-Salem in History*, published by Historic Winston in 1976 for the upcoming bicentennial celebration of the United States, explains the period from 1753 to 1789 through the Moravian archives:

> *Behind the apparatuses of the Rowan County government and that of Dobbs Parish, Wachovia developed its own theocratic institutions. Theocracy evolved in two phases—one during the brief life of Bethabara of the chief settlement and the other after Salem became the ruling center in 1772. Although the word seems to have been applied well after the system had been established, Bethabara's government and society revolved around the Oeconomie, the practice of common housekeeping. Similar in conception and practice to Carl Marks' notion of "commune," the Oeconomie was conceived as a temporary measure necessary to the founding of a large colony. At the outset of the Wachovia venture, at least, the Oeconomie afforded the settlement a means of providing labor for community tasks that otherwise have gone undone, in return for whatever food and clothing an individual might require. Without the regulation of both labor and consumption through the Oeconomie neither Bethabara nor Salem could have been built in the orderly, economical fashion that they were.*

The practice of common housekeeping that Oeconomie concerned itself with represented the material side of Bethabara's leadership. Oeconomie was controlled by a business manager, the vorsteher. Aeltesten Conferenz was a higher group of Moravians who were above the Oeconomie and controlled the spiritual side of the community. Aeltesten Conferenz was a central player and is mentioned throughout the Moravian archives. Their control of the spiritual affairs of the congregation was almost never questioned, even though the Conferenz's participants were not elected by the people, but rather were appointed by

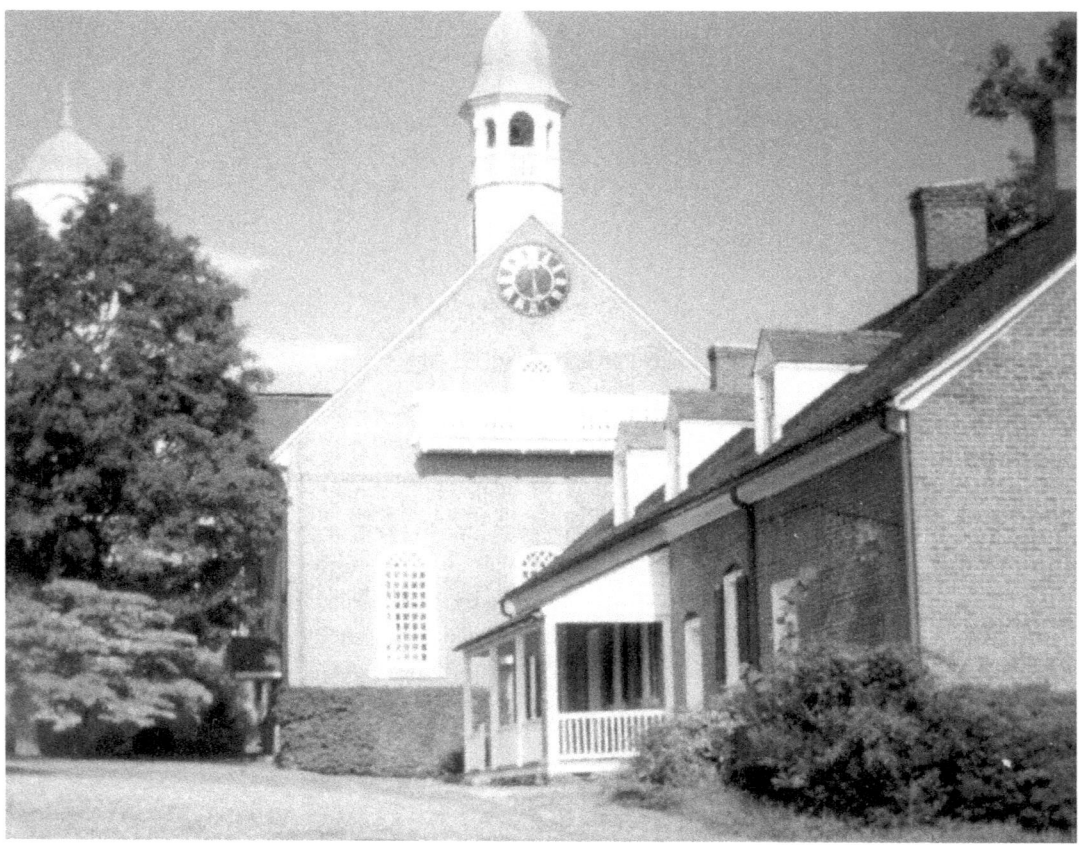

Home Moravian Church on Church Street.

individuals who held economic interest in the community. The Aeltesten Conferenz also took an active role in the planning of Salem. Since Wachovia was a theocracy, without a doubt the Conferenz had the greatest authority in the community.

The Conferenz stood alone in its authorization to interpret God's will for the Moravian congregation. By setting forward the Lot, the Conferenz hierarchy decided spiritual and material matters of the people. Community leaders also established themselves in matters beyond the spiritual and material. Helfer Conferenz, a higher group of individuals that was responsible for enforcing the Aeltesten Conferenz's Lot results, controlled legal matters and monetary funds. Creation of both the Aeltesten and Helfer Conferenzs allowed ministers and leaders from Germany to appoint the key positions to residents of Bethlehem, Pennsylvania. Another important feature of the Moravian lifestyle, guaranteed from those in control, was the adoptive "choir system," which divided the congregation by similarities of sex and age.

With the establishment of Salem in 1766, the Bethabara system became a grievance for the town's residents. In 1772, the people of Salem decided enough was enough. They felt that the way of Oeconomie was outdated and a more effective way of dealing with men and land had been practiced by another Moravian town: Bethania. Bethania had been established in 1759 by those who were unhappy with the Oeconomie in Bethabara, even though Frederick Marshall had begged the brethren and sisters to remain and stay true to the town's system. The residents of Bethania had established a system called "the Lease," which complemented the monopolies of Salem's business world by allowing the church to own the land while the residents leased it. Business and land were two commodities over which the Moravian leaders demanded complete control.

The Oeconomie was replaced by the Lease, thus beginning the second Salem system. At the construction of Salem in 1766, the minds of Salem's hierarchy were compiling information for the future town. The first decision from the Salem leaders was the separation of Bethabara from Salem. Bethabara was never intended to serve as the official town of Salem, so in 1767 it became purely a farming community. Salem leaders knew only one town could serve as the center of commerce and trade, and competition from surrounding outlot towns was out of the question. Bethabara, Bethania and the other towns in the Wachovia tract were all governed by Salem. Total command of the Wachovia tract allowed Salem to enter onto another path toward bettering its future—control of secular politics in and around the newly formed state of North Carolina.

In 1789, North Carolina was established as the thirteenth state of the newly formed United States of America, and the Salem theocracy was at the controls. For more than sixty years, the Salem leaders controlled the polls and voting block of the North Carolina General Assembly. Salem had learned a valuable lesson in government politics early on in 1776, when the State Assembly officially ended outside involvement by churches in government affairs. One could say the beginning of separation of church and state had arrived in that year. With that knowledge, and newly drawn county lines, Salem's brethren ignited their influence by their moral block vote. Beginning in 1789, and for the next thirty years, the theocracy vote allowed no candidate to win an election without the Moravians' nod of approval. Many of the Salem town leaders followed each other into the General Assembly and Congress. This list reads as a who's who of those fine Salem Moravians. Over the years, the General Assembly appointed George Hauser Jr., 1792–96; Gottlieb Schober, 1805–08; Charles F. Bagge, 1813; Emmanuel Schober, 1819–20, 1822, 1824, 1827–28; and John Butner, 1829. These representatives used their Moravian ideals to mold the government in an image that coexisted with the morals exemplified by the Moravian Church. The Bagge and Schober families sent a strong message to Congress that the servants of God and country were one and the same.

Moravians of Salem struggled with this new power in the government sector throughout the theocracy's sixty-year reign. First and foremost, Salem was the center of the congregational hierarchy of the Moravian Church in North Carolina. "Let us not forget" were the words conveyed by the Brothers to their government leaders, since the residents of Salem had been overrun by outsiders during the general elections, which they represented from Stokes County. The normally quiet, majestic town of Salem enjoyed the control, but despised the frivolities and crowds of secular politics. Throughout the first half of the nineteenth century, Salem had answered the call of its country and had represented it admirably.

Salem had struggled with the politics of the United States from the beginning. How could the theocratic institution of the Lease survive in such a world? A free enterprise system was growing in America with much more success. The world of economics was changing for the Moravians and for Salem. Competition, though kept from the congregational town, was arriving to the Moravians' customer base for trades and products. The 1820s and 1830s saw the economy of Salem decline and a more open competitive market arise. Industry of the day was producing more goods than could be produced by the individual tradesmen of Salem. Arriving on the industrial scene in the 1830s was an industry that changed the South: textile mills. Moravians learned that profits in excess of 20 percent could be gathered from textile production. These higher percentages on their investments overwhelmed them. Moravians began their own textile venture with the forming of the Salem Manufacturing Company in 1836. However, problems of outsiders flooding the town for employment made the Moravians extremely uneasy. Their way of life, with church and state entwined, could be in jeopardy. Demands of wealthy and influential brethren of the community pushed for the freedom in the pursuits of the wealth that could be gained from these highly profitable industries. The old theocracy could not stand the test to this arising Industrial Revolution, and the system of the Lease became history in 1856. New progressive Moravians ruled the day; however, another challenge was on the horizon—the Civil War.

Industry and economic conditions were not the only changes the Moravians faced in the first half of the nineteenth century. Moravians were very familiar, as were their Quaker brothers, with the opposition to war. Moravians were against oath taking or any allegiances to earthly causes. During the Revolutionary War and the War of 1812, their passive beliefs were respected. Their strength and representation in the General Assembly and Congress assisted the Moravians in forming the Society among the Brethren in Salem for Carrying the Military Load in 1815. This organization was created in order to start a Draft Fund, which "by united contributions the necessary money may be secured to pay substitutes for those names [that] may be taken in the lot."

The Draft Fund served the Moravians for more than fifteen years. Pressure from the General Assembly of North Carolina in 1837 finally succeeded in convincing its constituents to overturn all laws allowing the Moravians to avert the draft. Moravians were changing in their views of pacifism, so no challenges of the new law arose. Moravians took a giant step forward in their service to God and country and formed the core of the South Regiment of the Stokes Militia. This regiment served Stokes County well until 1861, when the state entered into the Civil War. North Carolina regiments, including those with Moravians, served valiantly.

The theocracy saw its institutions fall one by one, or at least change rather drastically, as in the draft laws. The Lot had fallen in 1818, but the elders' control over marriage was still a thorny issue. Since Salem's beginning, marriage by the Lot was the ultimate law of the Moravians. By 1801, cracks had formed, the Lot was overwritten and marriages of choice were allowed. General Assembly member Gottlieb Schober used his influence when his daughter Sophia was not allowed by the Lot to marry Brother Niemian Zevely. Even though Sophia and Brother Zevely were asked to leave the congregational town limits, their marriage stood and they moved to the Paper Mill Settlement in West Salem. In 1856, after the fall of the theocracy, it was decided that marriages were to be finalized only after the elders were made aware of it.

God and Country

One of the hardest battles the Salem Moravians faced was not totally fought on a conventional battlefield. It was fought against that then one-hundred-year-old adversary: slavery. The Moravian ideal was to isolate their community and live in harmony with the land as God had intended it. The Moravian archives of early eighteenth-century Salem show that the consensus of the brethren regarding slavery was soft compared to the rest of the South. Salem's early planner and leader, Frederick William Marshall, found "not many of our brethren or sisters have a gift of handling slaves without spoiling them." Did this statement refer entirely to African American men and women as children, or was there an underlying meaning directed at the white brethren and sisters? The Moravians' earliest

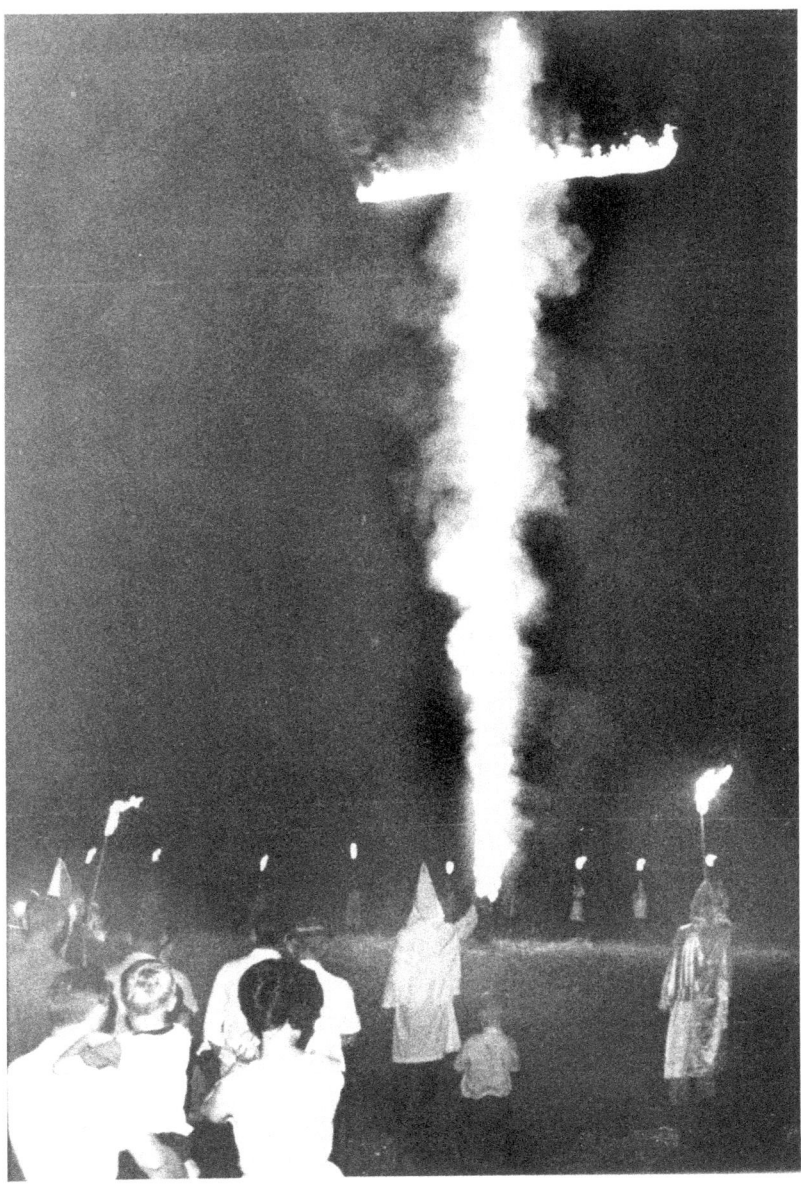

Years of work and understanding help to overcome a grim piece of Twin City history. There is still much to do.

teaching was not to let others do work for you that you can honestly do yourself, as this could be conveyed as slothfulness.

The Moravians of Salem found themselves facing this "spoiling" issue numerous times throughout the late eighteenth and early nineteenth centuries. Visitors and outsiders from other parts of North Carolina and the United States continually questioned the Salem brethren and sisters on the dress code of their slaves. The question on most of their lips was, "Why are they dressed like everyone else?" or, "Why are they not dressed in rags?" The Salem congregation answered with, "There is no call for any person of God to be dressed differently. We are all equal in God's eyes." The controversy of slavery in Salem continued mostly around those individuals being used in the Salem Tavern. Between the 1770s and the early 1800s, the Tavern alternately allowed and disallowed African American slaves as servants. In 1814, the congregational hierarchy determined to set a firm ruling on keeping slaves by adopting into law the earlier Moravians' belief that laziness comes to those who have another doing his or her work for them. According to the belief, this practice breeds sin. Harsh punishment followed slave owners who did not keep a code of honor for their behavior and their servants. By 1820, the Moravians had become like most of their fellow Americans in regard to slavery, both economically and domestically. Before 1822, the African Americans could worship with the white Moravians in Home Moravian Church; however, after the African American church was built in 1822, this was not the case. A separate but equal mentality in Salem had begun.

The progressiveness of the Schober family was sometimes just what the Moravians needed in addressing the controversial issue of slavery. Brother Schober had appointed an African American to supervise his paper mill for many years. The Paper Mill Settlement had a diverse workforce where whites, blacks, English, Irish, freedmen and slaves worked together hand in hand. Placing an African American in charge of all these men was as progressive as it could get when you weigh the surrounding landscape of the United States in relation to the slavery issue. History has documented that Moravian slaves were among the best treated, most religious and most highly educated in the South. If the Moravians had continued to follow the Schober family's lead in promoting progressiveness and replacing slavery with equality, the years after 1820 may have ushered in the second revival that the church had spoken of. Building on the strength of the Moravian faith, their political clout in the General Assembly and strong influences in Congress, the South and North conflicts could possibly have been avoided, thus saving the country from the horrors of the Civil War. If God and country had been allowed to mix with the Schobers' progressive ideals of a better world, a stronger America, instead of a divided one, could have been imagined. However, history is filled with many ifs in the outcome of our actions or inactions. Slavery and Jim Crowism may have been created by our inactions to this one "if" of which we speak. What is not an if, but a fact, is that Salem's view of slavery was different from most slaveholding towns. Unfortunately, the practice continued nonetheless.

The Lot, the Lease and the slavery issue were systems that the Moravians had to overcome. In addition, Salem's monopolistic economy and social order affected these previous systems and has continued to modern times. Monopolies were not an invention of the Moravians. Throughout history a few individuals, companies and countries have sought to create monopolies in order to destroy competition and make their customers totally dependent on their products and services. Monopolies served the Moravians with economic protection for their craftsmen and industries of Salem. However, by the 1820s, competition, the death blow to any monopoly, was growing around Salem's borders and throughout the newly established United States of America. Moravians realized their monopoly system was outdated and was destroying any chance of growth for their town's business interests.

For more than twenty-five years the issue of the separation of church and state was challenged by the Salem brethren. By 1848, the Elders Conference could skirt the issues of monopolies and Lease systems no more. In the summer of 1848, Salem attempted to close the books on these issues forever by abolishing the Lease and monopoly systems. The Lease system lingered with little usage or notations in the archives until disappearing in 1850. It had been intended as a means to keep people who didn't adhere to the Moravian beliefs out of the congregational town. The Lease restricted the Moravian brethren in their freedom of movement throughout the town lot and also restricted the right to construct larger homes, additions and new business establishments.

The monopoly issue was harder to silence than the Moravians thought. A year later, after much town debate, complete freedom of trade was finally agreed upon. In 1850, "The Rules and Regulations of the Congregation of United Brethren of Salem, North Carolina" was issued and on November 17, 1856, 103 years to the day after the Moravians arrived to settle Bethabara, the rules were officially adopted. From 1850 to 1856, the town bickered. The deciding factor was the transfer of Salem buildings and establishments to non-Moravians without any interference or acknowledgement from the Moravian hierarchy. Last of the theocratic ideals, "Seeking first the kingdom of God," had been agreed upon in 1850 as a rule and regulation. The congregation referred to the rule as follows: "Such rules are a voluntary agreement, adopted by all members of a congregation, nor can anyone be compelled to subscribe to them against his will. Neither can anyone be a member of the congregation, unless he asserts to and observes these rules." From 1820 to 1856, the theocracy had continued to rule Salem while battling the breakdown of its principles and rules. In 1859, the church issued the "principles and discipline, not rules and regulations, of the United Brethren Congregation of Salem." The theocracy was issued its final rites.

With the state and country accounted for, let us now turn our attention to God. Moravians set the religious base for the other churches, and government laws established according to Moravian traditions formed the base of the early city of Winston as well. The city has been blessed with good religious representation throughout its long history. Different denominations have added greatly to the diversity of our modern, late nineteenth- and early twentieth-century neighborhoods. Local government and city leaders used this variety of churches throughout the city to proclaim in the early twentieth century that Winston, North Carolina, had a church structure on every corner of the city. The earliest churches of the city were born in the town lot of Salem. Home Church, founded in 1771, is now housed in the structure built in 1800. Other Moravian congregations were formed on the outskirts of the Wachovia tract, in the neighborhoods of Bethabara, Bethania, Friedburg, Hope and Friedland. Others who were worshiping from other communities, both within and outside of the Wachovia tract, became the early settlers of North Carolina's organized churches.

Before we venture deeper into the history of the Twin City's churches, a few historical points must be addressed. Technically and legally, the first church in the future town of Winston-Salem was the Episcopal Church or the Church of England. Count Von Zinzendorf was a shrewd and enlightened individual. His insight led the Moravians on a journey to a new world and a strong church. In 1749, he persuaded the English Parliament to declare the Moravian Church an ancient Protestant Episcopal church. Anglican and Moravian clergy shared equal rights. Count Von Zinzendorf knew the Moravian world would never fully unite with the Church of England; however, the benefits of the alliance were many. Moravians had secured the rights as Englishmen. An Englishman in colonial America was at a complete advantage. By being known as Englishmen, not only would the Moravians be protected under the Crown with said liberties of the established Church of England, but they would also be granted rights that they held dear throughout much of their early days in the colonies and United States.

The Salem Moravian Church accepted the early churches of the Presbyterian, Quaker and Baptist faiths. However, differences in dogma and the isolationism they chose led the Moravians away from these congregations. Despite the similarities with the Quakers theologically—both were against war or judicial oaths—and the fact that their counties touched each other's borders, they rarely ever associated. Presbyterians were always welcomed to Bethabara and Salem. Presbyterians were so taken by Salem that they hoped to establish a central community and settle down there as well. A rift arose at the beginning of the Revolutionary War in 1776 between the Moravians' leader, Frederick William Marshall, and the Salisbury Presbyterians. The Presbyterian movement was growing, and Brother Marshall felt the Moravians' affairs could be compromised if the Presbyterians gained power in politics and religion after the war.

Baptists and Moravians shared the strongest allegiance of the three denominations. Both preached and ministered in each other's community. Again, the proverbial "religious boat was rocked" when several Moravian ministers who had regularly preached at the Baptist church on the Shallowford of the Yadkin River were asked rather vocally not to visit that neighborhood again. This unfortunate encounter between Moravians and Baptists in 1774 led to a more vocal concern by Moravians in Salem. In 1776, again at the beginning of the war, the vigilance of the Baptists' street preaching without the approval of the Moravian hierarchy was too much for the brethren to bear. Baptists were asked to leave the town and no Baptist church structure was allowed in Forsyth County for fifty years.

The early years of the United States saw religious expression and practice taken very seriously among its constituents. Salem Moravians continued to isolate themselves from other religious groups. The Revolutionary War and postwar period revealed a more open and progressive United States. Moravians thought change eroded their theocratic institutions of church and state. This unfolded in their relationship with another congregation known as the Dunkers, a German Baptist brethren seat derived from the same German tradition as the Moravians. Their beliefs and practices were similar. But the similarities ended when

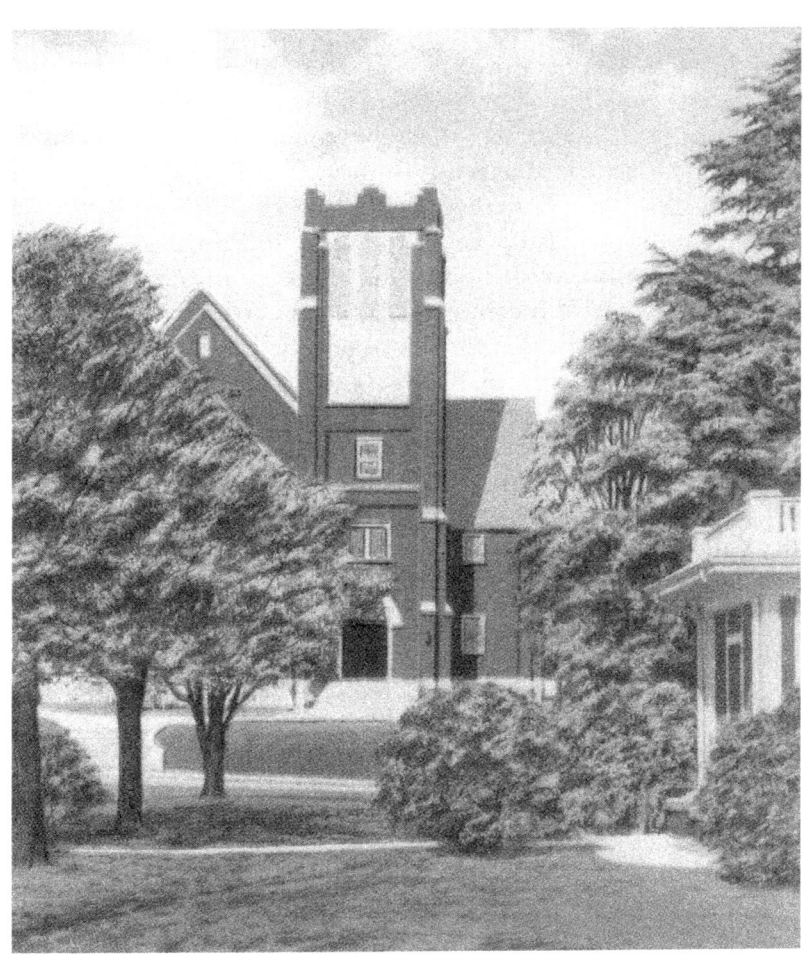

Salem Baptist Church on South Broad Street, with pastor's residence in foreground, circa 1940s. *Postcard collection, Michael Bricker.*

it came to the critical issue of baptismal rights: the Dunkers' practice is evident from their name. Another difference, which was a very important one for Salem Moravians, was the Dunkers' lack of theocratic control over business compared with the Moravians'. Dunkers were simple farmers. They had no meetinghouses and their minister was not paid. Dunkers shared the same feelings as the Quakers in that Salem Moravians' rituals were too elaborate for their taste.

An influential Moravian, Gottlieb Schober, led a movement that allowed another religious group to begin in Salem. As a North Carolina General Assembly member, Brother Gottlieb Schober's progressive ideas allowed the German Lutheran movement to be the first religious organization in Salem after the Moravians. Brother Schober's love of God and country touched not only the adults of Salem and the surrounding elders of the Wachovia outlot towns, but also the children he taught and ministered to. Moravian records of the early nineteenth century reported the children of Salem and surrounding townships were so taken by Brother Schober's interest in their religious and educational well-being that they followed him throughout the different towns singing and playing.

With this inspirational presentation by the children, Brother Schober's crowning moment was in his establishment of the Hopewell Sunday School in 1816.

With its next church, the Methodist congregation grew to be the largest of all the area churches during the nineteenth century. The first Methodist church that formed in the Wachovia tract was just to the west of the Salem town limits (the Methodist Children's Home on Reynold Road in Winston, in today's landscape). Protestant and Episcopal denominations of the Methodist Church began to gain more church ground in the 1840s. With the founding of the town of Winston in 1849, the Methodists became well established here. After the Moravian, Lutheran and Methodist congregations, the next congregation to establish in the area was Baptist. The first Baptist missionaries traveled throughout the Salem tract in the eighteenth and nineteenth centuries, never gaining a strong foothold early on, as Moravians and Methodists did. Their official arrival occurred after the Civil War in the 1870s.

Home Moravian Church was the only church structure in Salem town lot until 1822, when the African American church was constructed on the south side of Church Street.

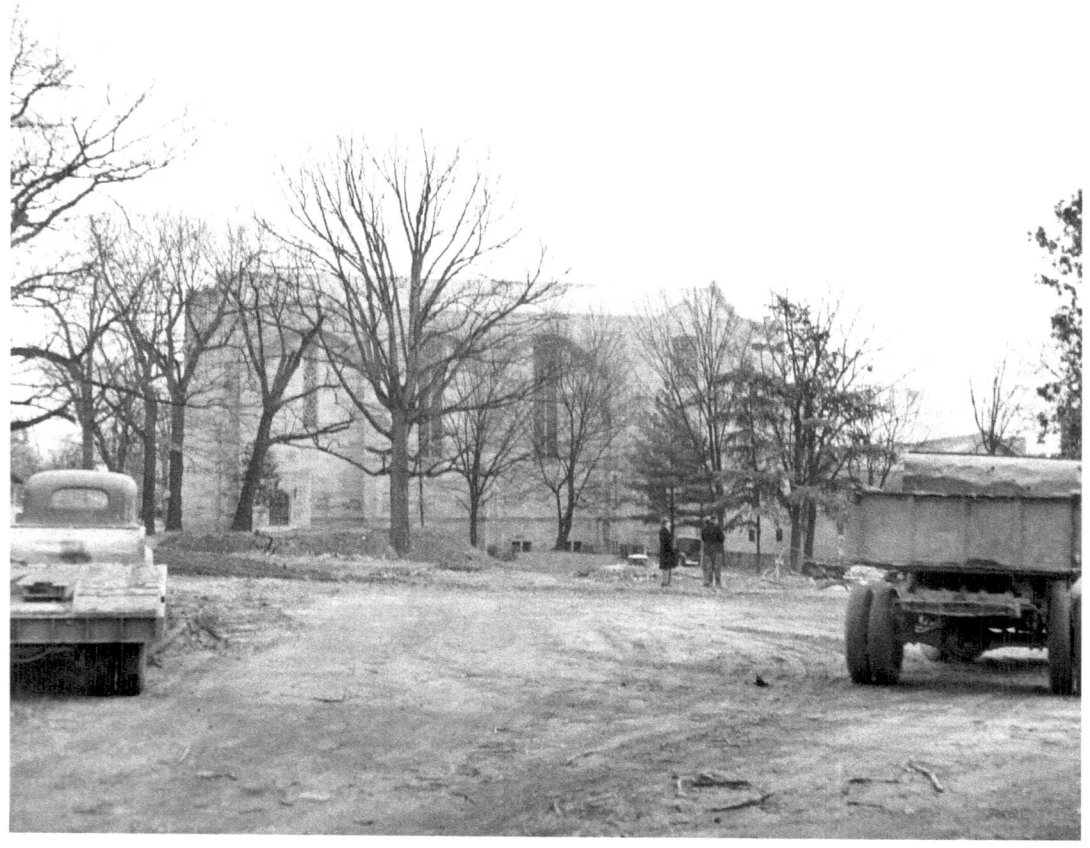

The R.J. Reynolds home on Fifth Street has been razed to make way for the new Forsyth County Public Library, circa 1950s.

God and Country

West Salem completed the other side of Salem's town lot with its own version of worship and churches. West Salem was blessed with good religious representation throughout its long history. Different denominations added greatly to the diversity of this neighborhood over the years. The strong precedence of the Moravians in Salem led to the establishment of the Elm Street Chapel in 1867 and Christ Moravian Chapel and Church in 1895. Later the Baptists, Methodists and Pentecostals arrived on the scene.

Even though an organized branch of the Moravian Church wasn't constructed in West Salem until 1867, the precedence of religion was still found much earlier in the neighborhood. Tent meetings, old-fashioned revivals and other types of gatherings occurred around the industrial area of the Schober Paper Mill as early as 1790, as well as on Moravian farms, such as the Krueser farm in 1817. Moravian ministers from Home Church in Salem traveled throughout the western neighborhood in 1800 sharing their message. Religious leaders from other denominations were also allowed to minister in this neighborhood. These other religious messages were allowed by the Moravians because most of the industry and farms were worked by aussenseiter. Workers consisted of English, Scots-Irish, Quakers, African American slaves and free African Americans. The African American church had its first organized beginnings at the Krueser farm in 1820. Two years later, in 1822, the St. Phillips first church was built on Church Street. St. Phillips is the oldest existing African American church in the United States. No solid structure by any religious organization other than the Moravians was constructed west of Marshall Street in the neighborhood until 1900. Salem Baptist Church was the first.

Salem's early years of church and politics were influenced by strong leaders who led Salem in both religion and government. One individual who best personified the strong bond between church and state was Brother Gottlieb Schober. Brother Schober (1756–1838) led both East and West Salem through his understanding of Moravian culture, religion and politics. In championing many causes for the Moravians through his law practice, including equality for all men—those in the east congregational town as well as those in West Salem—he pushed the limits of the Moravian Collegium's tolerance. Gottlieb believed free enterprise in business was the key to bringing all men and Salem itself to the prosperity he saw on the horizon for the nineteenth century. With Brother Schober's guidance, the paper mill had been allowed to run for many years with an African American foreman. The Paper Mill Settlement, along with outlots of English, Scots-Irish and even some Quaker residents, was growing. By 1830, the monopolies of Salem's early trades were over.

The last part of Brother Schober's life saw a complete about-face in his pursuits. His earlier accomplishments were laid to the side or given to his family members to continue. Gottlieb focused his thought and energies back to his core beliefs. He became ordained in the Lutheran Church as a minister, and he saw a chance to spread the teachings of Martin Luther. The resurgence of Lutheranism at the time is often spoken of as "the second awakening." A second revival in Christianity was taking place in the church. Brother Schober helped to champion the importance of children's education. Brother Schober's Sunday school led the way for children's education, both spiritual and intellectual, in Salem and the surrounding towns. He believed the Sunday school should teach the three Rs, as well as Bible education. Gottlieb was a pioneer and forerunner of the larger national movement of free schoolhouses in America and helped to set the standard for Calvin Wiley's public education programs after the Civil War. Brother Schober's daughter, Johanna Sophia, and son-in-law, Van Neiman Zevely, carried on the Schober progressive change in regard to the Moravians' lot and other business and religious ventures. Change could have been the Schober family's middle name.

An excerpt from the book *Three Forks of Muddy Creek* by Francis Griffin best summarizes the relationship between Salem and the Schobers.

> *The Salem experience showed the necessity of having rules and regulations, traditions and established practices; and to those who believed in and defended them. It showed also that human beings, no matter how carefully they are screened and selected, cannot be expected for long to react*

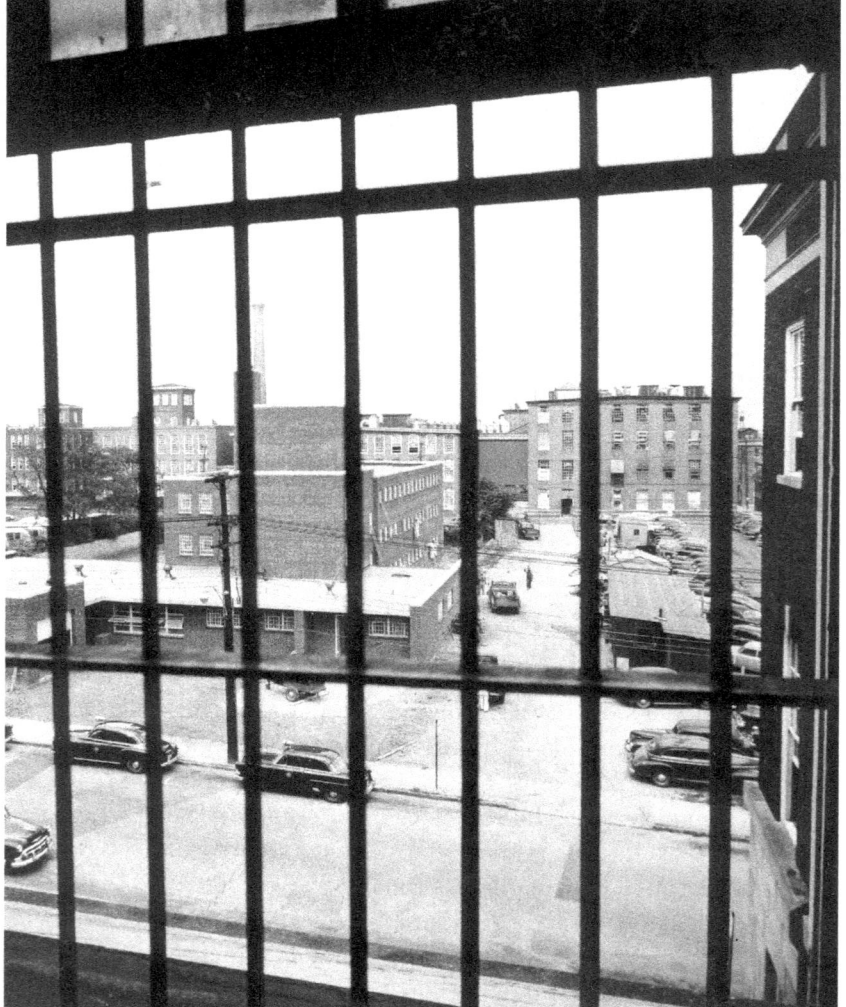

Looking from incarceration at city hall on Main Street toward the downtown jail on Church Street, circa 1950s.

God and Country

similarly to differing ideas and circumstances that arise. On the other hand, it showed that rules and regulations should not be regarded as immutable and even cherished customs in time may need to yield to legitimate aspirations. I hold for the theory that the conservatives did all right in sticking to their guns, that the rebels did well in gunning for change and that the moderates, who succeeded in tempering the inflexibility of the one by the untempered notions of the other performed a real public service. It is my observation that long, unquestioning adherence to the status quo tends to breed stagnation and to invite tyranny. With Thomas Jefferson, I hold that a little rebellion now and then, is a good thing. It is especially good when led by such people as Gottlieb Schober and his daughter, Johanna Sophia Schober-Zevely, who were intent not upon wrecking and destroying, but upon moderating and correcting. This makes the Schobers so great. They did not knuckle under, but managed to achieve their purpose without destroying a way of life. Brother Schober was much involved in the early beginnings of the Moravian evolution and epitomized its essence. He was not displeased with the development after his death and with the character, which the community and the church ultimately assumed. According to a newspaper of the day, he was last survivor of the early inhabitants of Salem. In spirit, perhaps, he was the first of a new generation of pioneers.

Once again God and country were joined at the hip in Salem. Salem theocracy encouraged this connection and drew on its power for many years. Although the theocracy became history by the 1850s, the decline of the theocracy's base in noncompliant judicial oaths, military service, slaveholding and free enterprise exposed a more important loss. Disobedience in the brethren's compliance with the church or God's law was devastating to the Moravians. The death of the theocracy brought about a spiritual death in the community as well. The loss of piety and a spiritual transformation occurred in these new Moravian Americans. German traditional pietism transformed into American practices, such as revivalism. From the beginning of the nineteenth century until the fall of theocracy, one saw a tightly controlled and closed community reborn as a secular American-born township. Revivals and tent or street preaching, as they were so named, intimidated and frightened the pietist Moravians throughout the first half of the nineteenth century. These Methodist revivals were, in the Moravians' eyes, a carnival show. By the 1820s, those carnival shows had spread throughout the Wachovia countryside and threatened to undermine not only the Moravians, but other religious groups in the area as well. Moravians and other congregations saw their attendances fall. If the spirits of the Moravians had not been dampened enough, the revivalists' ideals were spurred on by the progressive Moravian himself, Brother Gottlieb Schober.

In 1818, Salem allowed its Home Church to be used by a Methodist evangelist. By 1830, another Moravian practice met its demise. German pietism was replaced by Methodist techniques in evangelism. Moravians were quick studies and began to rival Methodists as evangelists. By 1842, Salem ministers added "Methodist tunes" to their wonderful Moravian compositions and went so far as loosening congregational rules for former Moravians, now Methodists, who wished to continue taking communion with them. When all was said and done, Brother Schober, a carnival show and revivalism helped the Moravians survive change. Survival of Moravianism was the prize.

Salem looked to the future with an uncertain eye. The old ways of the past and the new beginning of modernization brought a Dickensian quote to life for the American Moravians: "It was the best of times, it was the worst of times." January 16, 1849, was a day that changed Salem forever. Since the late eighteenth century, the residents of Salem had pushed the General Assembly of North Carolina to create their own county so that a place to practice their beliefs could be established in private. That day in January, ratification of the most sought-after event led to the creation of Forsyth County. These were the good times; however, the bad times were soon to follow, as the Moravians realized that their new northern neighbor, Winston, could bring many unwanted outsiders to the borders of their congregational town. Less than a year before the 1849 ratification, Salem citizens learned they were getting their own county and Salem was to serve as the county seat. Salem could not tolerate jury trials and the carnival atmosphere that accompanied them. Salem's county before Forsyth was Stokes County, which had its county seat of government in Old Richmond. Not long after Old Richmond was established as the seat, with all the frivolous events attached, a storm arose and a cyclonical wind literally blew the town of Old Richmond away.

Old Richmond regrouped and continued. Salem brethren, being very serious about their beliefs in God, felt this act was an omen. When their chance came to become the county seat of Forsyth, the Moravians felt God's wrath could fall upon them as well, so land to the north and west of Salem's town limits was used to create the town of Winston. Salem leaders believed if history repeated itself with another destructive act, perhaps Winston would be far enough away from Salem's congregational town and Salem would be spared. Winston obtained its official name in 1851, after the Revolutionary hero Colonel Joseph Winston. Between 1849 and the official naming of the town in 1851, the town was simply called Salem. With the political birth of Forsyth County came more decisions for the Americanized Moravians. Politically, residents of Salem had been staunch Whigs. The Whig Party later evolved into the Republican Party of today. Winston, on the other hand, acted from the beginning as a haven for the Democratic Party. The transition from the theocracy and the Whig Party's domination of Salem politics created a battle for the Moravians and their beliefs in God and country. The battle for identity of the American Moravians began in 1849, and lasted until 1880. The change had begun.

The three predominant congregations allowed the Forsyth County citizens to sample their religions before the years of the Civil War. Moravians, Methodists and Baptists were heavily represented. Both black and white congregations began to gain strength and their influence was found in government through that faith. Churches furthered their influence in nineteenth-century politics by adding more houses of worship to Winston and Salem.

Moravian circumstances in the political arena took shape in the 1830s with political parties. By the 1820s, national parties had existed, but were not recognized by the theocracy or the brethren. Joseph Winston, the namesake of Winston, was recognized nationally as a Jeffersonian Democrat, but in Salem he was identified as a candidate of the Moravian Party.

The Salem press touched on these party affiliations in the early newspaper, the *Weekly Gleaner*. John C. Blum produced the *Weekly Gleaner*, along with two other publications. The *Weekly Gleaner* and the *Farmer Reporter* were politically independent, while the third, the *Carolina Gazette*, was Whig affiliated. Salem's staunch Whig Party involvement led all of Blum's publications to become Whig affiliated by 1840. In 1828, the *Weekly Gleaner* reported a positive approval of the election of Democratic President Andrew Jackson. This Democratic endorsement was the last for the Salem media. No approval of any Democratic Party candidate appeared in a Blum publication until after the Civil War. Also by 1850, the Whig Party was led by the Salem industrialist Francis Fries (of F&H Fries Cotton and Wool Mills), Constantine Banner (of the Salem Manufacturing Company), Edward Belo (of the iron foundry and oil mill) and Israel Lash (of the cigar factory, oil mill, gristmill, tan yard and the Salem National Bank). These four individuals influence created an industrial market, which not only created a town, but created a town that grew in political, religious and national power well into the twentieth century.

Unfortunately for the congregational town, the Salem Whigs were not to be part of the political scene for long. In 1852, the National Whig Party fell into shambles and so did its replacement, the American Party, after 1856. By 1856, the Salemites had lost their party and their theocracy as well. Whig businessmen of Salem could look back at their crowning accomplishments of creating their own county of Forsyth and having the convenience of the county seat next door, but what was the future? Moravians of the congregational town knew they had to hold onto power or lose their control. Abraham Lincoln's Republican Party had arrived on the scene as an upstart political party. The Republican Party seized the opportunity with the demise of the Whig Party and became America's second mainline party. Was this the answer for the Salemites? No. Affiliation with the Republican Party was taboo for Southerners. The alternate answer was to join the Democratic Party. Remembering the carnival-like religious and political events associated with non-Moravians, the brethren resounded with a firm "nay." They wanted no part whatsoever with a political party of Southern radicals and secessionists. The old saying "Necessity is the mother of invention" spoke clearly for the congregation. The Moravians reached back to earlier, stronger, isolationists' beliefs for the answer. They created a party with no national party affiliation. The Independent Party had arrived in North Carolina by the simple politics of naming the Salem party as the "Old Whigs."

In 1859, Winston was incorporated, thus following the lead of its parent town, Salem, in 1856. In 1856, the Democrats succeeded in forming a pro-Democratic publication, the *Western Sentinel*, founded by Francis E. Boner and James Collins. The separation of Winston and Salem had begun. Not to miss an opportunity, Blum's Whig newspaper, the *People's Press*, approved all these appointments with a call to all citizens to put their blame for the war on "rabid Democrats." Another Democratic publication, the *Western Democrat*, retaliated constantly with labels of treason and traitors to the Southern war effort. As the battle waged on the battlefield, the dispute between Salem Old Whigs and Winston Democrats grew. Despite protest from Democrats, the Whigs continued to dominate Forsyth politics and, in the meantime, became more radical themselves. Disgusted with the war and pro-war Democrats of the South, the Salemites did what no one in North Carolina saw as an option: Old Whigs rushed to the party of Lincoln.

Winston-Salem

The governments of Salem and Winston were divided between Salem Whigs and the Winston Democrats, but the control of the two towns was in the hands of the Salemites. While the Salemites strongly opposed the War Between the States, the Winstonians embraced the old South and its prodigal son, slavery. By the 1850s, Winston and Salem had begun their magnetic relationship, with the positive and negative brought to Salem by the impending Industrial Revolution. Battles of God and country were played out in Salem and Winston because of their contrasts. Winston's saloons served alcohol as if there was no tomorrow, whereas Salem had severe restrictions on the sale of these types of beverages. Salem had a history of tradition in faith, arts and Moravian piety. Winston was the upstart, but inexperienced citizens and disorganization between the working class led to slow development in the town. In church, at work, in town politics and even in national Congress, the industrial bosses were at the helm. Some spoke of Winston becoming a large mill town. This was seen as a negative in Salem, since the Protestant ethics of thrift, sobriety and working "from dawn to dusk" ruled the day in

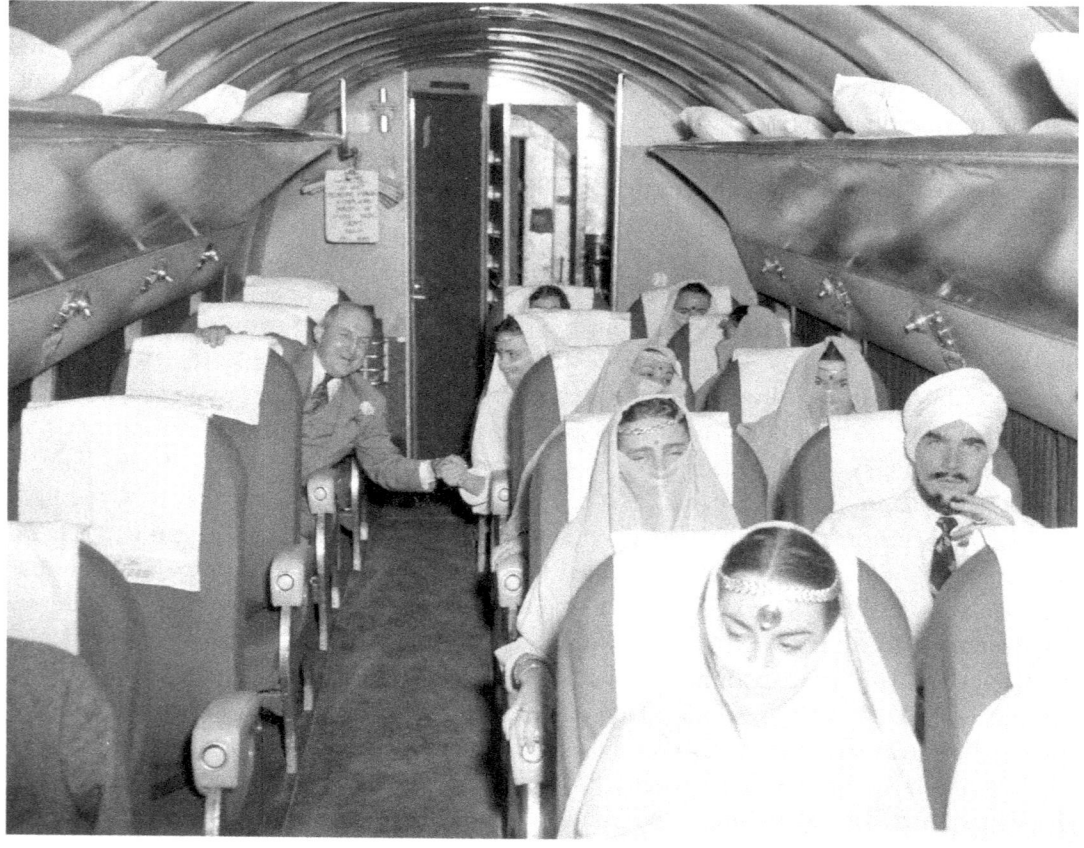

Mayor Marshall Kurfees was getting "a little too friendly" on his ride in a Piedmont Airlines aircraft. No, just a humorous stunt by local celebrity and artist Joe King.

God and Country

Winston. After the arrival of the Salem Textile Mill in 1836, Moravians knew what a mill town could do to their congregational town's control. The congregational town was not to be a farming or industrial center, but the controlling center of worship, politics and tradesmen.

The drive of the Methodist and the Methodist Protestants gave the millworkers the strength to carve out a niche early on in Winston. Winston, in its early years, was merely a few blocks of streets—Main, Liberty and Trade Streets in today's landscape. The closest non-Moravian religious organization was a small Methodist Protestant church, located in a small settlement town just outside the Moravian town lot. The town of Liberty had been founded in the early nineteenth century by Moravians who did not want to live in the congregational controlled town. The Methodist Episcopal church congregation built its church on Liberty at Sixth Street, a mere block from the Methodist Protestant church. The Centenary Methodist Episcopal Church was built on the site of the 1850 building. Wealth of the Winston businessmen aided them in building the premier church of the city. In a graceful and modern style, a prominent Richmond, Virginia architect designed what is recorded as "one of the most elegant churches in the South."

Winston's variety of church congregations gave rise to the expressions "a church on every corner" and "city of churches." The different denominations dotted downtown Winston. Sunday and Wednesday evening services saw a multitude of business leaders, government leaders and white- and blue-collar workers coming together for a celebration of faith and hope for their new town. Arrival of new denominations began in 1860 and continued until 1895. Moravians and Methodists were cornerstones by 1860, and for the next forty years every type of church imaginable arrived in Winston. Presbyterians were to arrive in 1860. The Civil War, unfortunately, slowed growth in all areas of the towns. Reconstruction brought its own hardships. Winston and Salem may have been out of money, but the communities were not out of faith. An individual arrived on the scene whose accomplishments were to be felt into the present time. Bishop Edward Rondthaler arrived in Salem in 1877. He became the pastor of the Home Moravian Church and served the Moravians for fifty years.

Reverend Rondthaler became the leader of the southern providence of the Moravian Church, a national honor. His leadership assisted the movement of church denominations of all beliefs to call Winston home. His book, *Memorabilia of 50 Years*, helped historians in Moravian and non-Moravian research to document year-by-year growth of the Twin City. A quote from the publication committee in reference to his 1927 book expresses a bit of history from the 1870s. "When you came to Salem in 1877, you found two quite small neighboring towns. You found a people poor and depressed by the trials of the war between the states, and the dread reconstruction days, and you found a Moravian congregation whose invested funds had been swept away in the general cataclysm." Reverend Rondthaler and the Moravians realized the war had not been the best option for the country; however, the brethren paid the price of the war nonetheless. When Reverend Rondthaler arrived to Salem in 1877, he found the train yard to be full of freight cars loaded with "dried berries." No industrial or consumer freight was visible. He thought this rather odd until he learned the "dried berries" were the only cash crop or sales item that existed in Winston or Salem. These berries had sustained the town during the Civil War and now were the sole economic product.

Winston's population grew from 443 in 1870 to 10,018 citizens by 1900. Winston had taken the lead as the central town. Salem's growth was a fraction of Winston's during this time period. By the late nineteenth century, Salem had taken on a retiree, suburban-type landscape. This suited the older Moravians just fine. In the modern Winston landscape, something much different had taken place. The 1880s ushered in the classes of people we know today. The rich, the middle and the lower classes were forming and the churches began to see their pews fill with these different classes of individuals. The wealthy Winston business leaders migrated to the Presbyterian and Episcopal congregations, while the other classes were predominant in the Baptist, Christian, Moravian, Lutheran and Catholic churches.

The landscape of the central business district of the Twin City in the twenty-first century is far different from its time as the "city of churches." In Henry Foltz's book, *Winston, 50 Years Ago*, published in 1925, he gives us a tour of Winston as it appeared in 1875. Through these excerpts of the book, a picture of churches and their locations is shown. "Proceeding westward on the north side of Second Street between Chestnut and Church Streets, one sees the partially constructed Baptist Church that will open its door in 1876." The First Baptist Church was the first organized Baptist church in Forsyth County. The Broad Street Church at Broad Street and Holly Avenue became the second organized Baptist church in 1889. Other Baptist churches were formed with Reverend Rondthaler's help. In 1901, the Marshall Street Baptist Missionary Church on South Marshall at Bank Street became the first Baptist church in the town of Salem. At the time of his retirement in 1917, Reverend Rondthaler was made pastor emeritus by eight Twin City churches.

Methodist churches dominated the North Liberty Street neighborhoods past Fifth, Sixth and Seventh Streets. Centenary Methodist, with its 135-foot steeple, was located between Fifth and Sixth Streets on the western side of North Liberty. Our journey in search of our next congregation will return to the center of town at Third and Main Streets. As we proceed west to the end of Third, we come to the prestigious church of the Winston businessmen and founders, the First Presbyterian Church on Cherry Street.

Leaving the entrance of the First Presbyterian Church, we head north along Cherry to the next block of Fourth Street. We turn left at Fourth Street to the next block of Marshall Street. St. Paul's Episcopal Church at the southern corner of Fourth and Marshall Streets saw its first incarnation in 1855. The church grew, and in 1908 a new edifice was completed one block east at the northern corner of Cherry and Fourth Streets, directly around the corner from the First Presbyterian Church.

The next home of worship found its beginning not in the Forsyth Courthouse, but in a neighborhood school. Winston Church of Christ launched its campaign in 1890 with the leadership of evangelist R.W. Stancil. The church was renamed the First Christian Church and began its services in the north Winston Union Grove School. In 1891, a temporary building was constructed, and in 1898 a permanent brick sanctuary opened on this site. This church was located due west on Fourth Street from St. Paul's Episcopal Church. In today's landscape, the site is occupied by a Winston-Salem parking deck on the southern side of Fourth Street near the intersection of Spring Street. The church moved in 1922, and the Hebrew Beth Jacob congregation purchased this structure. Winston's growing industrial workforce helped to found First Christian and three other denominations between 1890 and 1893.

The second industrial affiliated church was Augsburg Lutheran. In 1891, Reverend William A. Lutz arrived in Winston behind many Lutheran workers who had come to this growing city for employment several years earlier. The 1895 edifice of the Augsburg Lutheran church sits on the corner of Fourth Street at Spruce Street. The third church of the working-class congregation was St. Leo's Catholic Church. The Roman Catholic order of St. Benedict had entered North Carolina in 1870. North Carolina was to be a missionary territory between 1870 and 1924. Benedictine missionaries arrived in Winston in 1886, and by 1891, a missionary church was built at Fourth Street and Brookstown Avenue.

Our final church on the tour of the four blue-collar churches from the early 1890s is Calvary Moravian. Home Moravian on Church Street in Salem was the first church mentioned. Earlier we learned Winston was intended to be a Moravian town and to be under complete brethren control. But this did not happen, thanks to Democratic businessmen and Methodist endurance. A Moravian church in the Winston landscape was very important to the Moravian belief and the influential Reverend Edward Rondthaler was up for the task. Beginning in 1888, he worked diligently to see Calvary Moravian established and the building completed in 1893, by which point Reverend Rondthaler had risen to Bishop Rondthaler. Bishop Rondthaler presided over pastoral duties from 1888 to

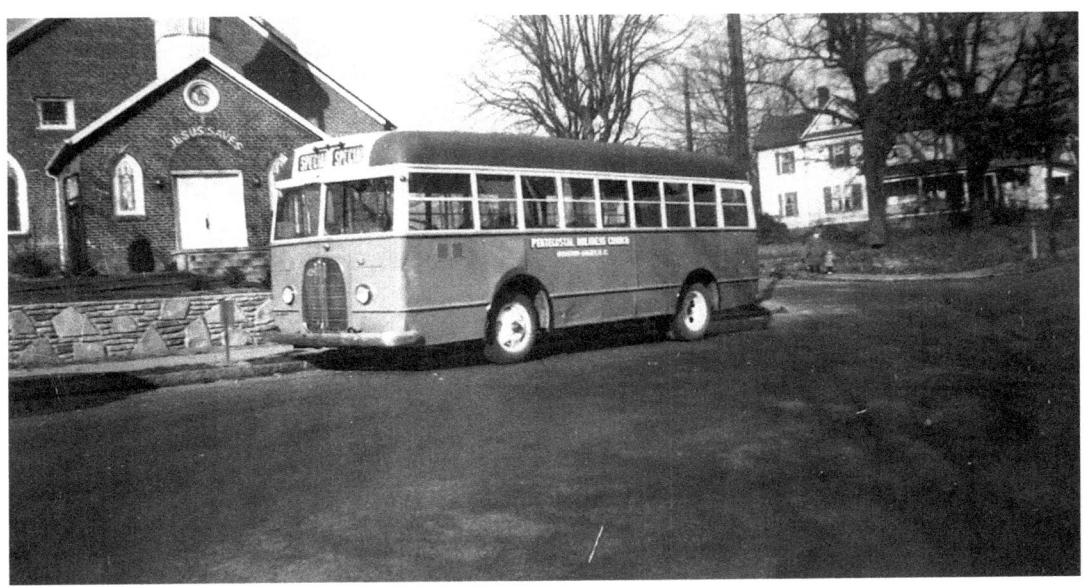

The Pentecostal Holiness bus awaits its passengers from their church at North Broad Street and Brookstown Avenue. The mansion house to the right was one of many that graced Broad Street between the West End and West Salem neighborhoods of 1880–1900. *Pentecostal Holiness Church Archives.*

1893. The congregation was fully organized on April 20, 1893, when direct Salem control was relinquished.

So far we have seen the strong connection between church and state, or God and country, through the establishment of the white industrialists and the white working-class churches in Salem and Winston. Now our journey will turn to the African American contributions to God and country. The beginnings of African American churches were found in Salem, or West Salem, to be more precise. Moravian, Methodist and Baptist preachers ministered to the African Americans in West Salem at the Krueser farm and the Paper Mill Settlement. Camp meetings were held in the early nineteenth century at the former Shuman plantation of Happy Hill. The creation of St. Phillips Church in 1822 brought a blow to Salem residents' Moravian belief of equality. Moravians had encountered the equality issue in regard to slavery with their exposure to the Quaker religion. Quakers relayed an emphatic "no" to the idea of enslaving any people. Moravians rationalized that slavery was not an acceptable practice because it allowed the slave owner to become lazy, which bred slothfulness, a sin. Perhaps if the Moravians had searched deeper into their faith, a firm no vote could have been obtained. But the town of Salem decided to compromise. Compromise was an early form of Jim Crowism, a separate but equal conclusion. The state had spoken and the church followed with the first segregated church, St. Phillips.

Segregation and the slavery issue found their way into Winston by a "splinter group" of the Methodists, a denomination called True Wesleyans, dating to 1842. They were a forbidden congregation in Winston. In 1847, abolitionist ministers from the sect came to Forsyth and Guilford Counties. In 1850, Adam Crooks and Jesse McBride, ministers of the True Wesleyans, were arrested in Salem for distributing literature opposed to slavery. In October 1850, the men were brought to court and the Moravian archives record the town's displeasure with them. "The preachers have come! The abolitionists are here! They ought to be lynched! They ought to be hung!" They were found guilty, but were released on bond. They were never seen in Winston again. The two ministers were not intimidated by the arrest and continued their crusade until they were run out of the state by angry mobs from Forsyth and Guilford Counties in 1851. If these events were not bad enough, the location where they occurred was worse. Winston's Forsyth County Courthouse was not complete when this event occurred, so the location of this melee was Salem Town Hall, which was a few blocks north of the center of the congregational town. Events similar to this occurred in Winston until the arrival of the event to end them all: the Civil War. Wars have a way of equalizing their participants. After the war and Reconstruction, the businesses, churches and everything else in town were bust. The prosperity of the African American church began to match the others. As their church grew, the African Americans' faith grew more. The strength of Jim Crow was also growing, and the history that followed for blacks and whites cast a shadow of indifference for both to face. "Separate but equal" were the benchmark words of Jim Crow. While this philosophy flowed throughout the South, Salem and Winston were always wrestling with this issue. Connection between God and country, along with its inseparable right of equality, seemed always at odds. The best way to discuss the black and white issue, the church and state issue and the Salem and Winston issue is by understanding the social order of all.

God and Country

The "social order" of Salem, Winston and eventually Winston-Salem has been shown to be rich in diversity. The diverse churches housed multitudes of denominations, both black and white. The governments of Salem and Winston had often been on different ideological pages with the Whig and Democratic Parties. Yet both cities were able to work together to form the Twin City of Winston-Salem. Social and orderly progression of the centuries culminated in a positive evolutionary outcome. The eighteenth century saw the arrival and founding of Salem. The nineteenth century saw the founding and development of Winston. The twentieth century bore the consolidated town of Winston-Salem. The societies of Winston and Salem were working toward consolidation long before it was officially achieved in 1913. Robert T. Gray of Winston said it best during a centennial celebration of the founding of the United States. On July 4, 1876, Gray wrote,

I speak of Salem and Winston as one place; would that I could speak of them under one name! They are one in identity of interest and future: the will of one is the good of the other, and whatever affects one injuriously will affect the other similarly. Am I venturing upon dangerous ground or taking a step too far in advance of public opinion and feeling when I express the desire and belief that the two towns will at some time not far distant, blight their troth, each to the other, and be united in the bonds of a happy union.

The greatest positive social change was in the growth of the churches of Winston and Salem after the Civil War. Denominations and their Sunday schools expanded throughout the two cities. By the 1890s, neighborhoods or suburban areas, as they were called then, began to appear. Churches and the city saw opportunities in the new neighborhoods of East Winston, North Winston, West End and Southside. The West Salem neighborhood had evolved from its nineteenth-century roots of farms and industry, and between 1880 and 1915 saw the development of West End, Washington Park (Southside), Granville Park and the largest of the suburban neighborhoods, Ardmore. Moravians, Methodists, Presbyterians, Episcopalians and Baptists, or as they are called by historians, the city's "first churches," organized and helped build the churches of these suburban neighborhoods. The largest and strongest church of Winston was Centenary Methodist Church, which was the grandfather of the Methodist church movement in Winston and helped to organize all Methodist congregations from 1884 to 1930. The Methodist Church created the Burkhead congregations in 1886 at 1010 North Liberty Street and Fifteenth and English Streets in North Winston. Other new churches were Groves Methodist Episcopal in East Winston at East Fourth and Woodlawn Streets, 1890; Green Street Methodist in West Salem at South Poplar Street, 1902; and Ardmore Methodist in Ardmore on West Academy Street, 1924. There were also the congregations of Central Terrace, 1900; Hanes Methodist, 1915; Hiatt Methodist, 1922; and Mount Olivet Methodist, 1925. First Baptist Church helped to create Broad Street Baptist in the West End neighborhood, 1889; Salem Baptist in West Salem, 1900; Southside Baptist on Sprague Street; and North Winston Baptist. First Presbyterian assisted in the founding of South Minster, 1912; Reynolda, 1915; and Covenant, 1947. St. Paul's Episcopal was involved in the creation of St. Stephen's, St. Timothy's and St. Anne's. Augsburg Lutheran sponsored Christ Church, 1957; and Epiphany, 1962. Salem Home Moravian assisted in the founding of Calvary,

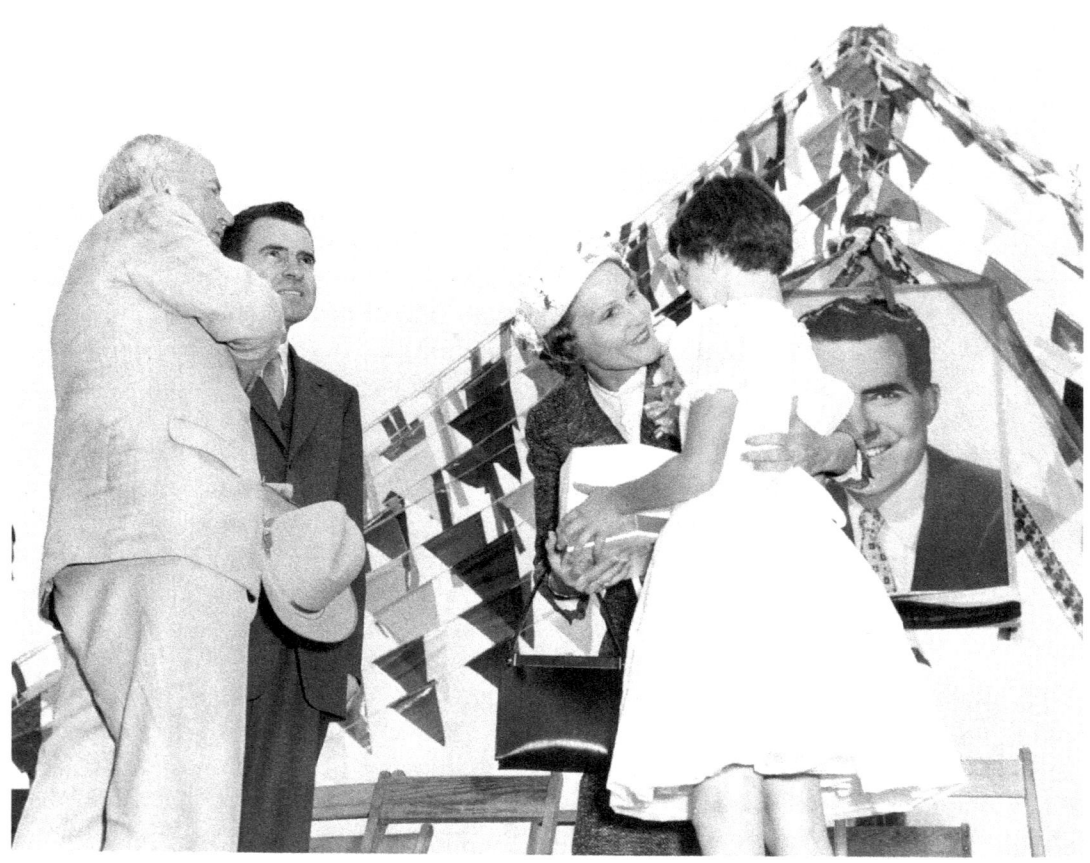

Celebration and public officials helped to grow the Twin City. A young Richard and Patricia Nixon are in attendance.

1893; Fairview in North Winston, 1895; Trinity in Southside, 1886; Christ Moravian in West Salem, 1896; and Fries Memorial, 1914.

    The 1920s ushered in an era of churches that crossed the line with a phrase that defined modern business, government and American economics: the all-American ideal of free enterprise. One may ask, how can a church be connected with a state of free enterprise? Centenary Methodist Church was that church. Competition between churches in Salem had existed since the first encounter between members of Moravian congregations and Methodist congregations. In 1909, a handful of Centenary elders and 135 members met in the West End Graded School, formerly the Winston Graded School before the founding of the West End neighborhood, to form the West End Methodist Church. In 1913, the members had designed and built the most expensive and uniquely designed church building in Winston. The neighborhood grew and many members were attracted to this unique modern structure. When West End Methodist became the largest Methodist church in Winston in 1925, a rivalry ensued with Centenary Church to draw members, establishing this period of church free enterprise.

God and Country

The end of the Roaring Twenties saw the two churches return to their roots and join to create the largest and most expensive church building in the Twin City's history, Centenary United Methodist Church on Fifth Street, in 1930. West Fifth Street had become the location of large cathedral-style churches. Joining the new Centenary Church were the new First Baptist Church and Augsburg Lutheran Church. The Great Depression saw a decline in church building as well as attendance. This trend continued until after World War II. The "social order" continued even with a loss of church members. The city's churches were spurred on with the New Freedom programs of President Woodrow Wilson. Social reform programs were being created by churches to help the increasing industrial workforce arriving to Winston-Salem. Between 1910 and 1920, Winston-Salem's population had more than doubled from 22,960 to 48,395. In 1916, Winston-Salem was honored with the award of being the farthest inland port of entry for trade. Since the nearest coastline was several hundred miles away, this acclaim proved the Twin City was progressing wonderfully and helped the city to become the most populated in the state.

The growth of the diversified denominations between 1930 and 1966 is reflected in the following list. These churches included both black and white members.

Denomination	1930	1966
Baptist	44	82
Christian	12	20
Christian Alliance	1	1
Christian Science	1	2
Episcopal	2	3
Friends	1	1
Greek Orthodox	1	1
Hebrew	1	2
Holiness	9	36
Lutheran	3	4
Methodist	25	26
Moravian	12	16
Presbyterian	7	11
Reformed	2	1
Roman Catholic	1	4
Seventh Day Adventist	1	1

Jehovah's Witness, Nazarene, Unitarian and Mormon denominations all arrived after 1950, with one congregation.

God and country were an awesome pair in early Winston and Salem. The balance between these two subjects set the stage for all that was to come in our city, as well as our state and country. Contributions from church and state combined to support charitable and government projects to better the city and its people.

As we continue our journey of the history of the Twin City, we will examine the people, the jobs they do and their social order. What we will find, rather than the melancholic "Winston is dead" type of expressions that were prevalent in the 1970s landscape, is a city of prominence.

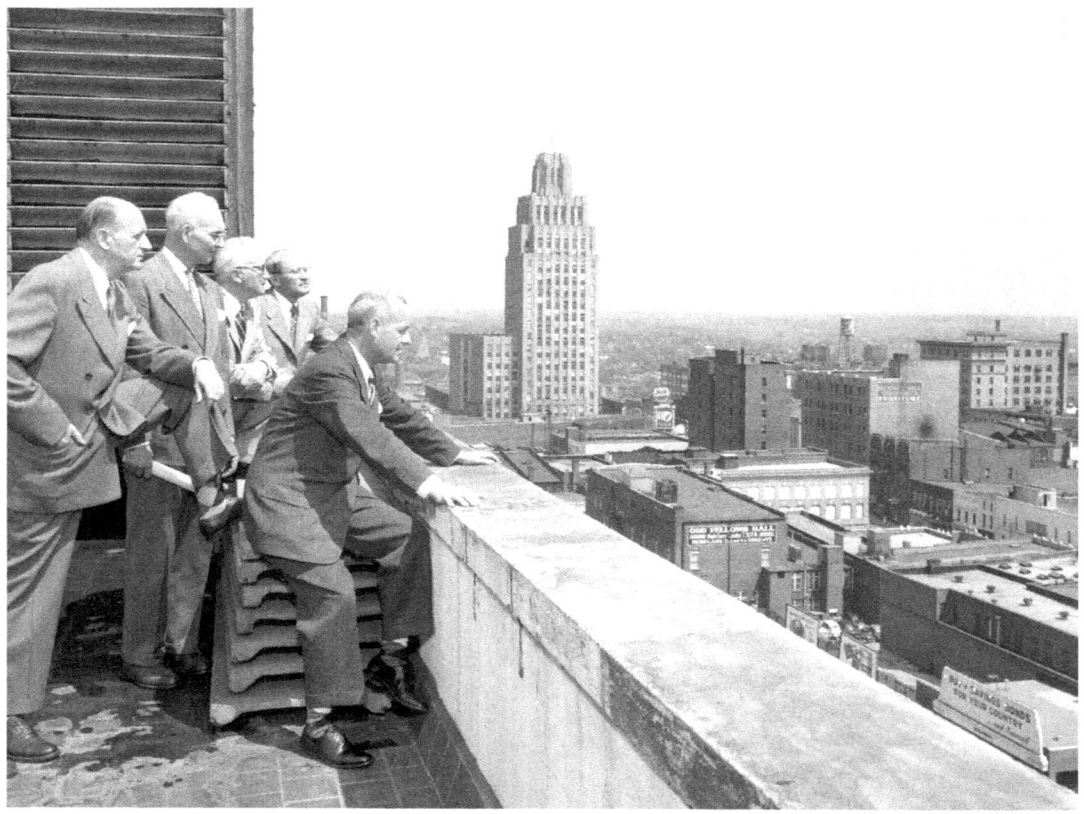

Community leaders and businessmen observe their city from the top of the Robert E. Lee Hotel, circa 1950s. Trade Street and Fourth Street is below.

CHAPTER 3.

The Jobs We Do

Our search for the jobs of Winston-Salem returns us to the roots of the Moravian town of Bethabara. With the arrival of the Moravians to Bethabara, church authorities had given the inhabitants self-supporting and communal instructions in the workings of the settlement. Moravian archives state it clearly: "Tilling of the soil and farming leads to self-sufficiency so that as soon as possible we may be able to eat our own bread." Fifteen years later, the brethren of Bethabara had moved beyond farming, which was still the principle wage earner of the vast number of Piedmont North Carolina residents, to the beginning of the main settlement town, Salem. Crafts, trade and industry were to be Salem's calling. Frederick William Marshall, the Moravian leader, wrote in 1765, and documented in the archives, "This town, Salem, is not designed for farmers, but for those with the trades."

The agriculture business was confined to the outlying Moravian settlements that surrounded the town of Salem. The direct agriculture interest of the town itself was planned in West Salem. Farmers residing in West Salem were of German stock, who were known to be the best farmers in the colony. Visitors and aussenseiter (outsiders) to the farms in West Salem and the surrounding settlements were impressed by the residents' agricultural abilities and stated such in the Moravian archives: "The thrifty, industrious and frugal brethren was honed by habit and training. Their diligence in agriculture is recognized by their Piedmont neighbors; however, imitated by few." The archive records continue, "The moment I, Elkanah Watson, touched the boundary of the Moravians, I noticed a marked and most favorable change in the appearance of buildings and farms; and even the cattle seemed larger, and in better condition. Here, in combined and well-directed effort, all put shoulders to the wheel, which apparently moves on oily springs." The West Salem outlots of farms produced crops, vegetables and herds. Livestock was raised for food, along with skins that could be traded. Grain, the first crop planted, was a staple for bread, followed by wheat and rye as the brethren's taste expanded. As the brewery business grew, the rye was used more in distillery than for bread. Gardens were planted with apple, peach and berry orchards throughout the western tract. These agricultural businesses continued until the Civil War period. Dried berry interest was one of the few that survived the war and Reconstruction.

The industries and farms that aided the congregational town of Salem, which was under construction, depended on the craftsmen who had come to Bethabara. Their unique skills had been gathered by Moravian elders for the purpose of constructing the permanent settlement. In 1753, the skilled craftsmen consisted of weavers, brick masons, millers, brewers, leather makers, gunsmiths, potters, ironworkers and tanners. The earliest craftsmen to arrive were Gottfried Praezel and John Birkhead, both of whom were premier weavers. Brother Praezel set his loom to weave cloth outright and is credited with beginning the first textile movement in North Carolina, in 1766. The same year, Jacob Mueller founded Salem's first industry, a brick yard. The brick yard had been assisted in its infancy by Wachovia's master mason, Melchior Rasp.

The early troop continued with Gens Schmidt, an ironworker; Nils Peterson, a brewer; Jacob Steiner, a miller; and Charles Holder, a saddle and leather maker. Valentine Beck was the first gunsmith. He worked between Bethabara and Salem until settling in Salem in 1772. The pottery business (founded in 1768) and the tannery business (founded in 1769) were already underway by that time. Gottfried Aust, a renowned Moravian potter known throughout Pennsylvania and Germany, opened shop in 1771. Brother Aust's pottery endeavor grew very quickly, thanks to his expertise and the abundance of yellow clay in the surrounding creeks of East and West Salem. Salem Pottery, in its seventy-five years of existence, had only three master potters: Brother Aust, Rudolf Christ and John Frederick Holland. Brother Holder settled in his trade as an expert saddle maker. This allowed Christian Frietz, who arrived from Germany in 1772, to specialize in leather gloves and other leather goods for the home. Brother Frietz expanded the leather business to include "dressed deer skins," which were a premium product of early Salem. With its export of these skins to Charleston, South Carolina, Salem's profit from this product allowed the town to purchase other products that could not be made or grown locally.

The tradesmen and craftsmen were applying their trades successfully and the profit margins were impressive as well. The Aufseher Collegium, detailed in Chapter 2, controlled all manufacturers. The collegium understood that strict control of the Salem craftsmen in the numbers of available "master-workmen" was imperative in continuing the craftsmen's monopolies. These "master-workmen" positions were limited and the numbers were set by the collegium. If others in the craftsmen positions arrived or were trained later, they were labeled as "journeymen" to their appointed craft or trade. Journeymen waited to be called only if there was an opening as "master-workmen" positions came available. Aufseher Collegium concluded the practice and assured there was no overproduction of said product.

In 1772, the system and the economic profit in Salem were well underway. That year, upon arrival to Salem, Matthew Miksch appeared to have no chance in the congregational town of craftsmen. His profession (the growing of smoking tobacco and snuff) was labeled by the Aufseher Collegium as having no need in the township. Brother Miksch decided to stay in the town anyway. He purchased a small house on Main Street and applied his craft, hoping that he would be able to create a market for his product. His product survived and became the pioneer of the National Tobacco Industry, which followed one hundred years later.

In 1773, Salem was recognized as an industrial center in the Carolina wilderness. The craftsmen began displaying signs on their businesses, which showed truly the business

The Jobs We Do

section of Salem had arrived. In 1774, the pottery, tannery, brick yard and community grist and flour mill shared the stage with new arrivals: a bakery, slaughterhouse and a small brewery by the Single Brothers. Also in 1774, the first community store was breaking ground, designed in a modern architectural style of uncut stone covered with plaster. Salem not only was an industrial center in the wilderness, but it also boasted a large central store selling various items, which was normally found only in larger coastal towns. Under the watchful eye of the collegium, the community store handled home-produced goods and imported ones. The customer base doubled, with individuals coming from miles away to trade at the store.

The Revolutionary War was on the horizon for the colonies; however, the town was enjoying the fruits of its hard work and sacrifice, with an abundance of jobs for its citizens. Within ten years of Salem's founding in 1766, the town had grown significantly. The borders of the congregational town were two streets running north to south, Church and

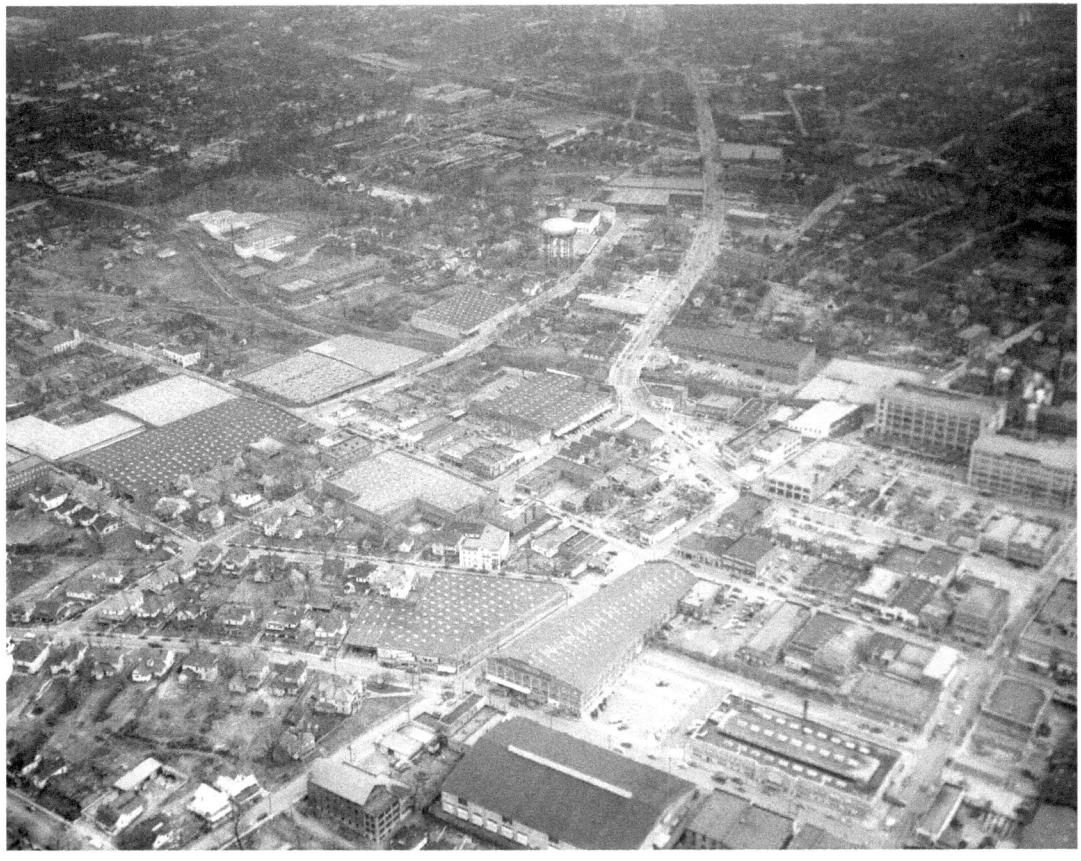

King Tobacco, King Cotton and downtown neighborhoods' workers helped tobacco and textiles to become kings in the Twin City. The streets surrounding the photo are North Main Street, Cherry Street, Trade Street and Liberty Street, circa 1950.

Main Streets. Intersecting streets running east to west were Maiden Lane (at the north end of town) and Fish Alley (between Main Street and the dead-end road that later was called Salt Street. Salt Street was developed and named for the salt business that was carried out in this area of town). The next connecting street between Church and Main Streets was Bank Street, which was farther south. South of Bank Street, connecting Church to Main Street and the dead end, was Shallowford Street. Farther south, connecting Church to Main Street, was West Street followed by Blum Street. Interestingly, after 240 years, the only name change of these early streets is that Shallowford Street was changed to Academy Street.

The following homes were extant at the outbreak of the Revolutionary War. The first house built (in 1766) was on the western side of Main near Bank Street. The second house (1767), the only two-story house that was built, sat at the western corner of Main and Bank Streets, beside the first house. The third (1767), the fourth (1768) and the fifth (1768) were built consecutively beside the first house, proceeding north. The sixth building was the pottery business (1768) at the western corner of Main Street and Fish Alley. The Schmit house and blacksmith shop (1768) was the farthest northern building in Salem. From the blacksmith shop we do an about-face and head south on Main Street. Arriving at the corner of Main and Bank Streets, the land on the eastern side of Main Street is empty of structures. This land was the original square of the town (1766). Borders of the square were Main, Bank, Church and Shallowford Streets. This square was replaced by the current square of today because the original one was too "high of ground" for proper water flow of the Salem Water System. Continuing our journey on Main Street, we find two buildings on the eastern side of Main Street near the corner of Shallowford. First is the Miksch Tobacco Shop (1771), and next door the Triebel house (1775). As we cross Shallowford on Main Street, we find on the western end the new square (1768) and on the western side of Main Street the Single Brothers' house (1769) and the Brothers' workshop (1771) directly behind it. South of the Single Brothers' on Main Street are the community store (1775) and the Anna Catherine house (1772), both of which are across the street from West Street. The most southern structure on Main Street was the Tavern (1784). The Gemeinhaus (1771) was on the eastern side of Church Street at Shallowford Street. The only other entity on Church Street was at the intersection of Maiden Lane and Church Street. This was the entrance to the Moravian cemetery, God's Acre (1771).

The sparse structures of the early town blossomed into a bustling township. The cornerstone of the industrial interest of the growing town was found in the Single Brothers' enterprises. Most of the businesses were confined to the Single Brothers' house and the Single Brothers' workshop. While producing goods for the congregational town, the Single Brothers also supplied the town with needed farmers, tradesmen and outside help. The schooling that was provided in these two buildings could be compared to that in modern-day technical and agricultural universities. The work and teachings of the Single Brothers extended to the outlying western neighborhood of farms and industry. West Salem was home to the Single Brothers' brewery and distillery, along with the slaughterhouse (along Academy Street between Salem bypass and Marshall Street, in today's landscape). Farther west of these industrial sites were the Single Brothers' farms. Single Sisters managed and worked the Single Sisters' gardens and apple and peach orchards to the northwest of the Single Brothers' farm in West

The Jobs We Do

Salem. In today's landscape, the terraced hills along Poplar and Broad Streets, north to First Street, were home to these groves and orchards. More farms and orchards extended along Academy to Granville Drive.

The first water system was controlled by the Single Brothers. In 1778, the central water system that made up the Moravians' water source was state-of-the-art and years ahead of any other town that existed in the western parts of the colonies. This was observed by President Washington himself on his visit to Salem in 1791. The beginning of the water system was located on modern-day Poplar above Brookstown Avenue. Another extension of the system was located on Second Street along the creek of Shady Boulevard to First Street. Both sites are part of the Holly Avenue historic district today. The original land existed in West Salem until it was divided between Winston and Salem in 1849. First Street was the dividing line of the two towns.

The Single Brothers' house was home to the future of Salem. Beginning at age fourteen, the boys were separated into apprenticeship positions after being assessed by the Single Brothers' elders. If the boys demonstrated high intellectual abilities, they were enrolled at the Moravian boarding school in Nazareth, Pennsylvania. At the completion of their training in Pennsylvania, these boys were awarded positions as ministers, lawyers, merchants and teachers throughout the congregation. However, most boys moved into their apprenticeship under the control of "masters," continuing a system that had been practiced in Europe for hundreds of years. The masters became just that in respect to control of the lads' lives. The masters' authority usurped that of the boys' own parents. This rule was not without some opposition from the parents. Congregational elders were quick to remind parents of the importance of masters and apprenticeships if the boys and their families wished to keep favor with the congregation and residence in the town. Also, the parents were required to give their children sums of money for clothing. A strict dress code by the masters came with a label: "No exceptions would be made." Upon completion of their apprenticeships, the young men began work in different shops of the business district as journeymen. Throughout these apprenticeships and journeymen years they were required to live at the Single Brothers' house as well as work there. Men had to apply to the elders in order to set up shop for themselves later.

The young men applied their trades with dedication, reverence and patience. Each trade shop was approached with the utmost respect. Trade shops in the Single Brothers' house consisted of the blue dyer shop, the joiner's shop, the tailor's shop and the turner's shop. The blue dyer shop received its name from the imported indigo plant grown in South Carolina. The joiner's shop contributed woodworking skills for skilled carpenters and cabinetmakers. The tailor's shop was one of the busiest, due to the interest of the customers who wanted the latest colonial fashions. The turner's shop found young men applying their trade on lathes. These crafts were supplements of the joiners' skills in carpentry and cabinetmaking.

Three craftsmen's workshops that were not physically located in the Single Brothers' establishments were the potter's shop, the tin and pewter shop and the weaver's shop. The potter's profession was carried out two blocks north of the Single Brothers' house. The tin and pewter business was carried out by other craftsmen in the town. For example, three generations of the Reich family molded and designed an array of tin and pewter products. From cookie cutters and candle molds to buckets, pots and pans and pipes, the Reichs covered the gambit of merchandise. The Reich family is an important part of the interpretive history of Old Salem. Several Reich family members were shoemakers as well. The Reich family extended into the West Salem neighborhood with a shoemaker's shop and residence located in the 600 block of South Poplar Street. John Reich purchased the John Ackerman home in 1840 and set up shop there. The shoemaker's shop, with later additions, is found behind the Ackerman house at 608 South Poplar Street. The Reichs' house and shop are currently in the Ruff family's possession. The home is owned by Bobbie Ruff and her business, B&B Wood Valley Art Shop, occupies the former shoemaker's shop. The weaver began in Salem, occupying the first house of Salem (built in 1766). The first weaver, Brother Gottfried Praezel, armed with his simple four-harness loom, created the simplest of weaves as well as intricate patterns and weaves.

Salem's economic success was not limited to the men of the community; women played key roles as well. Single Sisters, while residing at the Gemeinhaus, ran a school for girls, did laundry and tilled gardens. Vegetables and the laundry business were for personal, rather than commercial, use. Married sisters ran their own households with daily cooking, cleaning, sewing and mending and child rearing. Chores included meal preparation, manufacturing candles, lye making and soap making. Summer brought gardening to the forefront, along with the canning of fruits and vegetables. Women worked alongside the men at harvest time in the fall with haying and harvesting of grain. Single and married women were weavers in their own right. As children, they learned to sew and spin, and by the time they were teenagers they were able to make their own clothes. The laundry business proved the most lucrative of the early business ventures of Salem. The Single Sisters' Choir spearheaded its success into a major enterprise. Often the weaving and laundry business of the women saved the men's business interest at times when the craftsmen's enterprises were failing. Women also became educators alongside their male counterparts. The belief in educating all brothers and sisters was a benchmark rule of the founding Moravians from the town's very beginning.

By the early 1770s, the Moravians had branched out into furniture making due to the bountiful regions of forests in the Salem tract. The Revolutionary War was an economic disaster for most early American towns. North Carolina stores and shops, empty of merchandise because of the war, closed permanently. Adding to this mix the unstable currency, lack of raw materials and the hazards of transporting goods, many businessmen were left scratching their heads in disgust. When most of the North Carolina businessmen were throwing up their hands and calling it quits, the Moravians were taking business to another level. Salem's business manager, Brother Traugott Bagge, organized a group in Salem to rally North Carolina's new government and supply them and the rest of the American army with needed supplies to fuel their military mission. Brother Bagge became known as a "supply officer for the troops."

Salem Tavern also played an important part in Salem's economic successes. Moravians were able to balance the negative effects of a tavern of outsider influences with the positive fact that the business brought travelers to the town to purchase from the Salem craftsmen and merchants. The lodging and food brought more revenue. The Revolutionary War had brought the tavern new customers in the form of soldiers, both American and British. Salem

The Jobs We Do

became a post town for future settlements to the western United States and the tavern served many of those pioneers passing through.

Industry in West Salem progressed in 1791 with the opening of Salem's first paper mill, located on Peters Creek near the intersection of West Academy and Peters Creek Parkway. The tract became known as the Paper Mill Settlement, with additions of a paper mill pond, a rock and granite quarry and a sawmill, which were encompassed in the town lot. Farms, foresting and mills extended outside the town lot. Paper Mill Settlement lasted for more than eighty years.

Other trades arrived in Salem at the beginning of the nineteenth century. Often rivalries between craftsmen sprang up despite the attempt of the Moravian elders to keep this from occurring. Johahamn Ludwig Eberhard arrived from Germany to apply his trade as a clockmaker and silversmith. A young gunsmith apprentice, John Vogler, who had taught under his uncle Christoph in 1802, decided to expand his skills into clock making and silver smithing as well. The Vogler name became synonymous with the family's crafts throughout the nineteenth century. Another Moravian family that

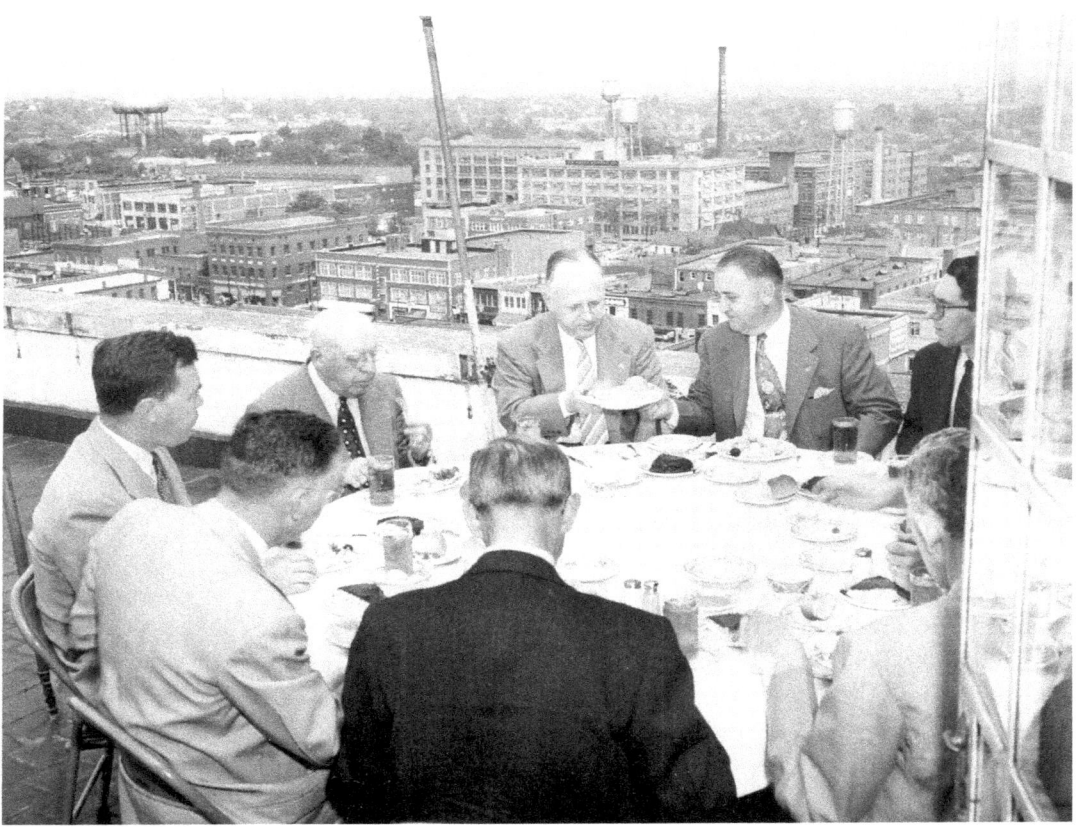

The meals served in Salem Tavern circa 1800 were enjoyed by dignitaries, settlers and government officials. Over 150 years later, this type of gathering is carried out on the roof of the Robert E. Lee Hotel. This scene overlooks the downtown area.

served the community for generations in the bakery business was the Winklers. The bakery business had been a challenge for the eighteenth-century community. The Single Brothers operated the town bakery and the Single Sisters had to purchase their bread from them—unchaperoned! In order to avoid this impropriety, an independent business had to be created immediately. After an unsuccessful baking business was started by Brother Thomas Butner, who became a major farmer and shoemaker in West Salem, the reins were passed to Christian Winkler in 1808. The Winkler family worked the bakery for more than 115 years, until 1926. The bakery has been restored to those earliest of years and sells its delicious wares as well.

John Vogler took the reins in becoming one of three individuals to begin a new generation of church and business leaders. Lewis David de Schweintz, administrator of Wachovia, and Dr. Samuel Vierling were the other two. These brethren had huge shoes to fill with the passing of Brother Bagge in 1800 and Frederick William Marshall in 1802. With this change in leadership, the stage had been set for more progressive ideas that manifested themselves in Salem's congregational and business world. New leaders, along with the likes of the progressive Schober family, initiated profound changes in the first half of the nineteenth century.

The Lot was eliminated and more choices were able to be made by individuals, and in 1823 the Single Brothers ended their choir house and communal business ventures. Competition was creeping into the town from outside businesses, and the Single Brothers' complex closed. The Single Brothers' house reopened shortly afterward as a traditional school. Brothers who left the Single Brothers' complex after its closing branched out into the neighborhood with small shops and houses. Workshops presented in today's Old Salem landscape are indicative of this time period of the 1820s and 1830s. By the middle of the nineteenth century, the mill had the title of "largest gristmill in Forsyth County." It prospered and existed into the twentieth century before burning in the early 1900s. The location of the mill in today's landscape was near the intersection of West Salem Avenue and South Broad, in the West Salem historic district. This spot intersects with the ongoing Southeast Gateway Project.

A Salem newspaper reported in alphabetical order the businesses of 1835: "Carriage makers, Meinung and Nissen Wagon Works, Chair manufacturing, two clock makers, several confectionaries, copperware producers, cotton manufacturing, three gunsmiths, three hatters, several joiners, a paper mill, two shoemakers, tinsmiths, tobacco industry, and toy makers." The Industrial Revolution had arrived in Salem. The technology that came with it helped to create the industry, along with the large complexes to house them. Three of these enterprises continued the dominance of Salem and later Winston as major national players in the nation's commerce undertakings. Cotton, tobacco and wagon making moved to the top of the list. American dominance in world economics had arrived.

King Cotton arrived on the scene in Salem in 1837. To tell Salem's cotton mill story, we must begin by returning to the eighteenth century. Textiles in West Salem were pioneered long before the mill concept was born. One such example was drawn from the Moravian archives and was recorded in the 1949 publication *Forsyth: The History of a County on the March* by Adelaide Fries. The archives state, "In 1789, a fulling mill was constructed in Salem by Abraham Loesch so the cloth could be properly shrunk and

The Jobs We Do

thickened. An insufficient water supply at the creek where he had located below Salem Hill forced Loesch to move his operation some two miles from the town on Brushy Creek." The original location of Loesch's mill was on Tanners Run Creek next to the new Old Salem's Visitors' Center. The moved mill, two miles farther west, was in the restored Langenhour Mill located on Salem Creek at Silas Creek. Another example was the Van Zevely Wool-Carding business (begun in 1805), located on the Petersbach (Peters Creek today) at the northwest side of West Salem near the present Hanes Park section of town. Van Zevely's homeplace (1810) was moved from this area in the 1970s to the corner of Fourth and Summit Streets. It was restored and now exists as the Zevely House Restaurant. The wool carding establishment was documented in many history books as a predecessor of the textile industry. The function of the wool carding trade can be defined in the following way: a metal comb or wire brush (card) for raising the nap on cloth, thus disentangling the fibers of wool or cotton to make ready for the spinning process. This was a simple but effective procedure.

The first venture for a textile mill in Salem came about in 1836. Originally the Moravians were hesitant to agree to allow such an establishment in the town, as they believed their way of life could be compromised with such a business. Unfortunately, the town's crafts and trade operations were not doing well financially, and the 15 to 20 percent profit by other textile mill ventures was enticing. Moravian hierarchy agreed to the venture, but only after strict control by Moravian elders was guaranteed over the mill operation. Also of note, in 1836, the Moravians allowed residents in Salem to only lease land. The church owned all the land in Salem, making Moravian control of land uncompromising. Life in Salem's first textile mill, the Salem Manufacturing Company, brought a new livelihood to West Salem. Of historical significance, the mill was the first steam-powered wool carding business in North Carolina. Remnants of the 1836 edifice are ingrained with the Brookstown Mill Complex on Brookstown Avenue below Cherry Street. Historians have pointed out in the past that West Salem was never a mill town; however, when one draws together West Salem's long history, it is clear that a "mill time" was present.

In the 1830s, farms in the Piedmont of North Carolina were devastated by drought, depression and failing crops. Many people from Stokes, Guilford and Davidson Counties came to the mill looking for steady pay and work. The workers who were hired were paid low wages with very harsh working conditions. These conditions proved inconvenient, but were tolerable due to the tough conditions the workers had came from back on their farms. Unfortunately, what the workers found intolerable and unworkable were the Moravian restrictions on religion and lifestyle forced on them after working hours. Moravians knew the background of their millworkers; however, they continued to control the workers constantly as if the workers were Moravians. This was a big mistake that assisted in the failure of Salem's first textile mill. Salem Manufacturing Company closed in 1849, after several declining years. The next textile venture was much more successful.

The Civil War brought havoc and chaos to the South. Reconstruction ushered in a depressive period until the boom of the 1880s. During Reconstruction, a massive rebirth of commerce and business had begun. Winston and Salem experienced the horrors of war as much as all their fellow Southerners. Scores of young men were killed in battle. Scores of others perished by sickness and squalor. The American Revolution had crippled the Salemites, but the Civil War was destroying it. Added to the loss of young men were once thriving factories and businesses. Shortage of supplies and the near complete depreciation of Confederate currency distributed to the Winstonions and Salemites a one-two punch. The Bank of Cape Fear perished, along with its branch in Salem, due to the worthless Confederate money. The Vogler business, a solid firm in Salem that was involved in clock making, jewelry and silverware business, was nearly destroyed. Winston and Salem may have been down; however, the Moravian faith and will to survive were not.

Salem had founded Winston in 1849, and by the 1870s the two towns had fought back financially, with the towns' residents working together for new-found success. The chance of Winston-Salem, one city, was beginning to be heard. Rebirth had begun with an unlikely pair—fruits and berries. These two foods were cultivated from the very beginning of Salem. With plentiful Salem crops and a Winston business called Pfohl and Stockton, the drying and shipping of fruits and berries had become very profitable. Pfohl and Stockton sold an astounding $50,000 a year in dried fruit. This industry became the switch that jumpstarted the Winston-Salem economy of the late nineteenth century.

After the Reconstruction period, the South, especially North Carolina, began to see a return to industry and commerce. King Tobacco was emerging, as were the mills. Textile mills grew largely due to the survival of the Fries Mills. Reverend Edward Rondthaler from the Home Moravian Church explains it best in his memoirs:

> *During 1881 our Salem Community has lived in quiet and has been favored with a fair degree of prosperity. We have persevered from accidents by fire and other causes. Improvement of our streets has continued and various new buildings have been put up. Among these the most notable, has been the completion of the Arista Cotton Mill erected by the firm of Mess. F&H Fries. The new building stands in a prominent and favorable location, is 160 feet x 70 feet, three-stories high with two extensive wings of two stories each. The edifice is brick-covered with tin and is built in the most substantial manner. It is said to be along with the Salem Woolen Mills the only manufacturer in the South lighted with electric light. Cotton, wool, iron, building and flouring establishments of our place have enjoyed a prosperous year and we may look forward with a fair degree of insurance into Salem's future as a town of varied manufacturing industries.*

Much like his relatives before him, Henry W. Fries built the Arista Cotton Mill in 1880. The Fries family continued its next generation of textile mills. At a cost of $125,000, the Arista Mill was constructed based on plans of the leading New England cotton mills. For the first time in Southern history, a cotton mill was lighted by electricity. Adding electricity helped Arista to produce cotton cloth in very large quantities. In the booming growth of the 1880s, the timing of this production was a welcome commodity to the city and the state. Also, the 1840 Fries Woolen Mill had taken its business to another level by pioneering the use of its gas works into its operation. Arista did the same with electricity. Between the two companies, they employed 240 workers.

The Jobs We Do

The twentieth century had dawned, and King Tobacco saw much growth in the first part of the 1900s. However, by 1903, the wealth and popularity of tobacco took a back seat to manufacturing. Cotton, iron, wool, flour, furniture, knitting and wagon making were the industries of the hour. The knitting industry, already the largest of its kind in the state, had expanded in the West Salem landscape through the building of the Carolina Knitting Mills on Brookstown Avenue. The cotton mills of Arista and its offspring, Southside Mills, were consolidated and were in the process of being enlarged.

The year 1904 brought yet another industry to West Salem. Wachovia Knitting Mills, a large, two-story brick building, had been constructed at the corner of Marshall and Wachovia Streets. By 1905, Wachovia Knitting Mills merged with the Maline Mills, keeping the name of Maline Mills. The mill expanded and doubled its size at the corner of Wachovia and Marshall Streets.

The last expansion of the textile mills was with Indera Mills in 1914, which was organized as a partnership between Francis L. Fries and his nephew, W. Ledourx Siewers. The name Indera came from an Indian princess whom Fries had met in Egypt in 1907. The princess must have made an impression on Fries. Indera Mills began small, with only seven employees, and rented space from Maline Mills. The company produced knee and elbow warmers and knitted slips. By 1925, Maline Mills had disappeared and Indera was growing and expanding. Indera Mills had taken over the entire building. Adapting to the demands of customers, Indera added rayon bloomers to its line in the 1920s and knitted swimsuits in the 1930s. The mill's brand name of Cold Pruf and Indera was known nationally, and the Indera Mill survived into the late 1990s. Mills of West Salem never achieved the status of the Hanes textile dynasty, although one should agree that from 1836 until the 1990s, over 150 years, West Salem textile mills held their own. West Salem mill time had been very successful.

The tobacco industry had its earliest beginnings in 1850, after the founding of Winston. The industry had died down in Salem after tobacco shops with a retail base lost ground. Plug and chewing tobacco were grown by James E. Ogburn four miles north of Winston. The Ogburn Station area, north of Winston, is named for this early tobacco pioneer family. Other tobacco interests began on the outskirts of Forsyth County. The tobacco industry gained much strength and variety after the Civil War.

With the dawn of the 1870s, the promises of a Twin City, Winston-Salem, was on the horizon, fueled by textiles and King Tobacco. With the war and Reconstruction behind it, Winston arrived at 1870 with its first tobacco business. Major Hamilton Scales opened Winston's first chewing tobacco factory in an old carriage house on Liberty Street. Fire had been lit and the demand for tobacco products was raging. In 1872, Major Thomas Brown opened his business in an old reconstructed stable not far from the Scales establishment on Liberty Street. Also in February 1872, which marked the one hundredth anniversary of the founding of Matthew Miksch's Snuff and Tobacco shop in Salem, the horn sounded for the first auction sale of leaf tobacco in the Piedmont. Tobacco production started running at its beginning and never looked back.

The 1860s had seen a loner tobacco man, James Ogburn, farming ten to twenty thousand pounds of plug at his home. By 1878, the tobacco factories and warehouses had grown like weeds and now totaled more than eight million pounds of plug. The period

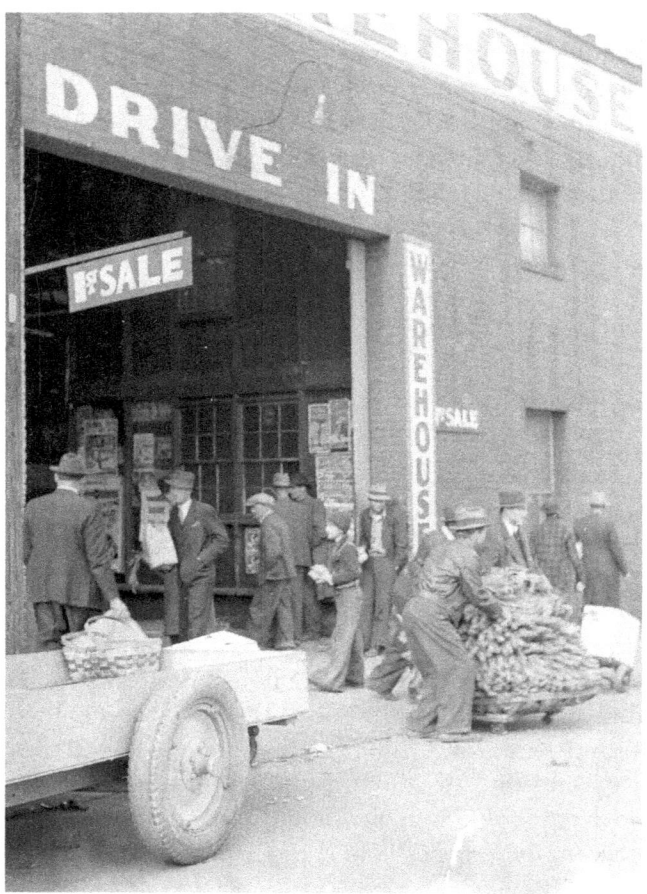

Trade Street was the business center of the tobacco market. The warehouses, auction houses and spectators participated in a carnival atmosphere unmatched in any other business venture in the Twin City, circa 1938.

from 1870 to 1878 also established the tobacco magnates who built Winston into the economic giant of the twenty-first century. Major Brown was joined by John W. Alspaugh and A.B. Gorrell to build a new warehouse on Church Street. This warehouse became the premier auction house of its time. History was made here with the first tobacco fair. In 2007, the Dixie Classic fair celebrated its 125th anniversary arriving from its humble beginnings on Church Street.

Pleasant H. and John Wesley Hanes also arrived to Winston in 1872. The Hanes brothers made a solid impact on the tobacco industry, but their involvement with textiles was known throughout the world. T.L. Vaughn and William A. Lash Jr. arrived in 1873. Also in 1873, the Planters and Piedmont warehouses served as mainstays in the city. In 1874, the future king of King Tobacco arrived. Richard Joshua Reynolds presented himself humbly with a small two-story factory that was no larger than a tennis court. The "little red factory" was its name. W.L. and R.D. Brown of Davie County arrived in 1876. Brown and Brother was their factory, and by 1878 they had the largest factory in Winston. By 1890, there were thirty-one tobacco establishments in Winston and Salem.

The Jobs We Do

In 1895, the Reynolds Tobacco Company was awarded first place for chewing tobacco in a national contest at the Cotton States and International Exposition in Atlanta. Old-timers boasted that "tobacco was not only King in Winston and Salem, but it tasted good as well."

By the 1890s and for the next three decades, the most important economic boom time of Winston and Salem's history was realized. The "New South," as coined by Henry Woodfin Gradey—editor of the *Atlantic Constitution* in 1887—so rightly typified the emerging business environment. The South saw new success in the abandonment of one-crop or one-business dependency. Variety was becoming the spice of life for Southern businessmen. Textiles, foundries, furniture and tobacco were a few of the many enterprises that emerged in this thirty-year period. The economic environment was perfect. Banks were strong for investment, the railroads were running successfully, the tax rolls had grown substantially and an abundant labor force and consumer base topped the scales. Steam and electrical power boosted the country into an emerging technological world.

Tobacco was combined with new technology to create the first cigarette machine, patented in 1880. Within ten years this technology was improved on by a Brooklyn, New York machinist, William Cyrus Briggs. In our own Winston landscape in 1892, in a rented area of Vance and Schaffners Iron Works on the corner of Patterson and First Streets, history was made. The cigarette machine Briggs perfected and his association with Richard J. Reynolds Tobacco Company catapulted the RJR enterprises to world notoriety. By the 1950s a motion picture was produced that touched on this occurrence, along with the battle to control tobacco by Buchanan Duke of American Tobacco Company that pitted Duke against Reynolds; the movie was entitled *Bright Leaf*. History is still being made today at the same location where it all started, Patterson and First Streets. Piedmont Research Park, with its advancements in science and technology, is another example of what greatness and success can happen on the streets of the Twin City.

Main Street between Second and Third Streets showed a growing business façade presented in just one year between 1878 and 1879. The home of the first Wachovia National Bank was found here. In succession were Ormsby Pianos, Organs and Sewing Machines; J.W. Goslen's publication, the *Union Republican*; the dry goods establishment of W.T. Carter & Company; George T. Foust, general merchandise store; and Clothiers, M. Stin & Company. At the corner of Main and Fourth Streets, across from the 1851 Winston Courthouse, was the cultural establishment of Brown's Opera House. The Wachovia Bank took over the entire block of Third and Main Street by building Winston's oldest skyscraper. This building is the only remnant of that bygone era.

Beyond the Depot Street (Patterson Avenue) of the freight yards was a new venture that had arrived in 1882. D.H. King arrived from Richmond, Virginia, with his ice and coal business, which he located at the corner of Third and Depot Streets. In 1887, he constructed a bottling works a few blocks south of his coal and ice factory. On Water Street, appropriately, he bottled mineral waters and flavored sodas. He followed later with beer brands entitled Vienna Cabineet and Tivoli. Always the entrepreneur, he fashioned all with their usage in his fancy venture on Main Street. The Soda

Fountain, one of Winston's finest, was located across from Winston's premier hotel, The Merchants.

The years 1886 and 1887 were full of growth in the housing market. Both years saw more building in the two towns than ever before. Reverend Rondthaler and the church leaders who had played an important role in the church and state connections of business, religion and politics saw a boom period in the late nineteenth to early twentieth centuries. However, there was a dark side to this progress. Companies and businesses were growing out of control in some of the larger cities. Reverend Rondthaler remarked,

> *When our constitution discontinued a title aristocracy, it did not mean that corporations should take the place of the greedy robber barons of olden times. No matter how good the constitution of a land or how favorable its situation, it could not remain free if given over to the lust of strong drink. The "liquor saloon" as the experience of our larger cities has already shown is an enemy to national liberty. It tends to bring communities under*

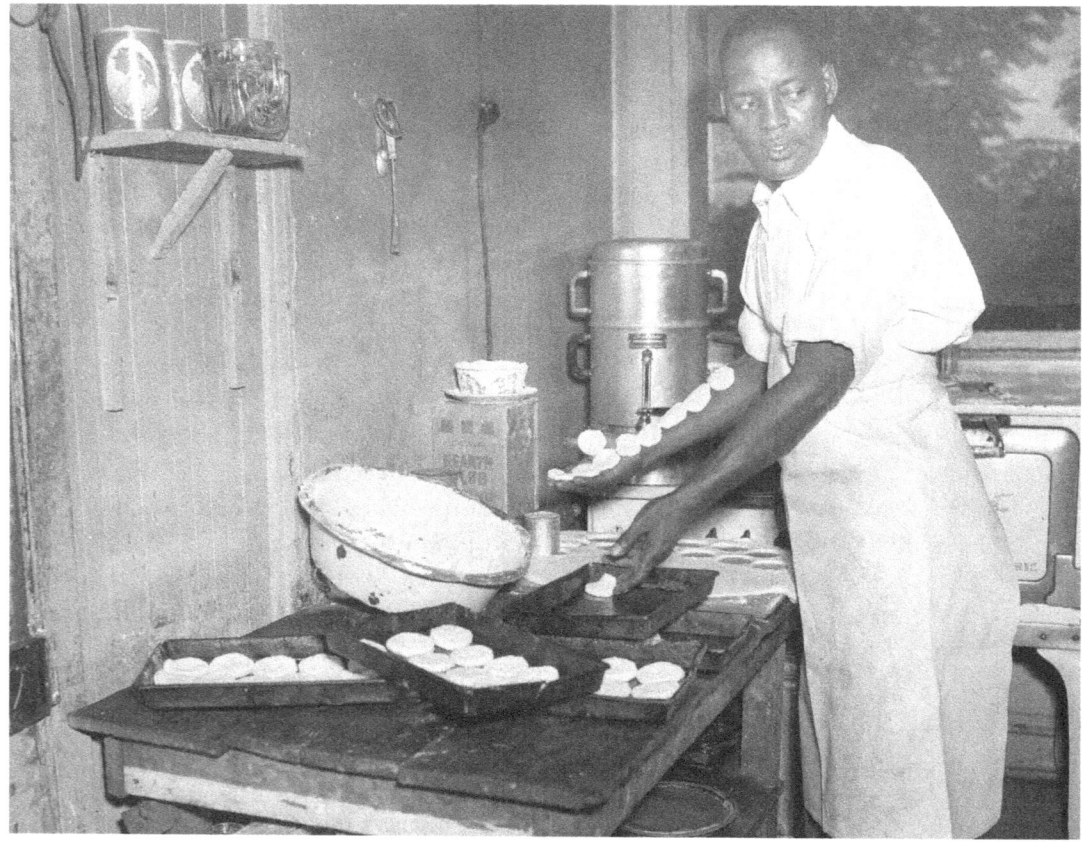

This circa 1950s photo depicts another bygone era, one that was experienced in the Depression and war years. Necessity is the mother of invention and this gentleman knows all too well of that.

The Jobs We Do

the tyranny of the wasteful passions of human nature. Where ever the saloon is strong, government becomes wasteful and injurious.

With these words, Reverend Rondthaler began the Temperance movement in Salem. Winston followed a short time later. The Prohibition era was on the horizon. Salem had its own history of prohibiting its people due to their Moravian beliefs. Prohibition of alcohol and what it could do was upon the town's mind once more. The saloon business was very profitable and the side effects of its wares were being felt throughout the populus. A clash between church and state soon arrived.

Our search of Winston and Salem jobs between the boom years of the 1880s and 1890s forward to the Roaring Twenties encompassed two time periods that saw the most growth and advancement in the town's businesses. Per capita, the growth of employees to employers was unmatched. Since this growth was riding on the back of the first Industrial Revolution in America, the baby boom job growth of the 1950s was made somewhat pale in comparison.

A summary of the events and establishments that marked these important time periods of Winston and Salem business are presented in chronological order beginning with the first period, 1888 to 1900. The list begins with the establishment and the year of conception.

Circa 1888
Ogburn and Son, circa 1850
Sullivan Factory, circa 1860
Beard and Brothers, circa 1866
H. Scales and Company, circa 1870
T.F. Leak, circa 1871
P.H. Hanes & Co., circa 1873
W.H. Leak & Co., circa 1873
T.L. Vaughn, circa 1873
C. Hamlen & Sons, circa 1874
R.J. Reynolds & Co., circa 1875
Brown & Brown, circa 1876
W.W. Wood & Co., circa 1878
Ogburn Hill & Co., circa 1878
Red Elephant Tobacco Works, circa 1878
S. Byerly & Son, circa 1878
Bynum & Cotton, circa 1879
Bailey Bros., circa 1880
J.M. Greenfield, circa 1881
R.L. Candler, circa 1883
Blackburn Dalton & Co., circa 1883
Reynolds Brothers, circa 1883
Lockett Vaughn & Co., circa 1884
Hodgin & Lunn, circa 1884

Brown Sapp & Co., circa 1884
S.J. Nissan, circa 1885
J.A. Butner, circa 1885
Model Tobacco Works, circa 1886
Lowrey & Stafford, circa 1886
Bitting & Hay, circa 1887
W.T. Gray & Co., circa 1890
W.A. Whitaker, circa 1891

Circa 1896 By 1896, textiles combined to expand and define the business environment of West Salem and the Southside neighborhoods. The Southside cotton mills of Henry Fries had extended deeper into the Southside neighborhood. The blue-collar factory workers' hard work had allowed the prominent citizens of Salem to begin building larger spacious houses and mansions in the future Washington Park neighborhood.

Circa 1897 This factory business was to become one of the largest in the two towns. That factory, the Southern Chemical & Fertilizer complex, appeared in the growing north Winston neighborhood.

Circa 1898–1899 In 1899, with seventy-five homes being erected, Reverend Rondthaler confirms the repeat of history. "The industries of the Twin City have been very actively pursued. There has been an increased output of manufactured goods, and a general rise in wages of skilled workmen, which we find from various interviews with leading firms to range from 10–20%. The demand for skilled labor has been so great that the home supply was not sufficient." With this increase of profit the success of the Twin City as it entered in the 1900s was secured. To quote Rondthaler, "The building operations for the year have been numerous and large. As many as 150 houses of all sizes have been erected, among which have been eight larger residences and a number of factories, stores and other industrial buildings." The base of commerce for the twentieth century was set with the following enterprises.

F.C. Meinung Store
  (located at Main and Shallowford, Brookstown)
Forsyth Chair Company
  (located at Sunnyside Avenue in Southside)
Fries Manufacturing and Power Company
  (located at Shallowford, Cherry and Salt; Marshall Street today)
The Furniture Store
Gilmore Brothers Wholesale Merchandise
Miller Brothers Lumbar Plant
  (located at Belews Creek Road)

The Jobs We Do

    Oakland Manufacturing Company
      (located at North Liberty and Patterson Avenue)
    R.J. Reynolds Factory Complex
      (located at Church Street between First and Second Streets)
    Salem Roller Mill
      (located on Mill Street, Broad and West Salem Avenue)
    Shelton & Dalton Box Factory
      (located on North Liberty Street)
    Southern Chemical Fertilizer Company
      (located on North Liberty Street)
    Spach Bros. Wagon Works
      (located at Waughtown and Glendale, Southside)
    Wachovia Roller Mills
      (located at New Shallowford Road, Brookstown Avenue)
    Winston Furniture Company
      (located at North Liberty and Patterson Avenue)

The textile and tobacco interests provided the principal jobs for Winston and Salem residents. There were also other jobs that allowed the owners to express themselves with advertising promises and creativity. A few examples of these follow, with 1898–1900 advertising:

A.C. VOGLER & SONS, MAIN STREET, ESTABLISHED IN 1858
"Furniture dealer and undertaker."

A. DAYE COMPANY, 412 LIBERTY STREET
"If you need clothing, shoes, hats of gents, furnishings, collars, this is your place."

BROWN ROGERS & CO., 3 WEST FOURTH STREET
"Machinery and agricultural implements, thrashers, mowers, reapers, stoves, oils, and paints."

D.H. KING, 209 EAST THIRD STREET
"Bottlers of mineral water, sarsaparilla, soda water, and ginger ale."

F.C. MEINUNG, SHALLOWFORD STREET
"Business and delivery wagons and express wagons a specialty—all kinds of blacksmithing and horseshoeing."

FOGLE BROS. BUILDERS, BELEWS CREEK STREET
"Manufacturer of building materials, mantels, tile, grillers, hardwood interior finish Salem, N.C."

Winston-Salem

Hughes Barber Shop, 107 West Fourth Street

Hinshaw & Mederias Company, Trade at Fourth Street: ladies', men's and children's store
"Wear them once and you will have no other kind."

H.W. Shore, Main and New Shallowford
"Dealer in heavy and fancy groceries, choice confectionaries, fruits, canned goods, fine imported and domestic cigars, and tobacco, crockery, glass, and queen's ware."

J.A. Vance, corner of First and Depot (Patterson Avenue)
"Iron works and Winston cigarette machines."

J.M. Woodruff & Co., 242 Main Street
"Make a specialty of women's outfits, up-to-date haberdashery in all forms or your money refunded."

Poindexter and Burge, 141 Trade Street
"Dealers in staple and fancy groceries."

Rosenbacher and Brother, corner of Liberty and Fourth Street
"Boys and children's clothing in varied styles—we carry the largest stock in North Carolina."

Salem Cotton Gin, Shallowford (Brookstown and High Street)

S.J. Nissan Co., Third and Depot (Patterson Avenue)
"Buggies, wagons, trucks, note the castle."

Southern Railway, Depot (Patterson Avenue)
"The only line in the South operating solid Pullman trains and dining cars. The only direct line to Florida, Cuba and Puerto Rica."

Dr. V.O. Thompson, 13 West Fourth Street
"Druggist can supply you with any article to be found in a first class drug store."
"Thompson's magic liniment is the best thing you can get for rheumatism, sprains, bruises, stiff joints, cuts, anything that hurts."
"The Thompson pink pill, Thompson's Cough syrup cures coughs, colds, bronchitis, sore throat, the croup, asthma, and relieves constipation, plus children like it!"

The Jobs We Do

The twentieth century arrived with every bit as much promise as the boom time of the 1880s and 1890s. In 1901, the assessed value of all taxable property in the Twin City and surrounding Forsyth County properties totaled $8.5 million. By today's standard, this taxable amount is small; however, the total taxable income of the entire state of North Carolina was only $300 million. The tobacco and textile industries fueled such an amazing amount of exports and imports for their products that an act of Congress was initiated in 1916. On June 16, 1916, a "Port of Entry" was established in Forsyth County. This designation had only been given previously to coastal cities until this date. Winston-Salem became the farthest inland port of entry in the history of the country to that point. Winston and Salem became officially the Twin City in 1913, after the merger of the two towns. The term "Twin City" had been batted around and voted on several times in the 1880s and 1890s. With the merger in place and the port of entry granted, the next distinctive label upon the Twin City was "Winston-Salem, a City of Industry, 1917."

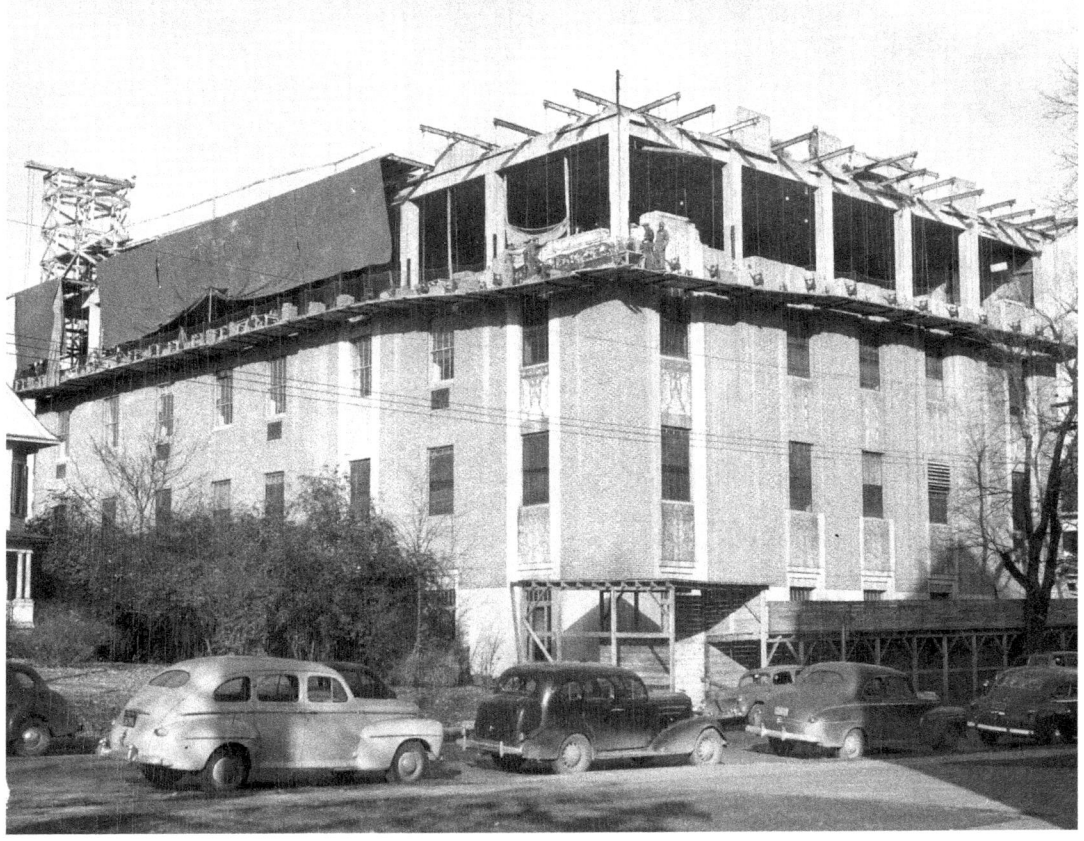

The Bell Telephone building on West Fifth Street, circa 1950s, rising from the landscape that once housed the aristocrats of early Winston. The Fogle Brothers' longstanding company played a part in its construction.

Winston-Salem

The City of Industry marked Winston-Salem's second time period of importance. The 1910s and 1920s gave the world its first view of a modern America. The following list introduces the public to the 1917 "City of Industry" business enterprises. The 1910s were responsible for giving the strength to the period that followed—the Roaring Twenties. First a few facts for 1917, which led the city to its prominence as a City of Industry.

- City of Winston-Salem leads the entire state in manufacturers
- 38 percent increase in population from 1910 to 1916, leading all North Carolina cities
- Leads the world in flat plug tobacco
- Leads the South in manufacture of knit goods
- Largest weekly payroll between Richmond and Atlanta
- Five banks among the largest in the state

The City of Industry produced very lucrative businesses that did not survive into the twentieth century. The following list is an example of those businesses and their advertisements with their proclamation of pronouncing the "City of Industry, circa 1917."

B. Swartz, 713 Main: Hide and Junk Dealer

Swartz is not only one of the largest junk dealers in Winston-Salem, but also one of the largest in the state of North Carolina. He is a buyer of all kinds of high-grade hides, tallow, beeswax, wool, furs, scrap iron and metals, and ships by the carload.

C. Gilbert Humphreys: Architect

Humphreys was born in London, England, educated at Cornell University, studied art in Paris for two years and came to New York, entering the offices of the late George B. Post, one of America's foremost architects. Humphreys also was with Bradford L. Gilbert, the designer of the first skyscraper erected in New York City at 50 Broadway.

Farrell Studio: Artistic Photography

Until recent years, an artist was understood to be a painter. Today there are more real artists who devote their lives to the profession of photography than people who are even passable painters. Artists may rack their brains for scenes, situations and compositions, but for intrinsic interests few things have ever excelled a good portrait and Farrell's portraiture shows the fullest values attainable.

Fletcher Brothers, Trade: Manufacturers of High-Grade Pants and Overalls, Wholesale Clothing, Hosiery, Shirts and Notions

The business was established in the fall of 1896. The business of the firm covers all the Southern states from Maryland to Florida, and eleven salesmen travel throughout this territory handling the firm's goods exclusively. This company puts out its pants and overalls under the brand of "Big Winston" and there are no better goods on the market.

The Jobs We Do

HOTEL PHOENIX: EUROPEAN PLAN
One of the good hotels here is conducted under the title of Hotel Phoenix. This is a European hotel quite well established, contains more than fifty rooms and is located in the heart of the city at the corner of Fourth and Liberty Streets opposite the courthouse. The hotel contains modern features such as electric lights, baths and bell service, and the rates are most reasonable. It is conducted exclusively on the European plan, but there is a high-class café in the building and several other high-class cafés nearby.

IDEAL PHOTOGRAPH COMPANY
There is no doubt that this is the most popular headquarters in Winston-Salem for what are considered popular priced pictures. Cleve Simpson turns out every picture and portraits of all sizes from the most expensive down to the penny pictures. He also specializes in enlarging of the best grade in watercolors, pastel, crayon and oil. Another special feature of the business is the Kodak Finishing Department. He does beautiful work and never fails to please the amateur. His prices are very reasonable: rolls or packs can be developed any size for ten cents and prints for three cents, any size. He is prepared to do all classes of commercial work as well as home portraiture. He has an automobile and will make trips to the country to make pictures, if desired. The Ideal Studio is complete in every sense of the word and is really one of the best arranged studios in the entire South.

MOTOR COMPANY INCORPORATED, 223 NORTH MAIN
In this concern, Winston-Salem can take pride in the fact that it is one of the largest institutions of its kind in the South. It has exerted a powerful influence in the growth and development of the automobile business of the state. The company served as the state agency for the Hudson and Elgin cars and was the local agent for the Packard, Dodge Brothers, Buick and also VIM trucks.

PIEDMONT CANDY KITCHEN, 527 TRADE
Only goods of absolute purity are handled and the stock consists of all kinds of candies, chocolates, fruits, tobacco, cigars, etc. The company also manufactures ice cream. This store is located near the post office.

RUSSELL AND MOSES PHOTOGRAPHERS, 413 NORTH LIBERTY: OVER THE ELMONT THEATER
Russell was formerly associated with leading studios in Philadelphia and Atlantic City and gained his experience in London, England. You get that something that is different at the Russell and Moses Studio; their pictures, while combining all the art qualities, are so perfectly plain and natural. They are true to life in every sense of the word.

SHORE TRANSFER COMPANY
This is the oldest and largest concern of its kind in Winston-Salem, the business having been established for the last fifteen years. It is devoted to transfer, storage and heavy hauling of all kinds, including freights, safes, pianos, baggages, etc. Shore is also responsible for the moving of household goods. They have wagons of all kinds, drays and moving vans suitable to each particular kind of article.

Winston-Salem

The Sweet Shop, 442 Liberty
This confectionary and fruit business is located opposite the New Auditorium Theatre. The business has been established for the past four years and has become very popular with those who are looking for quality and purity in the way of high-grade candies, chocolates, bonbons, etc. The place has a nice soda fountain and all the best drinks of the season are served. The stock includes a full line of fruits, such as apples, bananas and oranges. There is also a leading line of popular brands of cigars, tobaccos and cigarettes.

Vanola Company, 200 South Main: manufacturers of Vanola pure mints, eucalyptus cough drops and pepsin gum
A large number of people are employed in this plant, which is located in Salem at the corner on which the famous old coffeepot stands. The Vanola cough drops are becoming famous, being called by many "the greatest cough drop on earth."

Zinzendorf Hotel on Main
In the new Zinzendorf, Winston-Salem can boast one of the most charming hotels in the South.

Early ads from the 1900s began with many services and products for women. For instance, "Nothing makes a woman feel so hopeless as the many weaknesses and diseases so common of her sex. Pain and weariness are with her every hour. But Fannie May took just one bottle of my wonder tonic and was better in every way."

"St. Vitus dance can make a child conspicuous in public. No more the little one who is seen and not heard, but never fear moms, Dr. Green's nerve medicine could save the parents much excruciating embarrassment."

"The parents of little May Callah just 4 years old claimed she has been a healthy child because every time she was not hungry, had the sniffles or anything else I reach for the Ozomulsion [a fancy word for cod liver oil]."

Men had their share of complaints as well. Their complaints were simpler with their medicines for constipation, bad breath and sleepwalking. Drugs and remedies may have been the largest ads for the day, but advertisements for furniture, clothing and the like also arrived on the scene. The names in these businesses were Nading, Fogle, O'Hanlon, Rominger, Vogler's, Crim, Brown and Rodgers. A 1904 furniture sale at Rominger's and Crim's Furniture Store offered $0.60 manilla cane chairs for only $0.40 and a complete dresser bureau for just $9.50. At Rosenbacher's the ladies could buy china silk for as little as $0.39 a yard. Furs began at $1.25, and handbags were sold for $0.98. Brown and Rodgers and Company were selling a Peerless Iceland freezer that meant ice cream could be made without salt or oil getting into the container. One tiny illustrated ad showed a black, dark house with tiny white windows with the saying below it, "Fill your house with light. No house is modern without electric lights."

The following list contains the businesses of the blue-collar workers' two streets of commerce. The 400 block of Trade Street and the 400 block of Liberty Street at downtown

The Jobs We Do

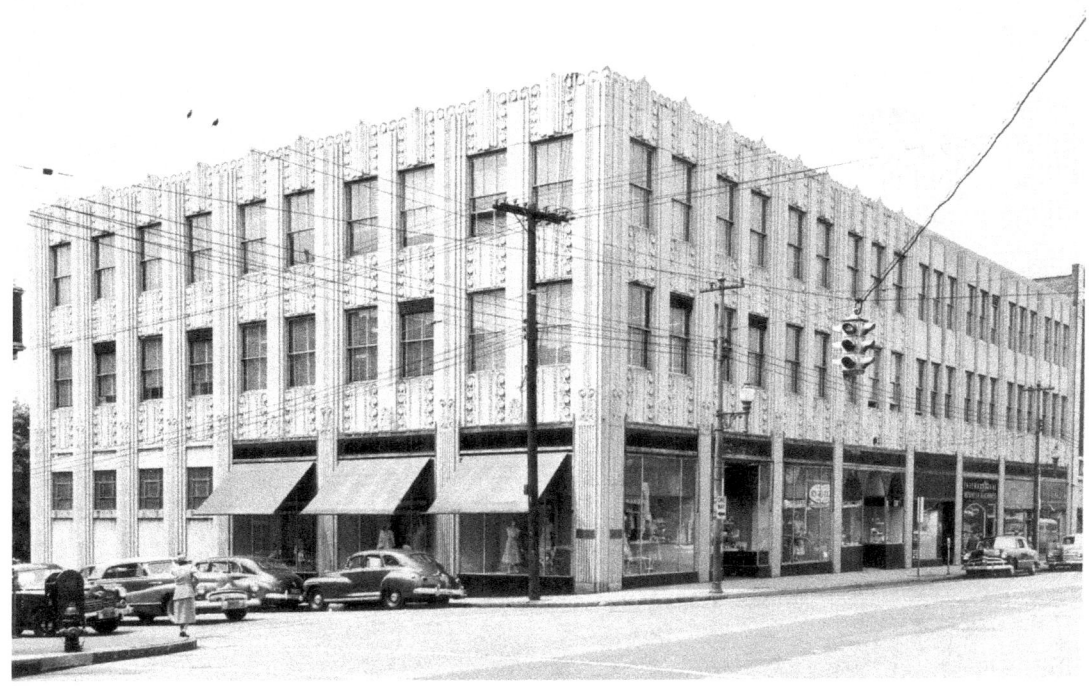

The Thalheimer's building at First Street and Poplar Street was indicative of the art deco architecture that graced our town in the 1920s and 1930s.

Winston were the centerpiece for shopping. Old-timers reminisced, "If it couldn't be bought within these two blocks, it ain't worth having!"

400 BLOCK OF TRADE STREET
The Adrmore Company
B.A. Miller & Company
Belk-Stevens Company
Bennett & Tesh Company
The Farmers Warehouse
Dr. Hedrick & Son, optometrist
Henry Rose Company
Red Star Sample Store
Russell & Moss Photographer, Silver Department
Trade Street Grocery Company
Tucker Ward Hardware
W.H. Marler Company

400 BLOCK OF LIBERTY STREET
A. Daye & Company
Antiseptic Barber Shop
Arcade Fashion
Broadway Theater
Colonial Theater
D.D. Schouler Racket Store
The Elite Bowling Alley
Fred Holtz Barber Shop
F.W. Woolworth
Gilmer's Department Store

Winston-Salem

G.R. Kinney Shoe Store
Ideal Theater
J.A. Neeley's Shoe Shop
Merchant's Bank & Trust
Myers-Westbrook Dry Goods
Rominger Furniture
Sosnick & Sosnick Store

Spry's Barber Shop
State Theater
The Sweet Shop
Thompson Drugstore
Wall-Huske Hardware
Watkin's Bookstore

The list of businesses for the Trade and Liberty Streets' blue-collar workers had the opportunity in 1989 to become part of the downtown Winston-Salem historic district. This wealth of buildings that had held such an amount of history for the city was unfortunately lost. The following is an excerpt from the historic districting report.

> *In 1989 a National Register nomination was prepared for the proposed Downtown Winston-Salem Historic District, which incorporated a larger body of contiguous historic properties related to the central commercial development of Winston-Salem between 1882–1930 and which retained sufficient architectural integrity to visually reflect that development. That district included part of the currently nominated Downtown North Historic District. Due to owner objection, the proposed Downtown Winston-Salem Historic District was not formally listed. In 1990, it was determined eligible for the National Register. With the subsequent loss of historic resources located north of Fifth were no longer physically connected with those to the south. Thus, the Downtown North Historic District—located north of Fifth, focusing on a particular aspect of Winston-Salem's commercial history, and having a period of significance that spans the years from 1907–1952—has been identified as a separate, distinguishable area of local historic significance and is therefore being nominated to the National Register.*

The nation's bicentennial celebration of 1976 had initiated the beginning of historic preservation for all of Winston-Salem. Nearly thirty years later, the loss of the 400 blocks of Trade and Liberty was incomprehensible when one considers the amount of history that was lost.

The economic collapse of 1929 brought many of the businesses presented earlier to an abrupt end. Most banks closed, with the Wachovia bank establishment being one of the few that survived. The Roaring Twenties had spun out of control in Winston-Salem as well as the rest of the nation, with the free-flowing credit that was being dished out to everyone. During the Depression, jobs were hard to come by. The 1930s were ushered into the Twin City with both dread and hope on everyone's minds. The city decided to adopt what the old-timers came to call "the Salem conscience and the Winston purse." The Moravian leadership and hope combined with the wealth of King Tobacco were thought by all to be the only way to weather this dark depression covering the landscape. The old-timers may have been right. Since the Gray, Reynolds and Hanes families had built the factories that employed most of the people, naturally these families did and should have run the Twin City. The Salem side of the Twin City had retired to allow the commerce and control in the government and business to swing completely to the Winston side. The Fries Cotton Mill

The Jobs We Do

Complex, which was so important in the King Cotton era, had reserved itself to the West Salem side of Salem industry. All important decisions of the twin towns were approved on the nineteenth floor of the 1929 Reynolds building at Main and Fourth. These decisions were not questioned by the populace or by the state government officials. You see, for many years, Reynolds Tobacco was one of the most profitable corporations in the world as well as the top taxpayer in the state.

With the help of Reynolds Tobacco, Winston-Salem weathered the Depression of the 1930s better than most cities. The dark side was felt most by those who were not associated with Reynolds directly. The speculation of many business ventures suffered an untimely death. One such example occurred in the automobile business. At the time of the introduction of Camel cigarettes (the most popular brand in the world in 1913), Henry Ford's automobiles, the model Ts and As, were the most popular lines. But variety was not among the features offered. Henry Ford often joked in his advertising, "You can buy our cars in any color you want as long as its black." A team of brothers decided in 1928 to bring other colors to the table for automobile enthusiasts in the Twin City. In 1929, their auto paint and detail business was just beginning to show a profit. Then, in October 1929, the crash of the stock market occurred and the demand for variety was history. These brothers, like many others, picked up odd jobs until the federal programs were initiated to put the folks who were not associated with Reynolds back to work. Innovative programs to put the breadwinners back to work included repairing run-down houses and schools, fixing parks and playground equipment and resurfacing roads. Two original programs, the Share a Job Plan and the WPA, kept many families from the poorhouse. One such plan sent hundreds of displaced families to work on old farms in the county. The Works Progress Administration helped thousands, including the two brothers in the aforementioned car manufacturing example. The brothers, along with others, constructed equipment throughout the city parks. Bowman-Gray Stadium was one of those projects. Hanging Rock State Park and Pilot Mountain State Park were two others.

The 1930s and 1940s presented dark and formidable challenges, but many companies still grew, with a few new startups. A list of larger ones brings us to the conclusion of the 1950s and companies such as RJR; Brown & Williams; and Nissan Wagon Works, which moved into furniture to begin the Unique Furniture Company; B.F. Huntley Furniture, which merged with Thomasville Furniture to become a national company; Fogle Furniture, which continued into the 1990s; the Bahnson Company (Normalair Company), which went global in the late twentieth century; and Salem Steel Company, which began in 1927 and continued throughout the twentieth century. The Bassett Company, Chatman Manufacturing Company, Western Electric and the like were strong into the twentieth century, until globalization began to eliminate domestic textiles and furniture industries. Some of the smaller hometown companies that became popular in the twentieth century, many of which still serve our town today, are L.A. Reynolds Company (1947), American Bakeries (1923), the Salem Company (1946), Sealtest Foods (1918), Carolina Narrow Fabric (1928), Royal Cake Company (1925), Container Corporation of America (1913), Champion Industry (1921) and Pepsi Cola Bottling Company of Winston-Salem (1908).

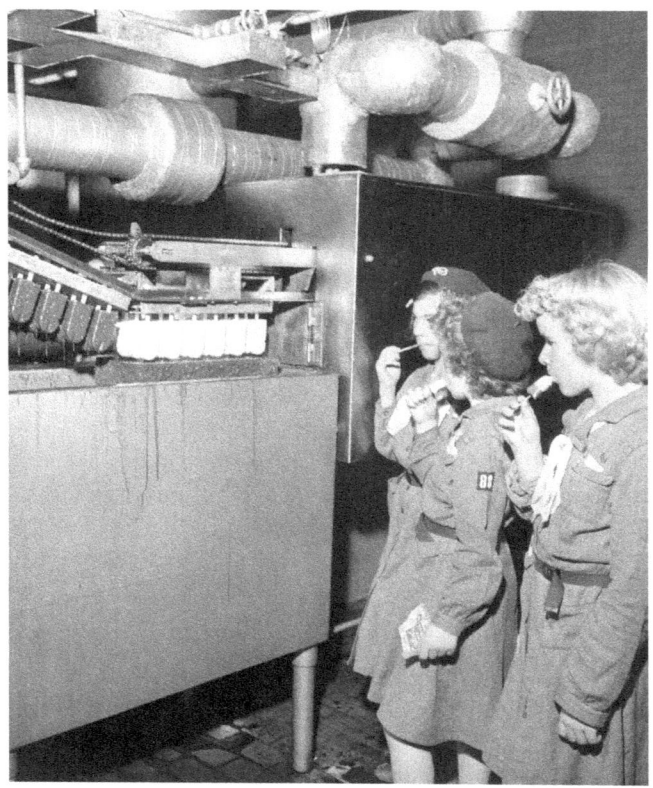

These Winston-Salem Girl Scouts are enjoying a bit of good taste at the Sealtest Plant on Patterson Avenue. *Michael Bricker collection.*

But the growth of business was happening in the surrounding neighborhoods, and by the 1970s, downtown Winston-Salem was considered an "old, worn-out…melancholic town." The repeated attempts to bring business back to downtown were foiled by the building of shopping centers and later the Hanes Mall complex. The shopping district was now confined to Stratford Road and Hanes Mall Boulevard. The downtown revitalization took another hit in 1990, with the loss of the 400 blocks of North Liberty and North Trade. A melancholy town of the 1970s that lets history be severed and divided throughout its township offers a disappointment of the past and a question for the future. What would the twenty-first century hold for the Twin City?

CHAPTER 4.

The People

The people of the Twin City who are often profiled in text and history have been associated with a handful of families: the Reynoldses, Grays, Haneses and Frieses. The Moravian story and its participants are trumpeted in print as well. In our search of the town's history, a more complete picture of the names and faces, movers and shakers, is presented. The different positions and impressions of these individuals played out over a more than two-hundred-year period of the city. Their stories cover rich and poor, black and white. Some I have known personally, while others have been researched, studied and admired. All the people with their concentrated efforts to impact and form the twin towns have a story to tell. Many will be presented for the first time.

In chapter 2, many of the early founders of the town of Salem were touched upon. Count Nicholas Ludwig Von Zinzendorf was an early savior of the Moravians and must be mentioned even though he never set foot in Salem. In 1722, he sheltered the Moravians on his estate of Saxony from the persecution of the Catholic Church. He organized the expansion of the Moravian missionary movement to America. The first settlers to arrive to Piedmont North Carolina were led by Bishop August Gottlieb Sprangerberg in 1752. The Moravians settled on a site of 100,000 acres in the foothills of the Piedmont. There were many early families originating from the first troop who arrived in this area in 1753. The early Moravian residents were John Beroth, Henry Bieffel, Gottfried Grabs, Balthasar Hege, Adam Kremer, Charles Opiz, Michael Ranke and Christopher Schmidt. Non-Moravians who arrived were George, Martin and Michael Hauser; Philip Schaus; Frederick and Henry Schorr; Henry Spoenhauer; and John Strup.

The Salem Academy was founded in 1771 as a girls' school. In 1772, Elizabeth Oesterlein came to teach girls in the Gemeinhaus. Sister Oesterlein's students ranged between the ages of two and eight. She taught reading, writing, knitting and weaving, as well as studying the Bible and musical hymns. By 1738, the Moravians began to admit girls from outside the town. Sister Oesterlein was involved in their education. The first non-Moravian boarders arrived in 1804: one from Caswell County, one from Fayetteville, two from Halifax County and four from Hillsboro. The yearly tuition was nearly $180. The course load consisted of arithmetic, English, geography, grammar, history, needlework and reading. An additional

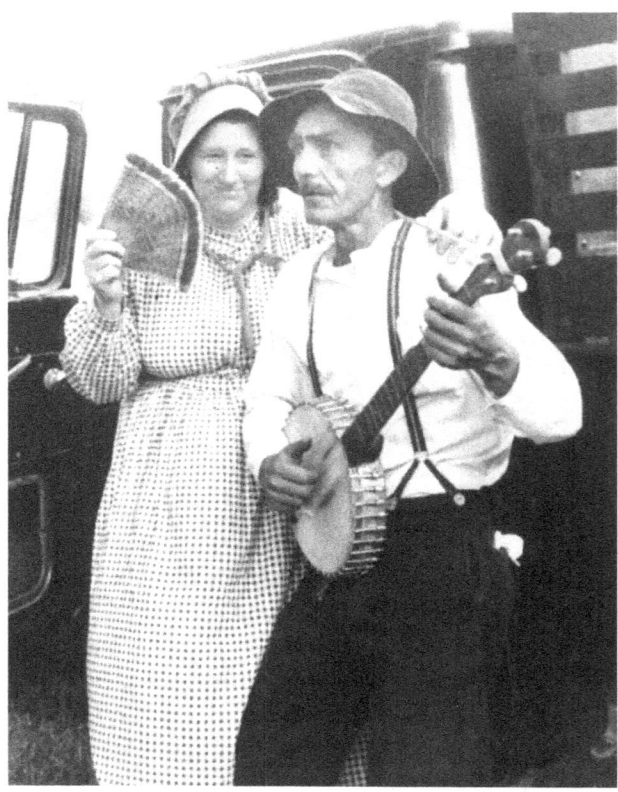

Old-time fun was had during the downtown celebration of the one hundredth anniversary of the founding of Winston in 1849. Photo circa 1949.

fee allowed the girls to learn drawing, music and more fancy needlework. The school's first inspector was Samuel Gottlieb Kramsch. The school became the choice of many families from the South. One of the most famous ladies to walk the halls of Salem Academy was Sarah Childress, who was from one of the South's finest families. Entering the academy in 1817, she began courting James K. Polk, who was then a student at the University of North Carolina. Childress left Salem in 1818 and married Polk, who became the president of the United States. Other famous students from that time included Mary Anna Morrison, who became the wife of Thomas "Stonewall" Jackson; Mary Denny Martin, the future wife of Senator Stephen A. Douglas; and Mary Pickney Hardy, who became the mother of General Douglas MacArthur.

By 1809, Wilhelm Fries had arrived in Salem and had set up a farm/plantation on the western side of West Salem. He began to use slaves as well as free blacks, not only for normal slave-type work, but he also began to teach them trades, much to the disapproval of the Moravian hierarchy. He often used the African Americans in other businesses, and due to the progressiveness of Brother Gottlieb Schober an African American was allowed to run the paper mill. Francis Fries, the son of Wilhelm, began the textile movement, but while he was a young man in school in Pennsylvania he often received letters from his parents expressing their disgust toward the church's negative stance on slavery. His mother, Johanna, referred to

The People

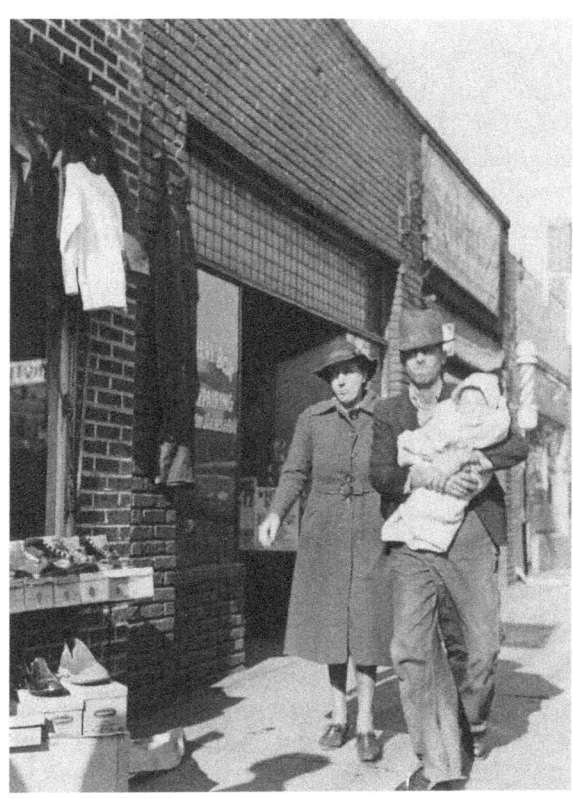

A Great Depression walk on Trade Street depicts a tighter time for many families.

the church as "silly. They are ridiculed in the village and think they are the only wise ones." The church board had demanded that Wilhelm sell his slaves. Wilhelm responded, "I prefer to go to the country where my farming plantation resides rather than to be part of the village where I now live." The atmosphere surrounding the congregational town of East Salem was different than what was found in the immediate West Salem. The issue of slavery arose again in the textile mills.

The 1840s brought much industrial realization to Salem. The prominence of the town grew to the point that the North Carolina General Assembly designated a new county, and the center of that county and the seat of government was Salem. This was a great honor for the Moravians, as they had sought their own county since arriving to the Piedmont. The problem at this time was that as the area grew and as many different types of people began arriving in Salem, being the center of a county brought even more outsiders to their steps. The Moravians decided that the seat of government should be controlled by them, but the business could not be carried out there. The Moravians appropriated land from West Salem to the west and to the north to be the new town of Winston. It had several residents already within its area, including a school that had been built in 1847, mainly for the workers of the textile mills. The town was incorporated eight years later and William Barrow served as the first mayor.

Nothing could compare to "court week" in the town of Winston, when people came from the surrounding cities and towns to talk politics and to exchange gossip. Many of the farm families rode in their Nissen and Spaugh wagons not only to view the festivities, but also to sell their wares. The selling by these farmers of their wares could constitute the first farmers' market in Winston. They arrived with their butter, dried fruit and eggs to sell and to mingle. The song and dance echoed throughout the evening at the campgrounds, which were at Liberty and Fourth in today's landscape. The O'Hanlon building, which still stands at this corner, was a festive time at the beginning of the Civil War. The stagecoaches originated in Clemmons and arrived by way of the Western Plank Road, which was Winston and Salem's link to the rest of the world. Mark Twain commented on traveling this plank road: "This ride would have been great if someone had not thrown down boards along the way." The road arrived in Salem in 1852 and connected the town in a way that no other thoroughfare had done before. The road continued to Salisbury and points south. By 1854, more than twenty thousand wagons used the road regularly. The road became known as "the Appian Way of North Carolina."

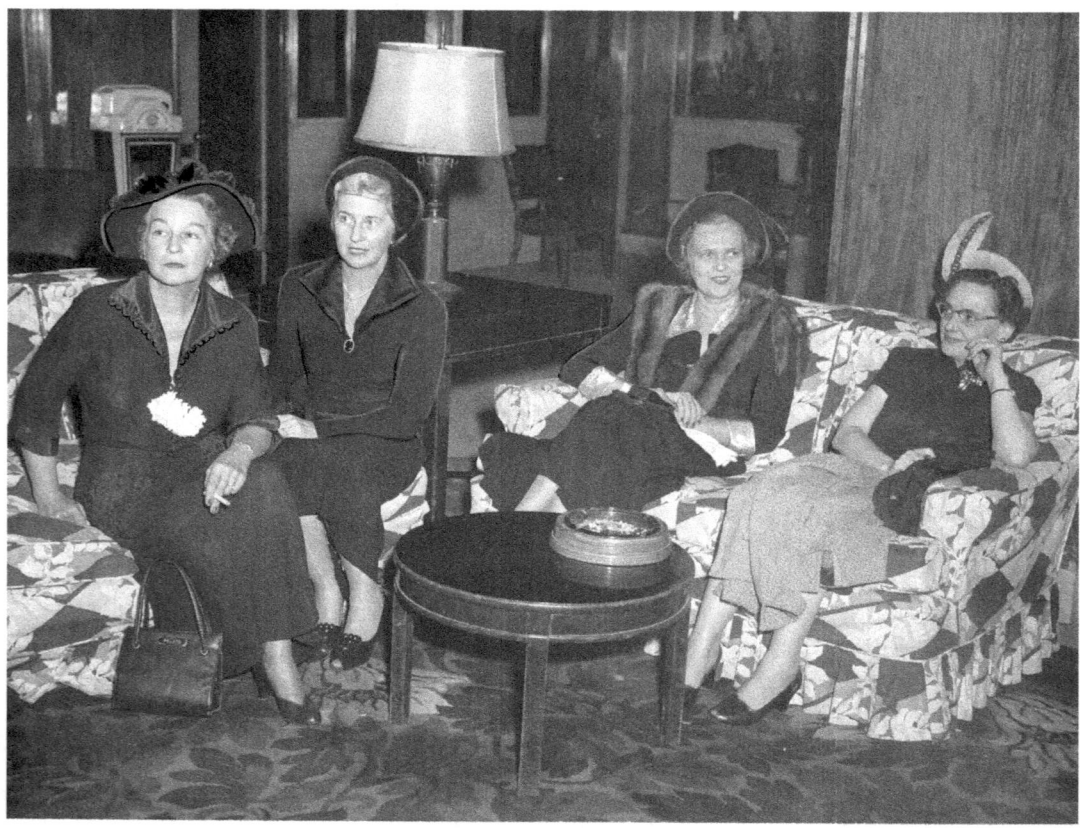

The Women's Club's contribution to a social time for all is shown here, circa 1950s.

The People

The education before and during the Civil War was regulated to Salem Academy and the Boys' School. The free schoolhouses were a product of the national movement to educate the masses who were unable to attend the private and affluent education systems. One such lady who made her way through the public school system was Emma Lehman. She was born in Bethania in 1841 and was the first lady to graduate from Oberlin College. In order to use the facilities, she was required to wash the male students' clothing, clean their rooms and serve their meals. It was a hard battle for women at that time in education. Emma's love of the outdoors and her love of literature allowed her to share her philosophy and poetry. This English teacher turned botanist discovered unidentified plants and was recognized for this. She attended the Salem Academy as well and began teaching in a country school at Bethania before eventually returning to teach at Salem Academy in 1864. The main hall of Salem Academy had just been built on the site of the former Geimenhaus.

During the Civil War, Emma was left with the task of supplying for and protecting three hundred souls at Salem Academy. In those trying times, she developed makeshift sources for food and clothing. Emma moved into the Single Sisters' House to begin further work as a Salem Academy teacher and began to abide by the set rules for the women of the congregation. "A single sister must be modest, retiring, humble, and steady. She will shut her eyes and ears against all evil and will avoid anything that might injure another."

Emma's interest in botany allowed her to be caught up in natural history and plant life. In her English literature, God's natural world became her preoccupation. Her writings and essays ascended to the stars and deep down into the earth. She had a wide range of interests; examples of the subject matter of her writings included the total eclipse of the sun, the invention of the telephone and recipes for fudge. In October 1909, she wrote, "Haley's comet will be clearly visible to the naked eye in the upcoming morning. For a few evenings it stood straight to the west and visible to one with good eyes." She described the eclipse of the sun, when "the moon's dark shadow began to creep over the sun's disc with barely three minutes of total darkness. The sky faded from blue to a dusky color. The earth seemed to be sinking into old age or rather perhaps all nature to stand appalled at the extinction of its Monarch, the sun." Her strongest fascination was with the plants, "for the infinite has sewn his name in the heavens in the burning stars, but on earth he has sewn his name in tender blossoms."

Emma taught junior English for many years at Salem Academy. She was always comparing male and female perspectives and discussed in 1922 her details on the male perception of women's roles. She remarked, "This school was begun with a very tiny seed. The rest of the world at that early day thought woman was fitted only to sew, to wash, cook and bake, to keep house, and to be a domestic drudge. Our fathers thought very differently. They had a wider vision and they planted the seed accordingly." Emma was very artistic and she enjoyed drawing many plants and often used paper art from clippings of the Sears & Roebuck catalogue to gain inspiration. Her painting *Sunset on Pilot Mountain* was included in a publication by the American Publishers Association in 1890.

A young student who arrived later to Salem Academy was Elizabeth Kapp, who was inspired by Emma Lehman. Kapp became a lifelong teacher who learned from her early years at Salem Academy and became the premier English teacher of R.J. Reynolds High

School in the 1970s. I was taught by Kapp as well. The most important contribution made by Lehman was found in the hearts of those who knew her and were taught under her. She served as an enlightened a role model to the female students. Her self-discipline, courage, commitment and independence allowed her students to grasp what she so fondly wanted to teach.

The Civil War created many problems for the Piedmont; however, it also brought to the forefront many of the Southern leaders in the surrounding areas. One such leader was General Robert E. Lee. Few figures in American history are as enduring as the general. He was happy not to commit himself to the North or the South in this war between brothers, but his duty to serve stretched through many generations of the Lee family. The following is from the personal remembrances of his descendant, Sara Ann Lee, a West Salem native:

> *Solomon Lee was my great-grandfather. These men fought in the war between the states. William, Solomon and Jackson Lee joined with the Calvary of Virginia and their Captain was their third cousin, Captain Robert E. Lee, third son of the Commander-in-Chief, Robert E. Lee, of the Confederate Army.*
>
> *Solomon Lee died in 1874 leaving three children, one Charles Solomon Lee, born in 1873, now living and my grandfather. He has a family of nine children, one my father, Clinton Andrew Lee born in 1905 in Forsyth County, NC.*
>
> *Great-grandfather Solomon Lee married Nancy Cook, who had a brother named John Henry Dewitt Clinton Cook, who was in the Infantry of the Confederate Army. My father was named Clinton after him and Andrew after his great uncle Jackson Andrew Lee.*
>
> *These men were large men in stature around six and one-half feet tall, being good kind men and liked and loved by everyone.*
>
> *My geology from my father Clinton A. Lee tells me that I, Sara Ann Lee, born December 20, 1937, hope to remember to pass on to future generations.*

The Lee family, through Sara's genealogical story, is but one example of the many ways in which local Winston-Salem relatives are connected in a national limelight. This example gives us insight not only to our state, but our nation as well.

For now, we will continue with life after the Civil War beginning with 1866. At the end of the war, Israel Lash headed the Salem branch of the defunct bank of Cape Fear. That year he reopened the bank under the name First National Bank of Salem. He added to his establishment a cashier, nineteen-year-old William A. Lemley, who had just returned from the war serving under the Twenty-sixth North Carolina Regiment as a band member. The period of Reconstruction after the Civil War was a grave one. The boom occurred in 1880, with the arrival of business fueled by the Industrial Revolution, which was gaining ground again after the war. Several men became important factors in Winston's rise. One of these men was A.B. Gorrell, who had served as a former mayor of Winston and was owner of one of the larger tobacco warehouses, the Farmers' Warehouse. M.W. Norfleet, also a tobacco dealer, began to enter politics as well.

Francis Fries and his brother Henry, who had established the Salem Woolen Mill before the Civil War, had created a large textile mill involved with several operations of weaving

The People

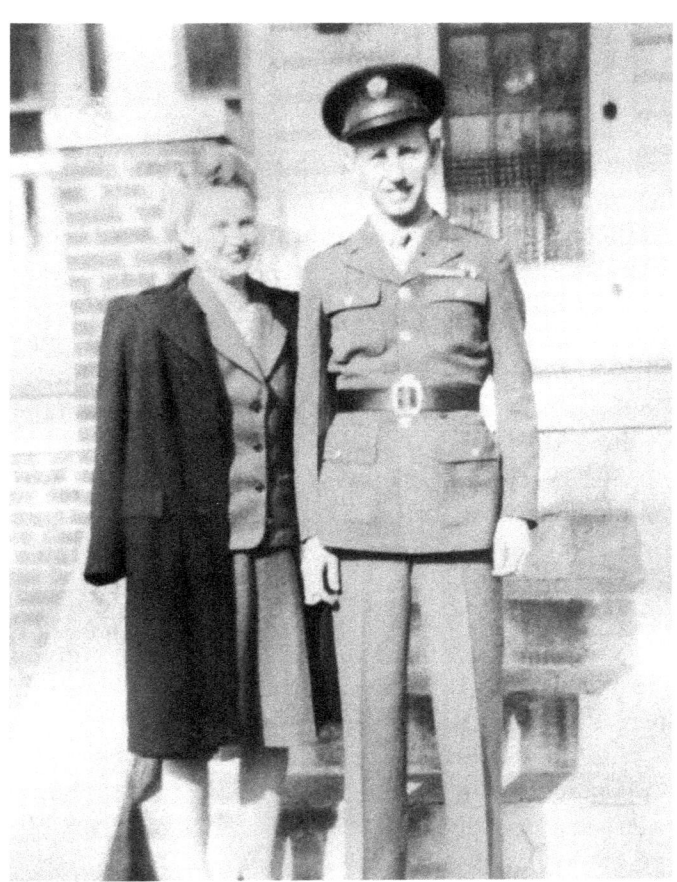

Mr. and Mrs. Branscome during Mr. Branscome's term in the Great War. *Branscome collection.*

woolen cloth, spinning cotton thread and yarn and grinding flour and cornmeal, as was associated with the mill enterprise. The Arista Cotton Mill that Henry Fries and his nephews built came with a complete electric power plant and was the first Southern cotton mill lighted by electricity.

The Industrial Revolution of textiles had come full circle with this mill and the association with electrical pioneers such as Thomas A. Edison and Frank Spraugh brought not only electricity, but also a new type of transportation: electric streetcars. The tobacco enterprises began to grow and prosper. By the early 1880s, the first West End neighborhood was completed in the areas of Fourth, Broad and Green Streets. The tobacco barons built houses in this area, with the first Winston Graded School located in this neighborhood. The families of Wyatt Bowman, J.M. Rogers, John W. Fries and W.A. Whitaker associated themselves with the city and economy. The directors who oversaw the tobacco board of trade were eight of the most influential men of the twentieth century: Henry E. Fries, C.A. Hege, C.A. Fogle, Richard J. Reynolds, Pleasant H. Hanes, E.A. Pfohl, George W. Hinshaw and J.B. Carter Jr. The tobacco board of trade enlisted the Chamber of Commerce to actively pursue better roads into the town and to secure money to bring the Twin City to a modern town of the twentieth century.

Winston-Salem

The year 1885 marked the first decade of R.J. Reynolds's involvement with tobacco manufacturing. In the short period of time he had been involved, his company's growth was the most dramatic of all the factories. In 1887 the Twin City had electric streetlights; by 1890 it had streetcars; by 1893, an intricate telephone system. During this period a rivalry had developed between the Reynolds brothers and the Hanes brothers. P.H. Hanes and his brothers had sold more tobacco than Reynolds, and they had also existed as a company before Reynolds. P.H. Hanes had decided to begin to diversify his company and had an eye toward textiles. R.J. Reynolds saw an opportunity to approach Hanes to buy them out. P.H. Hanes had already begun to invest his large tobacco profits in other businesses. One company he invested in was the Washington Cotton Mills. Hanes's involvement with this company associated him with the Fries family and their textile empire.

With the dawn of the twentieth century, the Twin City controlled textiles and tobacco on a national level. At the same time the Hanes and Reynolds empires were taking off, an association was beginning in Winston that led R.J. Reynolds to his ultimate product and national prominence throughout the twentieth century. William Cyrus Briggs's patented cigarette machine was being produced in a small section of the Vance and Shaffner Iron Works at the corner of Patterson and First in Winston. The association of Francis Fries and William and Henry Shaffner led Briggs to his association with R.J. Reynolds, and soon thereafter the cigarette industry was born.

With all of these major players coming together, R.J. Reynolds and P.H. Hanes saw no competition in building their empires. P.H. Hanes and the Fries family had worked together previously in textiles. The older members of the Fries family helped to mentor the Hanes family without competing along the way. The Reynolds family in Virginia was gaining prestige in the tobacco industry. Buchanan Duke founded the American Tobacco Company of Richmond, Virginia. His quest for domination in the tobacco industry went even higher than that of Reynolds. He pushed for the ultimate business enterprise: a monopoly. Duke founded the American Tobacco Trust and began buying up all the tobacco interests in the United States. The old tobacco men of Winston who had preceded R.J. Reynolds did not appreciate the audacity of Duke and his American Tobacco Trust. The old-timers joked that the trust was like a cancer on the industry, much like the cancers that appeared in the 1960s and were becoming more and more linked to cigarettes and tobacco.

This provided a twist to what was occurring between Reynolds and Duke. The old tobacco owners did not agree with the Trust, but they did not know how to fight the system without proper education. The tobacco men found their own resistance by appointing the younger R.J. Reynolds to be their spokesperson. Reynolds seized this opportunity and accepted buyouts from the other tobacco companies in the city. Even with these companies allied to R.J. Reynolds's tobacco interest, they were still small compared to the Dukes' empire. The shrewdness of Reynolds played out like no one, even Duke himself, could ever have imagined—R.J. Reynolds decided to join the Trust. To quote R.J. Reynolds, who was speaking to the other tobacco barons, "If you can't beat them, join them." R.J. Reynolds was working his plan from the inside of Duke's American Tobacco Trust.

The People

Within the first decade of the twentieth century, Reynolds's plan came together. By working with the Trust and only producing chewing tobacco, no one noticed as he prepared for the independence of his own future tobacco empire. Reynolds understood the future cigarette market and by aligning himself with Briggs, along with the help of the Hanes family, his cigarette market was huge. He reorganized his management team and created what became the future model for all twentieth-century big businesses. There were three key ingredients: a research department, a legal department and, most importantly, advertising. Old-timers at the Green Front Grocery Store at First and Broad often reminisced and argued about the two top products of Reynolds Tobacco. "Old R.J. introduced Prince Albert smoking tobacco in 1907, named after that prince or something, maybe a Duke. Others argued the best invention was Camel cigarettes in 1913."

Smoking tobacco was fine, but in 1913, the towns of Winston and Salem merged and the Camel was born, which had a two to one dominance over any other brand. Of note, Prince Albert smoking tobacco was named for Britain's new crowned prince of Wales, Edward the Seventh. The popularity of this brand caused a few raised eyebrows in the American Tobacco Trust and the Trust filed a lawsuit to stop any aggressive advertising for the product. R.J. Reynolds, with the urging of the old tobacco men, stood firm. In 1910, he hired a national firm, N.W. Ayers & Sons, to push Prince Albert onto the national scene. The Prince Albert brand became the first single brand of tobacco advertised nationwide.

The old-timers called R.J. by his nickname, Dick "Plunger" Reynolds. Plunger referred to his willingness to plunge head first into any risk with the hope of new ideas and boldly going where no tobacco man had gone before. His progressiveness also introduced the Reynolds clan to the high society of New York and entertainment. Between 1907 and 1911, advertising of tobacco arrived on the national scene with advertisements in *Collier's Weekly*, the *Literary Digest*, *Mauseys* and the *Saturday Evening Post*.

R.J. Reynolds's business savvy and down-home tactics helped to break the American Tobacco Trust. By court decree, the Trust was dissolved in 1911. Earlier in the decade, the standard oil monopoly had also been broken up. Distribution of all tobacco rights were dispensed to main members. Reynolds was the producer of the Trust Plug Tobacco, so he gained control of that market as well. Control of smoking tobacco and chewing tobacco was a giant leap for the company and its president. The cigarette market was dispersed to other trust members, but like the old-timers at the Green Front Grocery Store said, "We knew a few new products was added to the smoking tobacco and chewing tobacco dynasty and sell cigarettes as R.J. Reynolds' crowning achievement thanks to Camel's, Reno, Salem and Winston cigarettes, of course."

R.J. Reynolds died in 1918 at sixty-eight years of age. The tobacco industry grew after his death to a level even old Dick Reynolds never thought possible. Reynolds's brother Will took over the reins of the company, and not long after the death of R.J. Reynolds's wife, Katherine, Will took over the care of the four Reynolds children as well.

But our journey among the people of the Twin City does not continue with the Reynolds, Hanes or Fries families. The journey continues with a little young lady who arrived in the Twin City in the mid-1920s. The small young lady was Mattie Claude Lancaster, but the people of Winston-Salem knew her by her married last name (although she was divorced by the time she arrived in town) and adopted first name, Jacqueline Dorminy. At nineteen, Jacqueline graduated from the University of Georgia, finishing college in only three years. The year was 1926, and with a double major in art and drama she was well on her way to doing things her way. There was a custom at the university sponsored by a board member of the school. Mr. Pound, the president of the university, related the unexpected custom: "A bag of gold coins was given to the most outstanding and deserving drama student and Jacqueline was the winner for that year." But she had also broken a cardinal rule of the university: Jacqueline was the first student in the history of the school to keep an A average and a double major together—and double majoring was against university policy. In today's academic climate, a slap on the hand would serve as punishment for such a violation. In the 1920s, however, the scene could have been very messy. Jacqueline related to me years later the question that she asked the president: "Well, do I get the gold or not?" She got the gold, $500 in $5 gold pieces, to be exact. She took her education and money and never looked back.

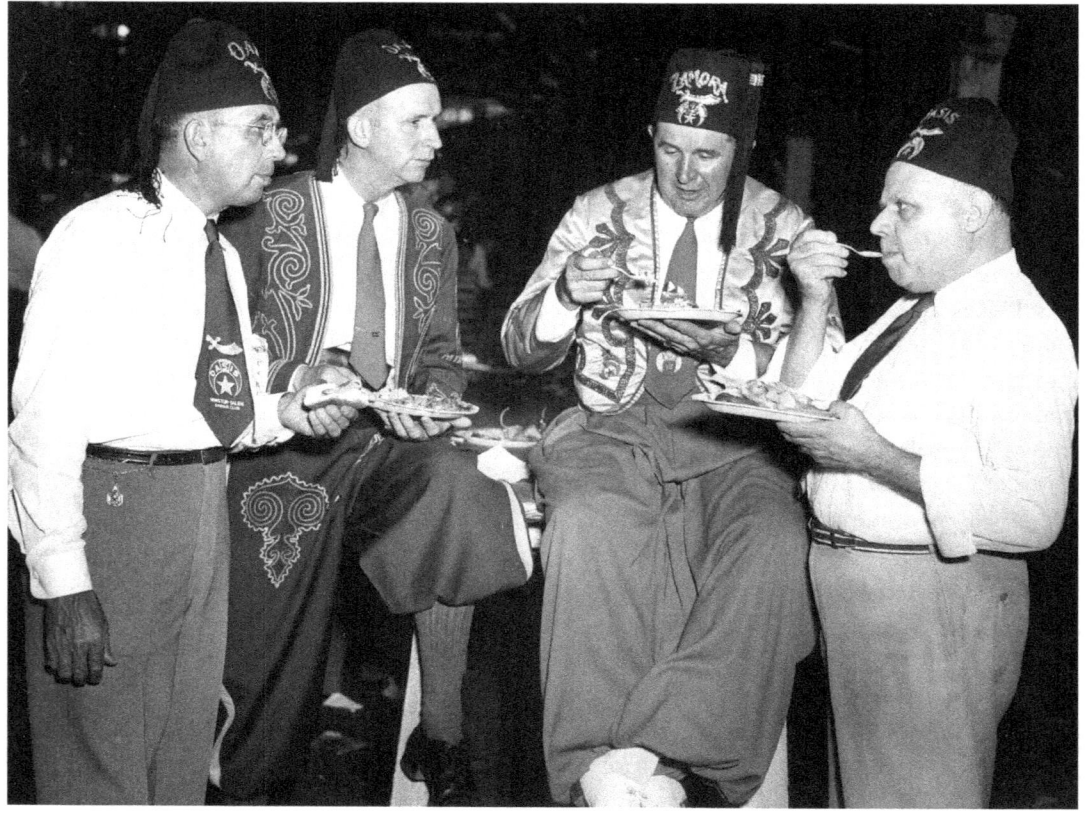

The Winston-Salem Shriners enjoy a quiet time. The Shriner Organization has been a positive influence over many years in the Twin City.

The People

Joining with the Royal Ballet of London and studying under Madame de Bellevoir, she began her true calling teaching dance and designing costumes. Arriving to the Twin City after the 1929 stock market crash, Jacqueline took over a dance studio at the glorious Zinzendorf Hotel on Main. Her client base grew to more than four hundred students. She also continued to dance and perform. To quote Jacqueline, "I have played from Maine to Miami and from the Atlantic to the Pacific Ocean." The combination of her etiquette and worldly travels made Jacqueline a pretty savvy lady.

When Jacqueline arrived in Winston-Salem to meet with the lady from whom she was to take over the dance studio, a piece of Twin City history was made. Jacqueline remembers,

> *I was waiting in the hotel for Mrs. Smith, the dance instructor, so I asked the bellhop where there was a good restaurant in town. He referred me to the close by restaurant, the Winsalt, I believe it was called. A nice establishment it was. I was enjoying a cup of coffee when the most boisterous group of unruly young people entered the establishment. I turned my back on the group and continued with my coffee. The group could have sit anywhere in the place since it was not lunchtime and there very few customers. However, they chose to sit at the table directly behind me. The rascals had inappropriate language for mixed company. Then, one of the young men, who appeared to be the ring leader bumped his chair several times into mine. That was the straw, which broke the camel's back. I stood up and turned abruptly around, tapped the man on the shoulder. As he turned with an obnoxious look on his face, I slapped him as hard as I could. I informed him and his group they were simply hooligans and need not come into a civilized establishment such as this. I noticed the owner turned a rather pale color. The hooligan informed me, "Do you know who I am?" I responded, "I could care less who you are since I know what you are." He continued to say he was Richard Reynolds, Jr., the son of the man whose company controlled the town. I responded, "If that be the case I have arrived to the town just in time" and walked away.*

Due to this incident, Jacqueline believed that her time in Winston-Salem would be short-lived. However, she was wrong. She began her school and taught dance as well as a private academic school for more than seventy-five years in the Twin City. In fact, the day after the café incident Jacqueline received a call from Will Reynolds, the patriarch of the Reynolds family, president of R.J. Reynolds Tobacco Company and uncle to R.J. Reynolds's children. Will begged Jacqueline to teach etiquette and poise to all the Reynolds children. She became their instructor and mentor until they became of age to take over their position in Winston-Salem society. She laments, "The boys became good students, hard-headed sometimes, but we worked through it." Jacqueline essentially became part of their extended family. In response to the question, "Did you have a favorite child of the Reynolds family?" Jacqueline's reply was, "Yes, Smith Reynolds." Jacqueline believed he was the one who lost the most, since he was so young when his mother and father died. "He was sometimes like a lost soul," Jacqueline said. An example of this lost soul persona was conveyed by Jacqueline during my last interview with her. She had returned from a business trip and was driving down Fourth at Marshall:

Winston-Salem

When I heard a loud crash of glass, I thought an accident had occurred, and then I heard another crash followed by another, realizing the origin of the melee was coming from up above. The Carolina Theater and Hotel was the origin of the commotion. I immediately knew what and who it was. A plate was sailing like a flying saucer out of the 12th floor of the hotel. I knew it had to be Smith. I stopped my car in traffic. I had no time to park. Someone was going to get hurt on the ground, so I just left my car in the middle of the street. I stormed into the hotel, entered the elevator and arrived at the appropriate floor. As I banged on the door, the door opened and standing there, barely standing I might add, was Smith cradling his baby. His baby was a jug of corn liquor. Problems with his ex-wife and new girlfriend. His ex-wife was a former Cannon and his girlfriend, Libby Holman. We talked for several hours with me standing between him and the window, so that no objects should be exiting the window. He sat in his favorite rocking chair with his baby. I explained how he had everything to live for, reminded him of his award winning airplane flight, his family. I told him if he tried to do any more stupid things tonight he would answer to me. Unfortunately, a short time later he died. I was out of town when his death occurred and it really hurt me when I found out.

The last question I ever asked Jacqueline was when my daughter was taking piano at her house on First Street. Jacqueline had been ill and could no longer attend her studio on West Fourth. In fact, the studio was being sold at that time as well. The question was, "Do you believe Smith committed suicide or was he murdered?" I did not know what to expect. The answer she gave was her opinion and did not play into the murder case at all. She responded:

Everything I knew of Smith over his short lifetime is in my perspective. He did not commit suicide. He had many opportunities to do that if he had wanted. I have traveled extensively around the world and I know people. He could not have committed suicide and I will tell you this, I never trusted Libby Holman and her friends and their intentions with Smith. I will speak no more of this.

Jacqueline Dorminy passed away not long after this last interview.

As a fifty-year resident of Winston-Salem, I have had the opportunity to meet interesting Twin Citians; here are a few I have known and admired.

Hal Church was a longtime resident of Winston-Salem. He arrived in 1939 after being transferred by his employer, Greyhound Bus Lines, as a bus mechanic. He and his wife and son resided in several historic houses over the years. Their first residence was 407 Washington Avenue in West Salem. Hal and his family later moved to a larger home on Marshall. The Marshall Street home, like all homes on Marshall, was torn down in the late 1960s and 1970s due to urban renewal. The historic village of Old Salem purged nearly two hundred homes and businesses from Salem, including the Marshall corridor, beginning in the 1950s. Hal's Marshall Street home was cleared for the expansion of

The People

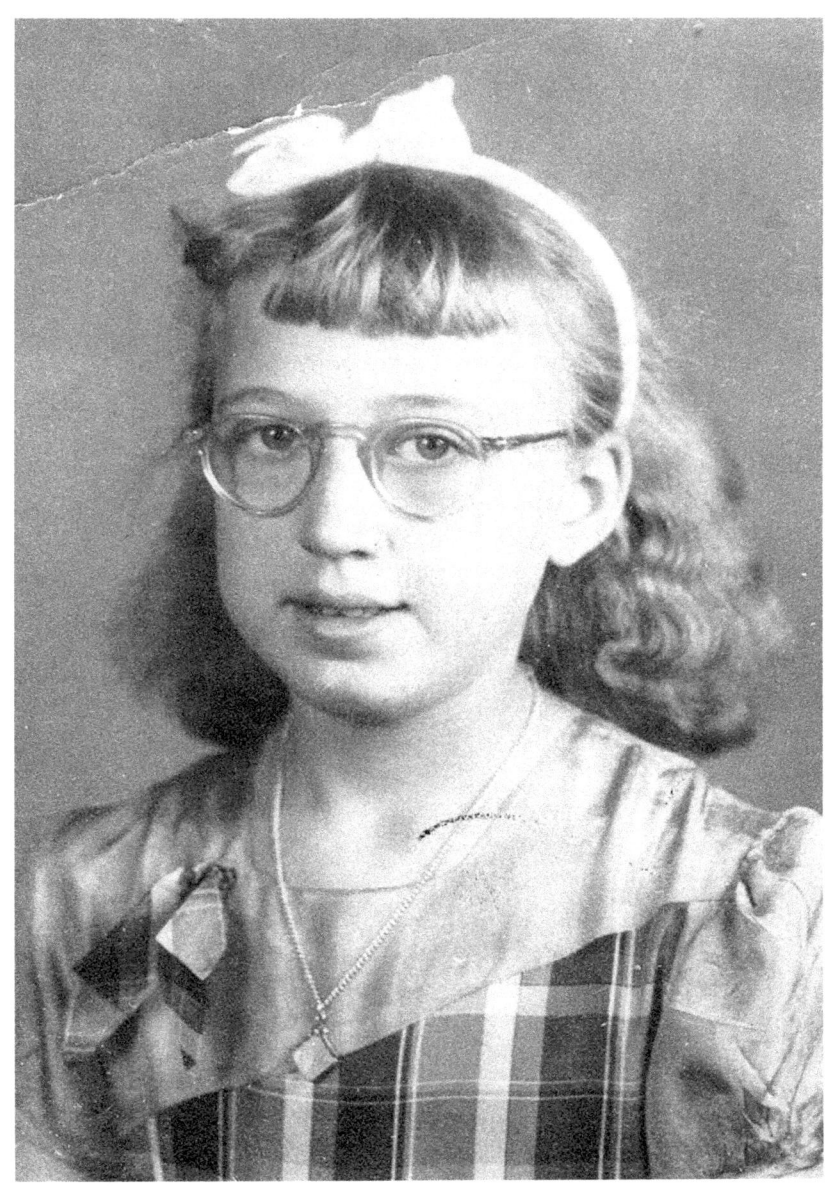

Miss Shelby Martin, daughter of Bob Martin. As a student of Granville School, her favorite playtime activities were cowboys and Indians and seeing the Saturday matinee. *Martin-Howell collection.*

the Coca-Cola plant. His family's last home was built in the Granville Park section of Winston-Salem. The house was erected in 1963 on Shober Street, which is named for Gottlieb Schober, an early leader of Salem. Schober ran the paper mill in 1790 and was also the first postmaster of Salem, preceding Benjamin Franklin's tenure as the first United States postmaster.

Hal remembers that most of the houses in West Salem were built before World War II. The West Salem area, around Granville Park and Hutton Street, had been dirt roads. "The World War II years were tough and lean times," he said. Rationing of food and gasoline supplies, along with practiced electrical blackouts, were regular occurrences during wartime. One experience that stands out in his mind during wartime was with reference to automobiles, buses and trucks.

> *All of these vehicles were required to have blinders on their headlights. The blinders helped to keep the light focused, so unnecessary light did not escape outward. In theory, this was done so no overhead enemy aircraft could spot heavily populated areas. Thank goodness we never needed it…Clothes, shoes, and groceries were very reasonable to buy back then. We could buy groceries for $8 to $10 and they lasted our 3 family members for two weeks. A gallon of milk cost $0.50. Our vegetables were grown in victory gardens. Victory gardens were a product of necessity during the war years.*

Hal's enthusiasm for auto, truck and bus mechanics led also to his detailed memories of auto information. "Our first car was a Chevy 24 model, 4 cylinder. It cost $150. Our first good car was a 29 model Ford. Standard cars built in the 1930s usually stopped running at or around 30,000 miles," he reflected.

> *Our entertainment centered around church and family. My wife and boy back in those days enjoyed walking to downtown Winston to Woolworth's Five and Dime store and eating at the lunch counter. They enjoyed taking in a movie at the Carolina Theatre where the movie cost only $0.10. How times have changed.*

In 1950, Hal worked for McLean Trucking as a mechanic supervisor. His wife worked for many years at Walgreen's drugstore on Fourth. He retired from McLean Trucking in 1975. A bit of Winston-Salem history parallels Hal's involvement with the trucking industry. His house on Marshall sat behind the first trucking terminal in Winston-Salem. Research has shown the terminal could have been one of the first multiuse terminals in North Carolina, meaning that several different trucking lines shared the same building. Hal's mechanical skills not only served his company well, but his neighbors too. Throughout his retirement and beyond, Hal was often called on to fix anything mechanical. Some woodworking was also required of him. He always responded with a smile and a helping hand. He also ran the voting precinct for West Salem at Latham Elementary for many years. Hal set a great example of citizenship for all residents to strive for. He has made Winston-Salem a much better place to live simply by his thoughtfulness and neighborly attitude.

King Joseph Brown Sr. was a pillar of the Winston-Salem community nearly all his life. Conversations with Brown have painted a picture of a unique resident. He was born in Winston-Salem in 1916, and he has seen the city grow and change. His portfolio reads as a who's who of Americans. He was educated in the public school system and graduated from Reynolds High School in 1933. After graduation, he worked at both Hanes Hosiery and Hanes Knitting. In 1941, he went to work as a civil servant at the Winston-Salem Post Office

The People

and retired from there thirty years later. He was called to arms in World War II and served as supervisor of the naval post office.

King was married and had five sons. He was always a family man, but it was his love of God that touched the community he so fondly called home. He was often referred to as the "Old Christian Soldier." He pedaled around the neighborhood on his bicycle, making sure all the young boys were awake and ready for church on Sunday morning. In 1934, Dr. Charles Stevens, pastor of Salem Baptist Church and founder of Piedmont Bible College, requested that King start a Christian book and Bible business. The business was believed to be the first all-Christian Bible and book service in the area. Upon entering the navy during World War II, King turned the business over to Salem Baptist Church, which established the Piedmont Bible Book Store. The store survives today.

For twenty-five years King served as chief judge at Latham Elementary school during elections, along with Hal Church. King's accomplishments could fill a book. In a historical way, he was a model twentieth-century man, carved from the same mold as Brother Gottlieb Schober and Brother Francis Fries, patriarchs of Salem.

Reverend William A. Cranford was born in the home of his maternal grandparents, Mr. and Mrs. Orville Pfaff, at 602 Hunter Avenue. William Cranford grew up in Winston-Salem and gave much insight into the evolution of the town. After the farms and industry of early years, families began to migrate to organized neighborhoods. The Pfaffs were one of the pioneering families to move to outlots of land west of Broad. Reverend Cranford said, "My mother's family came to Winston-Salem in 1884, according to family tradition. My great-grandparents were Francis W. Pfaff and Elizabeth Miller Pfaff. They built their house at 812 West. From a family of nine children, five sons had homes. They were Rufus, Thomas, Samuel, John and Orville." Samuel Pfaff's family carried the residence at 812 West while forming the Pfaff Glass Company, which still exists today on Peters Creek Parkway. John Pfaff established a large plumbing business and provided plumbing services for many residences and businesses throughout the city's growth. He resided at 118 Walnut and his plumbing business was less than a block away on Marshall, across from the Coca-Cola Bottling Company. Thomas Pfaff was also involved in the plumbing business. Rufus Pfaff was well traveled throughout the United States in sales. He built his family's home at 918 Academy. Orville Pfaff built a successful career at Taylor Brothers Tobacco Company.

Orville's grandson, William Cranford, attended Granville Graded School and, like many of the youth, learned to swim in the Granville indoor pool. He graduated from Reynolds High School. During that time he sang with a well-known, local quartet known as the Besper Singers, which had a program on the radio station WAIR (AM) on Sunday afternoon. The program was sponsored by B.O. Disher Furniture Company. On request the quartet performed at area churches. Reverend Cranford remembers: "One Sunday afternoon our program was delayed. Why? It was December 7, 1941. Pearl Harbor had been attacked!"

William attended and graduated from the University of North Carolina at Chapel Hill. While there, he roomed and became good friends with another Carolina native, actor Andy Griffith. Both young men sang in the choir at the University Methodist Church. Griffith was a soloist. They were both members of the Phi Mu Alpha honorary music fraternity. Reverend Cranford still keeps in touch with his friend with occasional visits. After graduating from the Moravian Theological Seminary in Bethlehem, Pennsylvania, William began serving in the ministry as the assistant pastor of Calvary Moravian Church in Winston-Salem. He also served as pastor of other Moravian congregations in other areas. He helped prepare for the publication of volume eight of *The Records of the Moravians in North Carolina*. After serving as pastor of Moravian churches in Ohio, New Jersey and

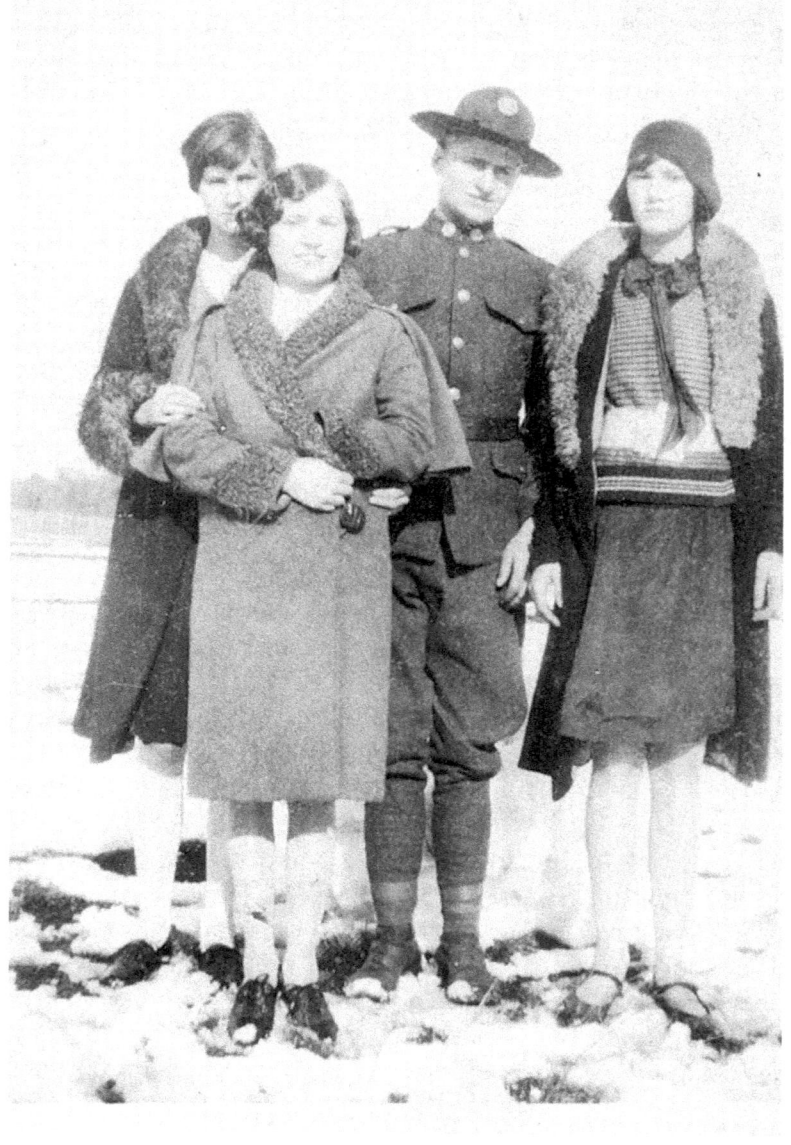

Mr. Bob Martin and family take a break from his war years at the beach. *Martin-Howell collection.*

The People

Pennsylvania, he retired in 1988 to his birth home in Winston-Salem. His life had taken him full circle. Reverend Cranford resided on the Board of Directors of the Wachovia Historical Society. He is also an accomplished writer, researcher and historian in his own right. He authored *The History of the Christ Moravian Church of West Salem*. Reverend Cranford has filed historical data in the Moravian archives at Old Salem and has helped multitudes of researchers from colleges and universities studying Moravian and American history to discover valuable information pertaining to Winston-Salem.

Thomas Holcomb relays growing up in Winston-Salem with his avid interest and great memories from his youth. In today's academic world, a young person's story is usually overlooked and given little importance. The heritage movement of all voices, young and old, is gaining strength, and rightly so. The citizens of the twenty-first century demand the whole story be told. Thomas Holcomb states the 1940s were the best years of his life and were the most enriching, historically. He was born in Martinsville, Virginia. At the young age of five, his family moved to Winston-Salem. Both his parents had family in the Piedmont area. In 1942, his family found a home that served as his lifelong residence. The house was built as a craftsman bungalow. The 1925 home brought magic and charm to the Holcomb family.

Thomas saw much change in his street and town as a youngster. World War II was on the horizon for America. The war efforts abroad and at home influenced the young as well as the adults. But, due to the children's innocence, the war was viewed as more of a fascination rather than in terms of the harsh realities that were bestowed on the adults. Thomas remembers the radio news announcements and the fireside chats by President Franklin Roosevelt. Through the media of the day, all the world's problems and actions were magically addressed and answered in a thirty-minute period.

Thomas and his boyhood friends were amazed and entertained by the newsreels and movie previews of the Saturday movie matinee playing at the State, Paramount and Carolina Theaters downtown. The newsreels ended and the childhood fun began with the movie fantasies of cowboys and Indians, space explorers and G men. The movie houses on Liberty and Fourth also had live stage shows. The State Theater, being the oldest at the time, had begun by showing vaudevillian performances and silent movies in the early twentieth century. In the 1930s, 1940s and even 1950s, movie stars and Hollywood cowboys graced the stages of these local movie palaces in order to entertain their young audience. Hopalong Cassidy, Red Ryder and others joined the list of earlier performers such as Hoot Gibson, Rudolph Valentino and the greatest magician of all time, Harry Houdini, in playing the hallowed halls of the State and Paramount Theaters.

Thomas recalled a live stage moment as vividly as if it had happened only a day ago. Lash Lerue, a unique cowboy star, performed not with a six-gun, but with his patented bullwhips. The whips were used in his motion pictures to disarm and catch the bad guys. Lash, like many of the older cowboys, performed his own stunts; many were excellent marksmen. Lash was no exception with his mastery of the bullwhips. Another cowboy star with modern-day notoriety was a child actor, Little Beaver. Little Beaver was a character Indian sidekick to Red Ryder, another well-loved cowboy. Little Beaver often assisted Red in apprehending the bad guys or helping to rescue the damsels in distress. Little Beaver was an excellent marksman with a bow and arrow. He demonstrated his ability on stage, and since the ages of the children were close to his own, the applause was deafening. Today, we know Little Beaver as Robert Blake, who played in Little Rascal comedies and was recently cleared as a murder suspect in the killing of his estranged wife. "Another reason to dwell in the past instead of the present sometimes," says Thomas Holcomb. The movies, World War II, cowboys and Indians had an impressive impact on the young boys of the 1940s.

When a birthday, Christmas or special event came around, Thomas, like most boys, hoped for a present. The war had made toys, bubblegum, etc., rather rare or downright obsolete. Thomas recalls the war's impact on his own gift one year. His birthday had arrived and he had his heart set on one present the whole year: a "nickel plated Gene Autry pistol." He had admired the prize at Silver's Department Store on Liberty Street, which was often called a five-and-dime store. Silver's Department Store, later renamed H.L. Green's Department Store and McCory's Department Storewere, along with the Woolworth five-and-dime, was one of the last department stores downtown. Thomas said a boy or girl could get lost in time and space in this store. The store was unique and was normally only found in much larger cities of that day, as it had four floors. The top-level entrance was on Trade and the second-floor entrance was on Liberty, plus two more levels below ground. Silver's had been built in the early 1900s on the site of one of Winston's largest nineteenth-century tobacco warehouses, the Farmer's Warehouse. Thomas was always fascinated by the Liberty Street entrance because the pavement out in front of the entrance was covered with a four- by four-foot steel partition cover. At certain times throughout the day the partition rose up from the pavement and a man appeared, as if by magic. The event, of course, was not magic, but the loading ramp for receiving stock.

Silver's Department Store had everything a child or adult could need or want. It even had its own miniature grocery store tucked away on the third floor below Liberty. "The magic of the downtown hustling and bustling with customers and merchants was lost with the entrance of the shopping centers and later the Hanes Mall," said Thomas. He remarks, "The old downtown shopping wasn't as fast and efficient as what is found in today's market, which includes the Internet buying, but again, much more magical." Unfortunately, there was no magic for Thomas in regard to that nickel-plated Gene Autry pistol. The war made the pistol too expensive. He did receive a pistol; but the affordable one he got was made from pressed sawdust. Thomas relays, "It was not the same."

After the war, things changed for Thomas and his family. The ration stamps for all the food necessities and non-necessities, along with a plentiful gasoline supply, made life easier for all. The small neighborhood grocery stores of the city could stock their shelves once more. Winston-Salem was no exception. There existed seven mom and pop grocery stores along the 100, 200, 300 and 400 blocks of South Green Street, related Thomas. At the corner of Green and First, there was even an A&P store, a national chain. The building was recently razed for a new Warthog's baseball stadium downtown. Thomas reminisces,

The People

We did not have any idea that the chain food stores—the A&P was the first arriving in 1917 on Liberty—which [would help] to destroy the "ma and pa" stores we so dearly loved. The magic of ordering your grocery list by phone and having it delivered to your door by auto, truck or even a boy on a bicycle made our family feel special. I was driven to Western Auto downtown in 1946 and presented a brand new red Western Flyer bicycle. I now picked up our groceries by myself. I was proud. Also, I graduated from the play pistols to my first Daisy Air Rifle and guess what, I did not shoot my eye out.

Thomas references the 1983 movie version of *A Christmas Story*—one of his favorites. The Christmastime theme hits home to a boy who grew up in 1940s America.

When Thomas turned into a teenager at the close of the 1940s, the downtown took on another meaning. "With the opening of the first mega department store, Sears Roebuck & Co. at Fourth and Broad, the '50s had arrived," said Thomas. "I was old enough to see what became my perfect movie—*The Outlaw* with Jane Russell." A story for another time when we are a little older.

The stories of Winston-Salem personalities could fill hundreds of books. With every door one opens on an individual, many more persons appear. One such door was opened to me at a young age. While growing up on Broad near First Street in the 1950s and 1960s, the old dividing line between Salem and Winston was my backyard. The 100 block of South Broad and Shallowford Street, the last remaining part of the original road that connected the eighteenth-century Old Shallowford Road and nineteenth-century Plank Road of Brookstown Avenue, was occupied by houses dating from the eighteenth and nineteenth centuries to the early twentieth century. Several of the houses along Shallowford had been razed in the mid-1950s to build a modern ice cream restaurant, Parker's Drive-In Eatery. My residence was at 119 South Broad Street. Several large houses in the 100 block of this street were constructed in the 1910s. The houses of the 100 block replaced a farm and farmhouse that had been built on the road to Salem, Old Shallowford Road. The houses in this block were heated with what was referred to by old-timers as "the best heat for any modern house built after 1900." Steam heat, by way of old-fashioned radiator and boiler systems, fueled these once aristocratic homes.

As I was enjoying a game of kick the can as child, I learned the homes had a hidden mystery. All of the homes had been built on a ridge that towered over several stories from the front of the homes to the back of the property lines. Terracing and ravines was how the early Moravians referred to the landscape of Winston-Salem. As I played I noticed a figure moving in the basement of one of the houses. I looked in a small utility window of the basement to investigate further and, shocked, I thought I had found a burglar. This was no burglar, but an old gentleman who had worked for all the families in the area for many years. The African American gentleman, who called himself Uncle George, had worked "firing the furnace," as he called it, in most of the "rich folks'" houses since they were built. His knowledge of the area and homes transcended nearly fifty years. I was told a doctor had built the home in which I lived. According to Uncle George, the doctor had a very large family that spread throughout the whole the house, which by my accounts was around five thousand square feet. I tried to coax Uncle George on more than one occasion over a period of six years to give me his last name. Later, as an adult and researcher, I tried to find out more about Uncle George, but to no avail.

This story reminds me often of the need for the African American history of the city to be brought forward with extensive research by those who lived it. When a history of all diverse individuals is shared and recorded, a more complete knowledge of our past can be understood by all. Only then can we begin to live in a more harmonious world. This is the challenge I leave with my readers and the people of the Twin City.

CHAPTER 5.

How Does Our Garden Grow?

To answer the question posed by this chapter's title is to look deep into what makes the Twin City unique: the arts, music, architecture of its buildings and transportation provide Winston-Salem with a garden of town experiences that are rich and fruitful for body, mind and soul. Exploring these four subjects demonstrates why history is so important in keeping our garden strong, thus never forgetting the past that made us this way.

In alphabetical order, our journey begins with the architecture in the Twin City. Much like the link between church and state, Moravian architecture reflected the values and ideals of individuals, groups and government within the church and governing agencies. The Twin City followed the same ideals in expanding the city physically as well as spiritually in the design of buildings and structures. The transition to brick construction brought the traditional Moravian architecture of Salem more in line with English and American buildings.

The church congregation conformed its congregational buildings to existing structures, particularly those found on the square. The Girls' School (1805) conformed to the influence of the Home Church with its hooded entrance and ironwork. The inspector's house (1810) was located beside the Boys' School, so it was built to reflect the structure of the neighboring edifice. The inspector's house compared in style to both the Home Church and the Girls' School. The structures of the surrounding rural area outside Salem before 1800 were impermanent. These early structures, although not worthy of comment in respect to the town, were to be recycled into future buildings after 1800.

The Krueser farmhouse, later to become the Brietz plantation, had its beginning in 1818 in West Salem. The house's Federalist style did not match the typical old South plantations. Dr. Frederick Schumann arrived in Salem to form a plantation with more than two hundred slaves, but he was forced to leave the immediate congregational town and begin his plantation at what was to be called Happy Hill. He later changed his stance on slavery, believing it to be immoral, and deported his slaves to Africa. In 1860, the rural area of Forsyth was inhabited by few farms with very few slaves. Most of the larger old South plantations of western North Carolina were located in Davie County. Most of the remaining residents of the surrounding township were small farmers, and none owned slaves.

Winston-Salem

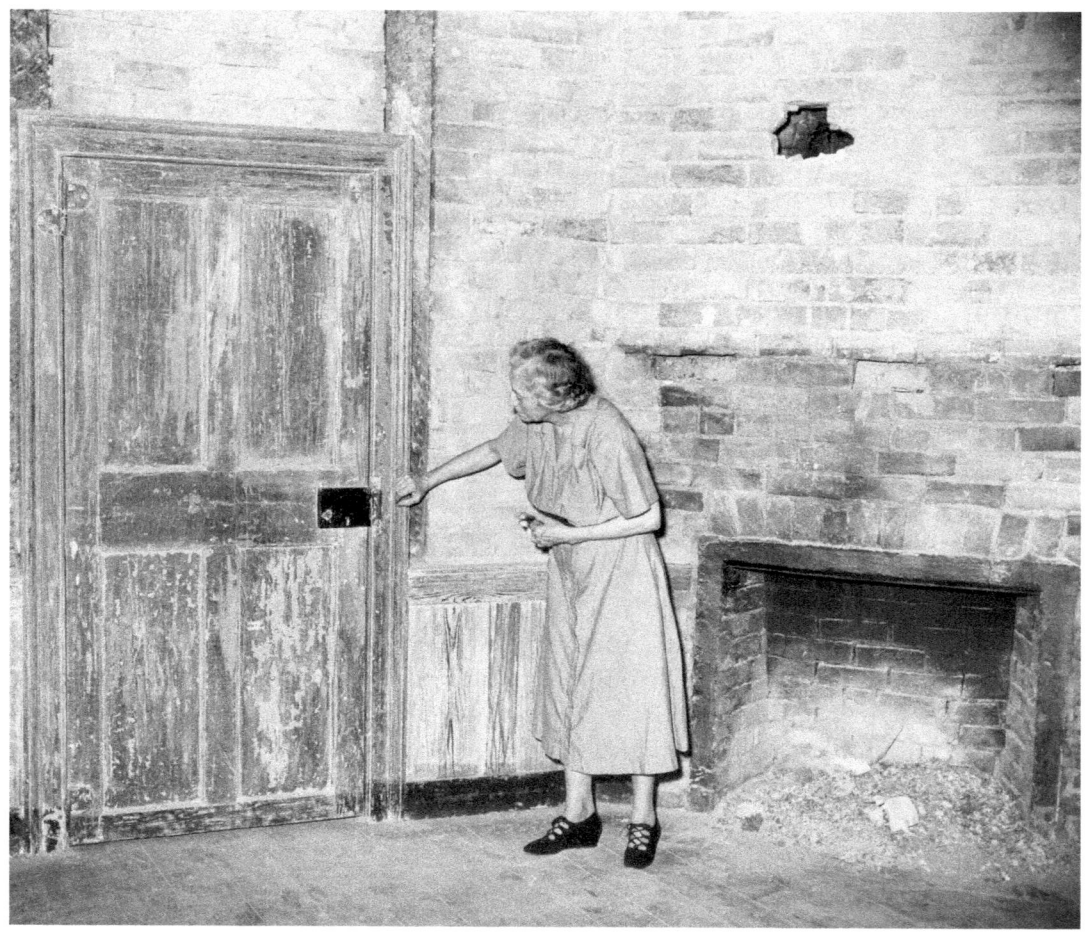

Old Salem Inc. began to reconstruct the Moravian Salem in 1950. Many houses, such as this one from eighteenth-century West Salem, were razed and much of their parts were used in reconstruction in the historic district.

    The only building that survived the eighteenth century was the Adam Spach 1774 "rock house" at Friedberg, which was built with the assistance of Salem's masons. It was a fieldstone structure over a spring with a large basement into which the cattle were driven. Portholes for guns were located around the outer walls. This particular type of structure was found in West Salem near the Peters Creek area in an earlier settlement known as the Lagenauer settlement (1740). This home was built in a style similar to the "rock house," portholes and all. The structure along Peters Creek is often omitted from written histories of Winston-Salem because of its earlier time period, before the founding of Salem. In past histories of Salem, few buildings of comment appeared from the West Salem landscape.

    The twentieth-century increase in office buildings, factories, churches, homes and governmental halls was directly linked to the financial success of the Twin City. Between 1915 and 1929, before the great stock market crash, the amount of building in the town

How Does Our Garden Grow?

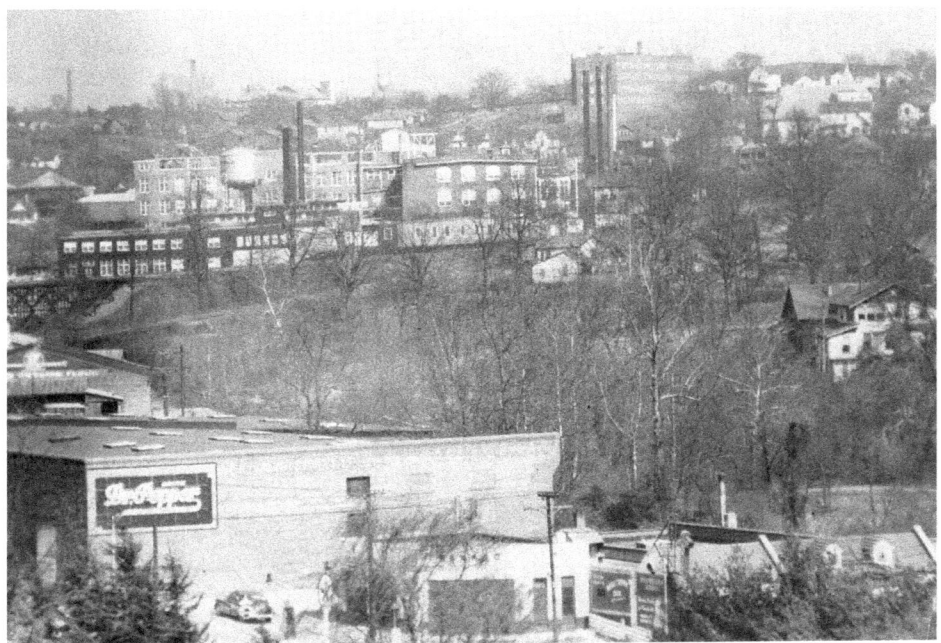

Chatham Mills is shown in this circa 1950s photo in the West End neighborhood above the shops along Reynolda Road at Northwest Boulevard.

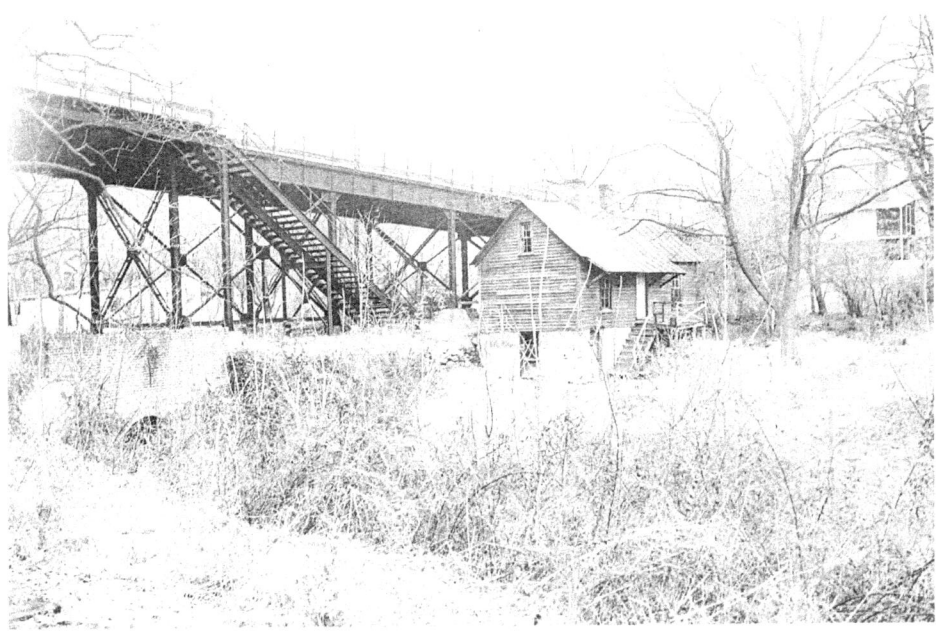

The bridges of Salem and West Salem connected the two neighborhoods over the Southbound Railway, circa 1910. The Bank Street Bridge and the eighteenth-century outbuilding of early West Salem are now history.

Winston-Salem

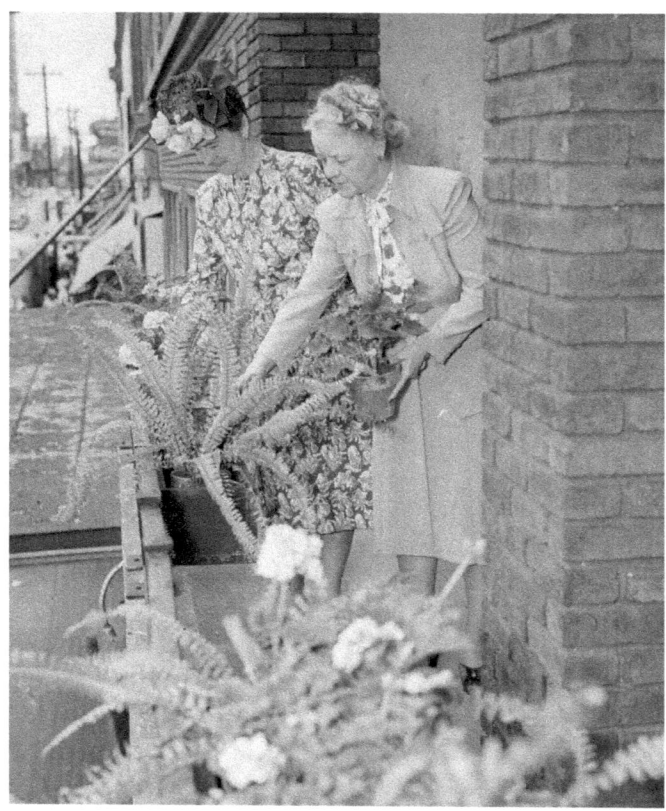

Many storefronts along Trade Street had small apartment and town homes on their upper decks. Here, two ladies are bringing their garden to beautify the tobacco trade street of the 1940s.

had increased by more than 800 percent. At the same time, the city was expanding, first from the center core and then through the newly created suburban housing developments. The first residential developments—East Winston, North Winston and West Salem—had appeared in the 1880s with the arrival of the concept of neighborhoods. The largest suburban development, Ardmore, appeared in 1914. Ardmore claimed a record of building one home a week for twenty-two years. The Southside and Waughtown areas arrived in the mix in the nineteenth century, but were not part of the city limits. The expansion in the 1920s included Reynolda Village, the Granville Park area, Crafton Heights and Melrose. The West Highlands, Westover, Westview, Reynolda Park, Forest Hills, White View, Bonair and Konnoak Hills followed. Also in the 1920s, at the height of Jim Crow, the city's largest and most restrictive development began in Buena Vista and Country Club Estates. Alta Vista, a substantial restricted suburb for African Americans, arrived also.

Building and construction firms also grew between this period, from 17 contractors in 1910 to more than 39 by 1924. By 1966, Winston-Salem was home to 112 general contractors, not including the subcontracted firms, which doubled that number. This was a large jump, considering the town had started with only the Fogles and the Millers earlier. By 1910, two architectural firms were established. By the 1920s, six separate and very large firms called the Twin City home. There were many buildings and developments that rose beginning in the 1920s and on into the 1960s. Examples of these are the

How Does Our Garden Grow?

Reynolds Tobacco Research Laboratory (1957), the Vienna School (1957), Northside Shopping Center (1958), Parkway Plaza Shopping Center (1959), Wake Forest University (1950s), the Hanes Community Center (1958) and the Western Electric office building on Reynolda Road.

The styles of the late nineteenth century that helped to create the modern-day neighborhoods were outmoded when the wealthier families moved to the west. The buildings and houses, adhering to classic revival styles such as Georgian and Italian Renaissance, arrived to the scene with a mixture of column and pilaster and open columnated façades. An example of this was in the new post office on Fifth Street, with its huge columns giving the effect of an open courtyard leading to the main entrance. A crowning achievement of the 1920s was the Richard J. Reynolds Auditorium and Reynolds High School. This school became known as Society Hill and the Georgian design was led by Winston's most popular architect, Charles Barton Keen. The design used Corinthian columns based on the same proportions as the Roman Pantheon. The exterior was colonial brick with Indiana limestone cornices and trimmings. Before the Depression, the last substantial building to be built was the Reynolds building in 1929. The building trends after the Depression were mixed, and culminated in the 1970s with designs that were of little architectural interest.

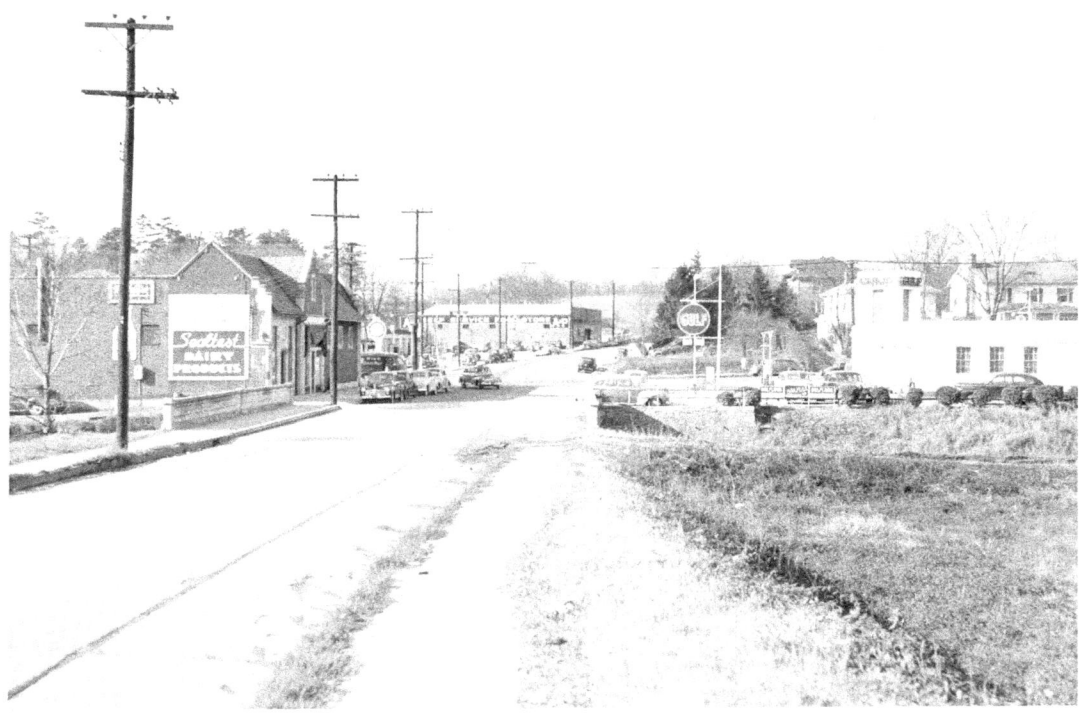

The bridge over Peters Creek at First Street is visible, circa 1950. The bridge connected the West End neighborhood and the Ardmore neighborhood.

Winston-Salem

"The City of Arts" has become the catchphrase of the Twin City. The quality and diversity of the arts, with the likes of the School of the Arts as an example, rival that of much larger cities. The list includes the Winston-Salem Symphony, Chamber Music and Piedmont Opera Theater. The new Trade Street Arts District has been growing and evolving every day. The arts, including music, dance and painting, are expressed throughout the Twin City from its earliest years to the present. Our first stop on the arts tour, an institution that promotes and presents all of the above, is on Reynolda Road.

Reynolda House and Gardens is a magical place where beauty, history, fashion, art and painting come alive in the former estate of R.J. and Katherine Reynolds. The house is one of a few early twentieth-century American country homes that still exist in their original forms. Located a mere three miles from the central business district of the Twin City, Reynolda was Reynolds's attempt to create a world of his own. Whether you are rich or poor, visiting Reynolda today will remind you of our own garden that has grown throughout our lives. Early in the 1900s, the founder of R.J. Reynolds Tobacco Company began the construction of buildings to support his 1,067-acre estate. The community consisted of state-of-the-art dairy barns, a church, school, greenhouse, central power plant, laundry, icehouse, carriage sheds, blacksmith shop, smokehouse and cottages for staff and their families. The architectural design was to resemble a quaint English country village.

Reynolda House is currently used as an art museum, but the house looks as it did in 1917; the gardens are an approximation of the ones created eighty years ago. Visiting Reynolda gives you a sense of the past that occurred in the 1910s and 1920s in the early city. Katherine and R.J. conceived their country place to have a wealth of gardens and recreation facilities and to be a beacon of light in agriculture and community life. Reynolds did not live long in the country house, as he passed in 1918. Katherine and R.J. had developed an enthusiasm for rural life after their honeymoon in Europe. After reading pages of American magazines depicting country homes, this was the place where both wanted to be. James B. Duke, the tobacco tycoon who had battled R.J. earlier, had developed his own country home. Duke developed a farm in Summerfield, New Jersey, which encompassed 2,200 acres. It featured a half-mile racetrack for harness horses, a diary for 250 Guernsey cows and spectacular gardens filled with rare trees and flowers. Duke's country home could have had an influence on R.J., fueling their rivalry that had been created earlier.

In 1936, Mary Reynolds and her husband Charles Babcott bought out the other heirs and Reynolda was under one ownership once more. With the Babcotts' help, Reynolda House flowered anew as it became a museum for all to see and love. Much like the twenty founding families' experiences in the early days at Reynolda, now the rest of the Twin City could experience this garden into the present and beyond.

One of the most enduring structures and parks was a culmination of the work of the Reynolds family and the Hanes family. Richard J. Reynolds High School and Reynolds Auditorium were dedicated in May 1924 in honor of tobacco magnet R.J. Reynolds as a gift to the community from his widow, Katherine Reynolds Johnston. The same team that built Reynolda was responsible for this structure. The school and auditorium overlooked the new Hanes Park. This land was given by the Hanes family

How Does Our Garden Grow?

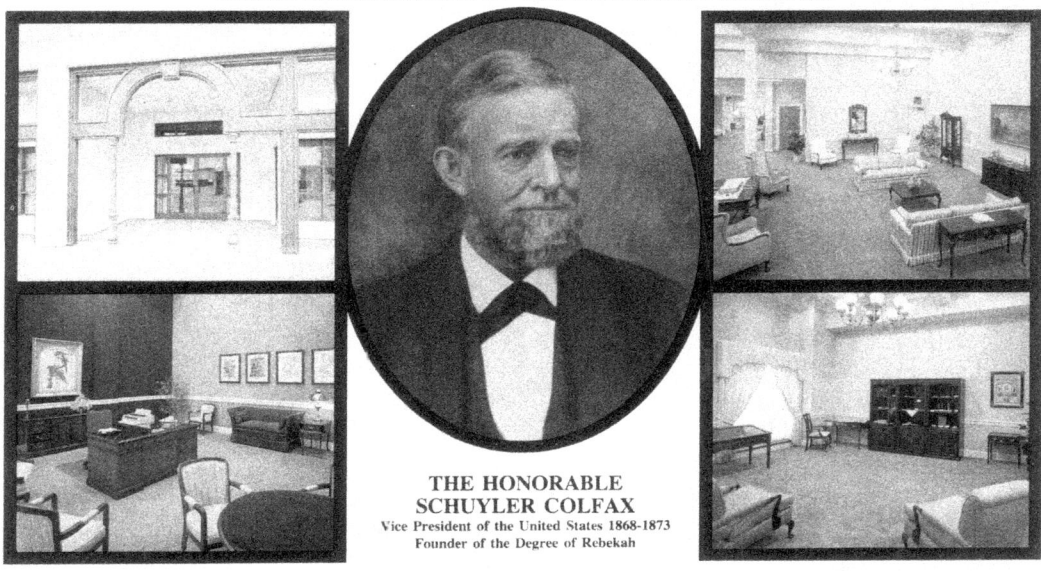

The Oddfellows building on Trade Street is home to the Sovereign Grand Lodge International Headquarters and International Rebekah Headquarters. The international museum of the Oddfellows and Rebekah Organization is located in this building dating to the nineteenth century.

to the people of Winston-Salem for recreation and play on the edge on the West End neighborhood. The grounds of both were landscaped with flowers and trees to match those in the Reynolda area. Today this natural beauty is enjoyed by many generations of the Twin City.

Military bands arrived on the scene in the 1830s and progressed until the Civil War. The bands were used to drill and to perform "martial music," which was used for parades. The band rendered marches and classical selections while retaining woodwinds as a sweet reminder beside ringing brasses. Ceremonies commemorating the signing of the Mecklenburg Declaration of Independence were composed in honor of George Washington, General Thomas Polk and Governor David L. Swain. From the early beginnings, music had been woven into the rituals of the Moravian Church as well as into daily life. The Moravians had brought the first trombones to colonial North America and had built the first organs. Salem musicians played for church services and for special celebrations. On Easter Sunday, they played in God's Acre to celebrate the Resurrection. The Salem Sunrise Service is one of the longest continuing services in the country and celebrates in the same way it has from the very beginning. The Salem Military Band entered the Civil War as part of the group of musicians known as the Twenty-sixth Regiment Band of the Confederates. After the war, they returned and formed the Salem Band. Some of the band members marched and played in most of the parades and

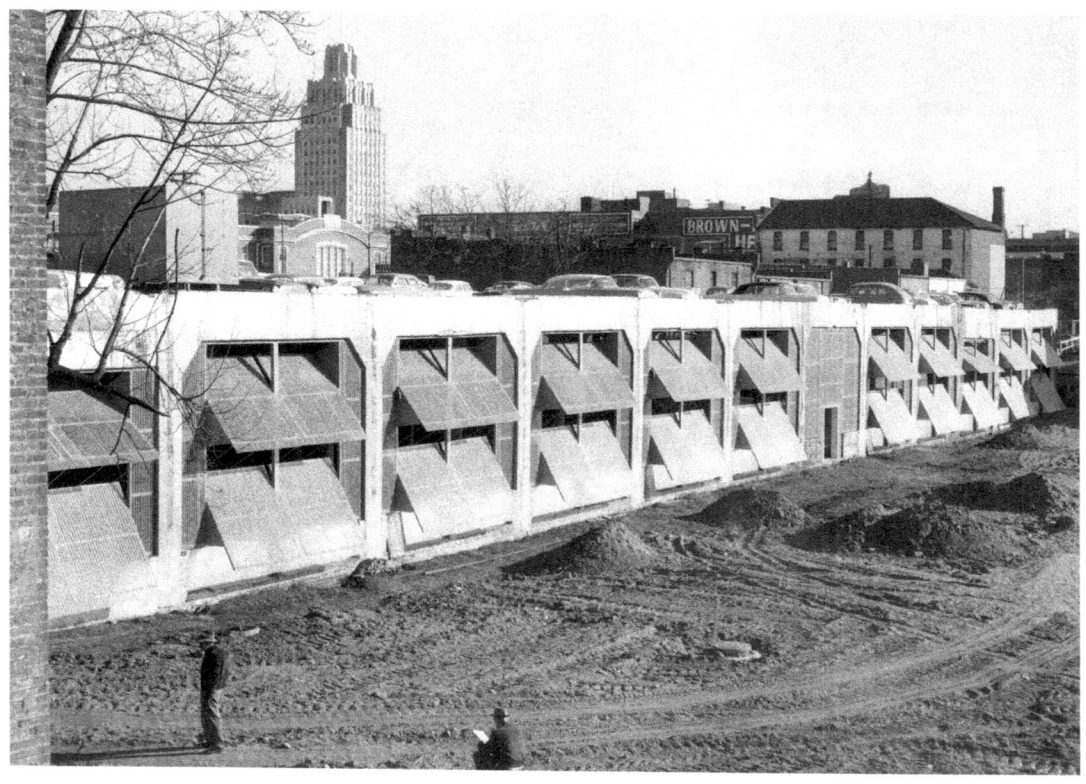

Modernization in the 1950s had arrived in a new necessary parking deck along Trade Street.

events until the early twentieth century. Some of these men were James M. Fisher, A.C. Meinung, Julias Leinbach, Daniel T. Crouse, Augustus Hauser, William Hall, Joe Hall, A.P. Gibson and Samuel Mickey. Some of the members of the 1912 Salem Band were children of the aforementioned. These were Robert Ormsby, William Ellias, Ralph Pfaff, Henry Hanes, Douglas Rights, Clarence Leinbach, John T. Stockton, Charlie Vance, Francis Grunert, Sam Brewer, Harry Mickey, Ollie Peddycord, Sidney Brietz, Bernard Pfohl and Walter Kern.

Turning from music, we turn toward literature with the Moravian writers. The Moravians had always kept good records and the archives from the late eighteenth century include many examples. Gottlieb Rueter, surveyor, wrote explaining the landscape: "No matter where I stand, it is possible to go to any other part of the land without crossing a stream, though the path may resemble the moves of a piece in a game of draughts." His writing explained the mountains and streams and the difficulty of acquiring good direct roads into Wachovia. He wrote, "Willows make pretty trees in the bottoms and the umbrella tree would be an ornament to any lawn." The writings of the Moravians were extensive day-to-day accounts. In 1855, after the formation of Forsyth County and the beginnings of Winston, English had replaced German as the official language of Wachovia's church and community records.

How Does Our Garden Grow?

The first book published in 1857 gave an account of the community. *The Moravians in North Carolina*, written in English by Levin T. Reichel, was the first publication that brought the church and town records together in one form. Edward J. Steadman founded a magazine that he felt spoke for the whole intellectual South. These publications were found in several issues of Winston's *Western Sentinel* in the late 1850s. After the Civil War, a literary figure came to Winston. His name was Calvin H. Wiley, and his cultural influence was felt throughout the South. He became the first superintendent of North Carolina's Common Schools. He nearly singlehandedly built the state's public school structure before the Civil War. He was also an accomplished writer, writing romances published in America and England. He also edited and wrote for the *Southern Weekly Post* and other literary journals. He had also written textbooks for the schools.

Emma A. Lehman arrived to Salem Academy as a teacher and her poetry was published in European circles as well. Her collection of poetry, *A Guide to Forsyth County*, included "Sunset on Pilot Mountain." Lehman is the example of an educated woman of the South. The next literary person to arrive was young Adelaide Fries, a Salem College graduate, in 1896. Her true calling was history and her extensive scholarly research made her the first and foremost historian of the Twin City. In 1898, she published a local history of Forsyth County based on records between 1753 and 1898. Wiley, Lehman and Fries set the stage for one of the most brilliant and famous literary figures of the Twin City in the last half of the nineteenth century.

John Henry Boner was a tall, fair-haired twenty-year-old, who because of health problems had avoided military service during the Civil War. He founded a newspaper, the *Salem Observer*. It was a literary gem in relation to former papers published in the area. *Whispering Pines* was Boner's first volume of poetry, and it was published in New York in 1883 and included sixty-five poems. With these poems, America learned about life in Salem and North Carolina. He sent many of his poems to Edward Oldham, owner of the Winston *Western Sentinel*, who published them as well. The fulfillment that Boner received from his poetry carried through the years. Boner passed away of tuberculosis in 1903, at the age of fifty-eight. Bishop Edward Rondthaler wrote in the church memorabilia of his burial: "The poet of our graveyard, the late John Henry Boner, with notable appreciation." His poetry succeeded him and was praised by national critics for years to come. On the basis of his fame, he was considered the foremost North Carolina literary figure of his time. At the beginning of the 1920s, with the arrival of Richard J. Reynolds High School, the school's literary newspaper adopted Boner's *Whispering Pines* as its official name; the name still exists today.

Winston-Salem's history of transportation begins with wilderness roads and clumsy wagons and ends with modern airports and fleets of trucks. The first roads of the Twin City began in 1753. Wachovia was a tract of streams, meadows and woods in Rowan County, but no navigable stream flowed within miles. A normal trip to enter the Wachovia tract took several weeks and the road was very bad. The journey to Bethabara was followed by some good roads from Pennsylvania, but upon reaching the wilderness of Maryland the trip became very bad.

In the Salem of nearly two hundred years ago, the modes of transportation were detailed in many varieties: horses, buggies and trains are a few examples. The roads

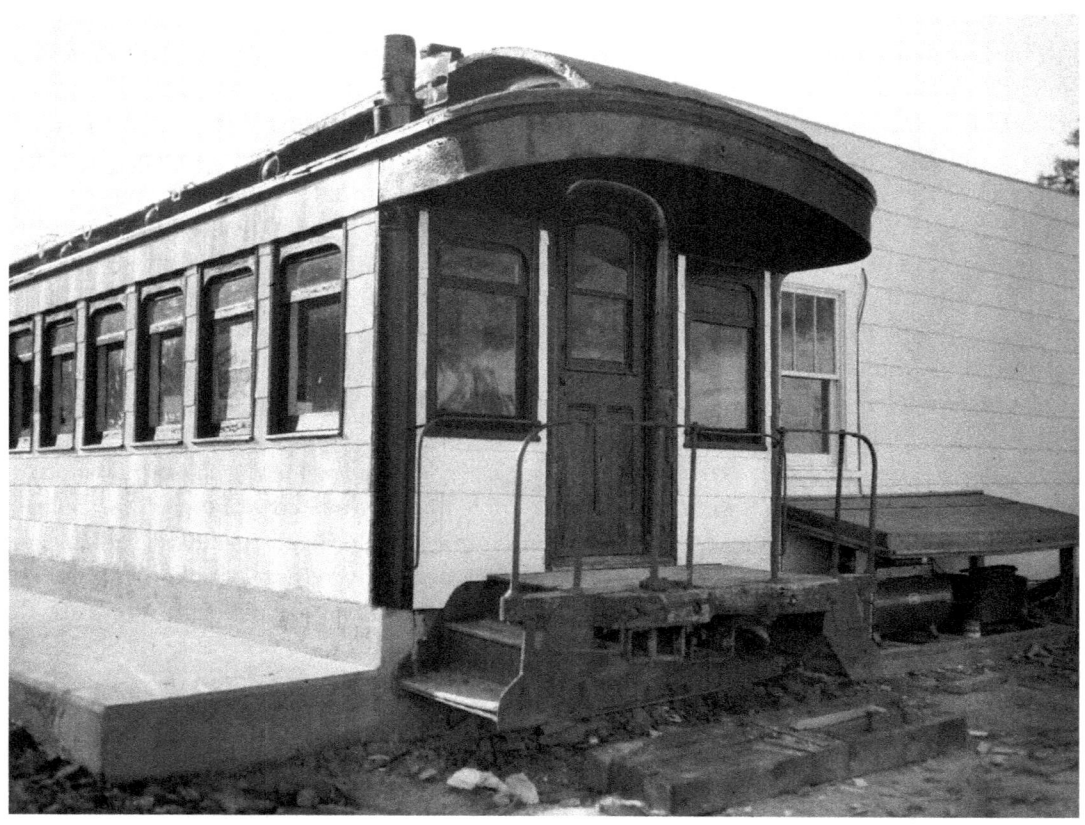

One of the last city trolleys from the nineteenth and early twentieth centuries was recycled for a time as a restaurant downtown. Ollie's Trolley was the restaurant's name.

and bridges that were traveled throughout the Salem neighborhoods were lined with ravines and valleys. Early roads throughout central North Carolina have a connection with much older Indian paths. Several of the colonial roads were found near Salem and helped to connect them to the outside world. The most important roads were the King's Road, the road to Shallowford, the road to Salisbury, the road to Cumberland and Plank Road. The town of Salem was connected to all of these roads. The connectors ran through West Salem so as not to clog the congregational town.

National distinction arrived in Salem by way of President George Washington's visit in 1791. President Washington was impressed by what he saw and experienced here. After he finished his journey across the United States he sent out public officials to set up "post towns" throughout the country. The post towns were towns that were decreed important for trading, commerce and refueling for further settlers. Usually the most modern towns for the times were chosen. The officials arrived in Salem about 1805. Salem became an earmark for those traveling north, south and to the west. The post town of Salem was for many years the last major outpost for settlers heading west, northwest and southwest in order to colonize future states of the country. The settlers resided and refreshed in Salem, preparing for their long journey westward.

How Does Our Garden Grow?

Another part of the roads that gave the citizens and visitors trouble was due to the steepness of the hills and the drop-offs of the ravines. For example, Paper Mill Road (1795), which connected the industrialized area of the paper mill to the congregational part of Salem (Old Salem), had an elaborate arched bridge over Petersbach (Peters Creek). Buggies and light wagons could travel over the bridge easily. Before the bridge was built, the terrain of Petersbach was virtually impossible to cross except by foot traffic. The bridge served the community and westward pioneers for more than fifty years. Unfortunately, in 1850, a major flood hit the area, washing out all the bridges. More modern bridges followed. The historical bridges that still exist in the Twin City and especially in the former town of Salem are important because they carry the remnants of that bygone period. One such bridge is the Wachovia Street bridge (1894), which was constructed in a horseshoe shape. The arch is common bond brick, while the abutments are cut granite block. This type of masonry bridge was very rare in the South, particularly for a non-railroad bridge. The architecture of the Wachovia Street bridge, along with that of a bridge on Academy Street at Factory Row and a third bridge on Brookstown Avenue, is extremely unusual in this region.

The primary mode of transportation in the late nineteenth and early twentieth centuries was by far the most enjoyable for many of the residents, as this period was the age of the trolley. In 1890, the city decided to study the idea of bringing a trolley to Winston. The trolley was scheduled to run from city hall in Winston to the Waughtown area. The plan revived an area of the city's history that had flourished from 1890 to 1936, with the trolley being the primary transportation. The Thomas Car Works in High Point was one of the largest builders of trolleys. Today it is known as Thomas Built Bus and provides buses for the schools. The trolley ran down South Main, crossed the bridge on Salem Creek and then turned at Waughtown onto Sprague. Adjoining lines took the cars into other areas. When the first trolley rolled down Main on July 14, 1890, it marked the opening of only the third electric railway system in the country. The Winston-Salem Street Railway was incorporated March 11, 1889. Its organizers included Thomas A. Edison, Frank J. Sprague, W.H. Wingate, Edward H. Johnson and J.H. McClement. Sprague was given credit for designing Winston-Salem's system, and with that Sprague Street was named in his honor. The trolleys were kept at what was called "the car barn" at the corner of Church and Second. When the foundation for the new federal building was dug, remains of this trolley facility were discovered.

In 1891, the Winston-Salem Street Railway and Winston Electric Light and Motive Power Company consolidated to form the Winston-Salem Railway and Electric Company. The railway handled hundreds of passengers daily. In 1900, the Fries Manufacturing and Power Company purchased the railway and lighting system. Between 1900 and 1926, the railway was prominent, with very few buses existing. In 1935, Duke Power had purchased the trolley system, but it disbanded in 1936. With the Duke Power buses taking over all the routes, the trolley system was history.

The coming of the trolley system also instigated the beginning of the horseless carriages. By the mid-1920s, jitneys had begun serving local counties. These were early buses and were owned by the African American community. The jitneys expanded in 1926 to become the Safe Bus Company. The first officers were H.F. Morgan, president;

J.F. Hairston, vice-president; and C.R. Peoples, secretary. That same year, John L. Gilmer bought up several county jitney services and began the Camel City Coach Company. In 1930, the Camel City Coach Company merged with the Blue and Gray Lines of West Virginia to form the national Atlantic Greyhound Lines. The Greyhound lines have continued to serve up to the present date. Several bus stations appeared on the scene beginning in the 1920s, when one was located on Marshall Street in the industrial area of Winston-Salem. A new bus station arose in the downtown area of Winston near Cherry and Marshall in the 1940s. An example of the Greyhound Bus history was given in an advertisement dated 1935, when the bus station existed at 935 South Marshall. The motto of the Greyhound in Winston was, "As grows Winston-Salem, so grows Greyhound." In 1925, the company began with 6 buses, 5 stations, 25 employees, 192 route miles and 1,800 passengers per month. By 1935, it was advertised that they had grown to 205 buses, 318 stations, 585 employees, 5,481 route miles and 249,000 passengers per month. The Greyhound was a total success.

As the trains, Model Ts and trolleys were phasing themselves out, the roads were beginning to get larger and faster. The brand-new Interstate 40 link snaked through Winston-Salem in the mid- to late 1950s. Many old-timers remembered the road almost as a family member

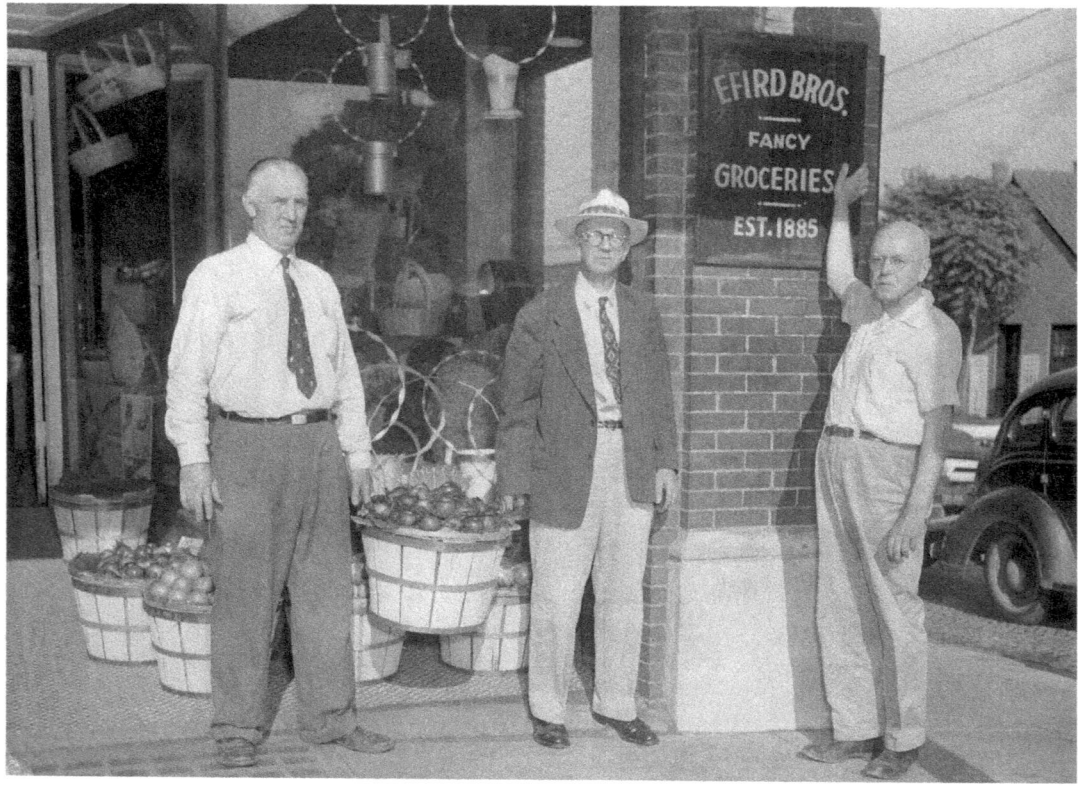

The Efird family had established itself early on in the grocery business. The family also expanded into retail and early tobacco interest.

How Does Our Garden Grow?

whom you wish had never come to visit. The highway was obsolete the day it opened. It also had a dark side, as it took away many of the homes of Salem. The highway cut a path of destruction through the East and West Salem communities and split neighborhoods in the west. With this split, the isolation of the northern part of West Salem from the southern part aided in the decline of the 1960s of many of the neighborhoods, from West End in West Salem to Holly Avenue. In the city of Salem there were nearly two hundred homes and businesses that were lost due to the highway. Both black and white suffered. The highways and parkways of Winston and Salem created many losses at the same time that they increased the pace for the twentieth century that has never slowed down. When we look at the past of transportation, we find a certain amount of humility in a slower pace than that which is found today. Many are beginning to wonder if the downtown area and the neighborhoods surrounding it should adopt more of a green space with more foot traffic and bicycle transportation.

The last garden we will touch on is one that everyone who has lived through generations of the Twin City can remember. The grocery stores of Winston have served as meeting places, learning places and places that have nourished us. In 1918, in a few-mile radius in the downtown and older neighborhoods there were many mom and pop grocery stores.

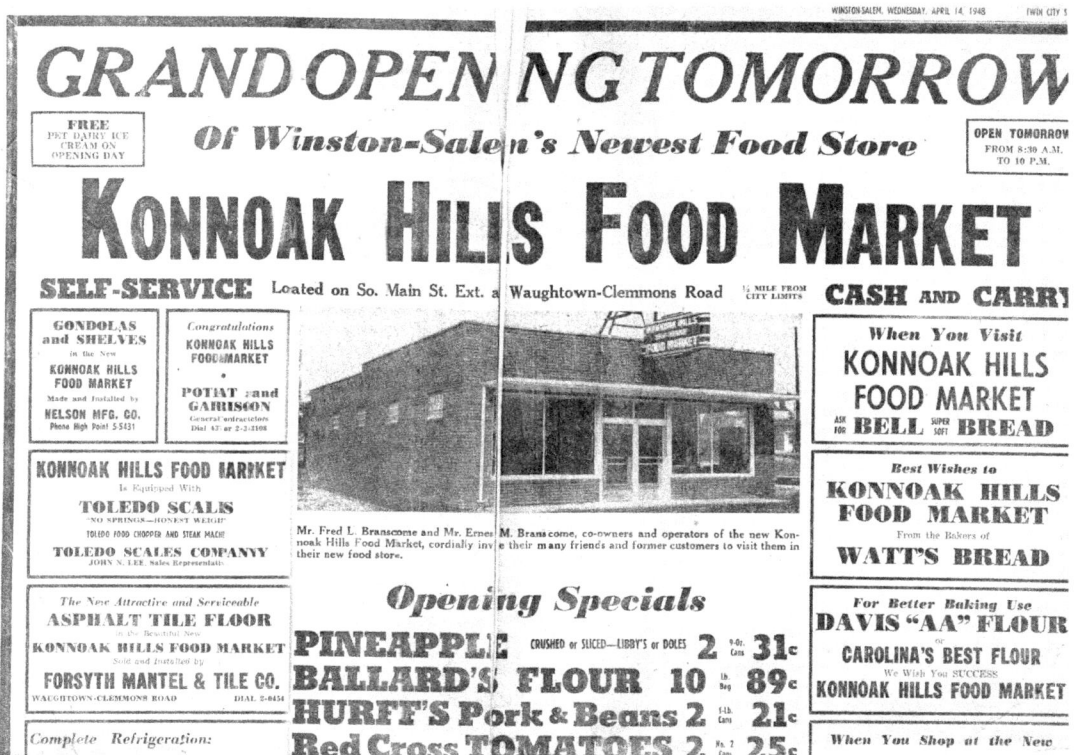

The Konnoak Hills Food Market was begun by the Branscome brothers. This mom and pop grocery store was beginning to update to a larger store in order to compete with the national chain grocery stores. *Branscome collection.*

There existed that year 150 types of establishments. This literally gave us a grocery store on every corner. Bryant Lee, a resident of an older downtown neighborhood, was asked, "Where did you and your family shop for groceries in the 1920s, 1930s and 1940s?" He responded, "Our neighborhoods were sufficient. Very seldom did we have to go to the downtown for groceries." A few grocery store chains had arrived. One of the first was the A&P Grocery Store at 100 South Green Street, near the dividing line between Winston and Salem and West End and West Salem. On Green Street there could be found about seven grocery stores. Example of these were Tesh's Grocery Store at 104 South Green, Barney's Grocery Store at 326 South Green and one of Bryant's favorites, the Hot Dog House at 406 South Green.

Mrs. Marilyn Ruff of Poplar Street relayed the experience of many Salem youngsters and the places they liked to hang out and go to. Two of the drugstores that were very popular were Wellfare's and Gooches' Drugs. Krispy Kreme Doughnuts could be had at the original location on Main, and if you wanted something a little bit cooler, Peerless Ice Cream—a little bit farther down on Main Street—could satisfy you. Several meat markets existed. One of the popular ones was the Salem Meat Market on Main. This store became a victim of the Interstate 40 route during the 1950s. Prior to the interstate's arrival, children could play and run in those days and not worry about problems that are had today. Many families, as in Mrs. Ruff's situation, were allowed to have many animals. Around the city one could find goats, horses, sheep and chickens, and, of course, dogs and cats. The area around the Peters Creek Parkway was a wilderness for many of the older people to hunt and for many of the youngsters, such as the Ruffs, to ride their horses along some of the paths and thickets that were part of the Paper Mill Settlement of more than one hundred years before. As we study Winston and begin to look at the neighborhoods in chapter 7, we will touch more on what special quality each neighborhood had and what it had to offer for its citizens.

CHAPTER 6.

The Three Rs

Reading, writing and arithmetic have been the staple learning exercises for America since the Blue Back Speller of our great grandparents' days. In searching out the three Rs of Twin City history, we arrive at three subjects to outline this chapter's journey: education, medicine and publications. These three subjects will highlight our schools of higher learning, our hospitals and medical teaching facilities and the media of publications.

The Moravians who settled the Wachovia tract in the 1750s were heirs to time-tested educational procedures. With this tradition the communities chose their leaders to conduct worship and industry while beginning their culture. The congregation adhered to the choir system and married members, single brethren and single sisters were separated from one another, as were the little boys' and little girls' choirs. Danish-born Hans Petersen was appointed schoolmaster for Bethabara's boys in 1762. He died shortly thereafter, only serving one year. Many other ministers and settlers became willing teachers to the young boys of Bethabara until finally Salem was established in 1766. The town was the center of church and governmental activities, controlling the trades, commerce and culture, but schools were not brought in until 1772, when the first families with children arrived and the Salem Girls' School was founded. Girls were not normally provided with education in colonial America, but the Moravians in America and abroad had realized the necessity for instruction of both sexes. Boarding schools had already been established early on in Bethlehem, Pennsylvania, as early as 1749.

The Single Sisters' quarters of the Geimenhaus were home to many of the first pupils. They were the daughters of the town leaders: Misses Bagge, Meyer and Schmidt were taught by Sister Elizabeth Oesterlein. Sister Oesterlein had arrived from Bethabara and taught reading, writing, household skills, sewing and weaving. No math was taught. Her successor in 1780, Sister Catherine Sehnert, added mathematics to her curriculum. Payment for teachers' salaries was provided by the parents and additional congregational funds; however, this often came up short, given the intense involvement of the teaching. The educational group solicited the residents in order to provide the added monetary funds. Many teachers were encouraged to take on part-time jobs to supplement their meager incomes. Sister Elizabeth Miksch and Sister Sehnert adopted a part-time craft in glove making. By 1788, more money had been appropriated and twelve girls had been added to the roster. Salem was ready to expand, with more girls coming to the boarding school from around the area; however, the difficulty lay in the number of good teachers they could find. The school operated on a limited staff until the end of the eighteenth century. Requests were sent to Pennsylvania in order to recruit new headmasters and teachers. The church leaders realized a meeting was necessary with the dawning of the new century.

The boys were not left behind in education by any means; their school also opened in 1772. The older boys in the choir houses attended formal writing and arithmetic classes. The school nearly closed in 1775, due to a lack of pupils. With the beginning of the Revolutionary War, more boys were brought into town and the school continued. The war, unfortunately, had weakened both the Girls' and Boys' Schools due to loss of revenue, but the congregation overcame these problems and continued on. While many of the other students remained day students, several were allowed to be taught at home. The house at which these youngsters were taught was expanded in 1784, and maps and textbooks in German were brought into the system. More boys from neighboring towns were brought in. Brother Frederick Marshall noted, "The snail is about to outgrow its little rented shell," and with that they began to push for bigger quarters.

By 1790, Samuel G. Kramsch became the principal of the Boys' School. He began to have classes not only in German, but in English as well for the older boys and the Salem men. The schoolhouse for the boys was again becoming too small. In June 1791, a monumental event occurred. As the boys were doing their daily work, laboring away at the curriculum, a tall stranger appeared at the door. President George Washington was paying Salem a visit. The schoolmaster was overcome, as was the class, and the schoolmaster immediately wanted to continue the class. One student read from his spelling book, "A cat may look on a king." This got away with President Washington and he appreciated the selection. After this encounter with President Washington, the congregation believed it was time to put aside enough money to construct a new church and a new school. The current Boys' School that exists in the Old Salem restored village was dedicated in 1794, with much celebration from trombones and choir singing.

Up until that time the boys who had finished school became apprentices upon entering their teens. With the new establishment, more thought could be put into new courses, such as bookkeeping and surveying. Newly created advanced classes in writing, history, geography, geometry, Latin, Greek, French and art were added. The modern world of teaching and subject matter had arrived. In 1795, the studies began to fall away due to the fact that the pupils were finding it difficult to acquire apprenticeships. The craftsmen of Salem wanted apprentices who were less sophisticated than the graduates of the school. What they may have learned is that education breeds freedom and with more freedom comes less time for your job. Many of the craftsmen felt the new students were lazy. They believed that music led to more dissatisfaction in their work. Enrollment began to fall off and the classes were moved from the building to the Single Brothers' house in 1800. The eighteenth century ended with no Boys' School at all.

The beginning of the new century in the Wachovia tract was ushered in with the arrival of a new bishop in 1802: Bishop Gotthold Reichel. The bishop brought with him a true interest

The Three Rs

in education; he had founded Nazareth Hall, a boys' boarding school in Pennsylvania. The first girls' boarding school was located south of the congregation house on the east side of the square. The cornerstone was laid on October 1803, and the building stood the test of time and is now part of the Old Salem experience. The pupils generally ranged in age from eight to twelve, but no one could remain after the age of fifteen. By 1804, the "boarding school for female education in Salem, North Carolina," taught regular classes in reading, grammar, writing, arithmetic, history, geography, plain needlework and German. Extra courses included music, drawing and fine needlework. The school grew throughout the early nineteenth century and by the end of the first decade the academy had eight teachers and eighty-five boarders. The girls came from Virginia, South Carolina, Georgia, Kentucky and Tennessee. The girls who were taught here returned to their parents with an education that helped in the settling of the new United States.

By the mid-nineteenth century, the academy had gained a national reputation through its expansion and growth. The Civil War was on the horizon and the academy saw new importance during the conflict. Education of the boys was primarily limited to younger pupils approaching their teens, and most graduates entered apprenticeships at the Single Brothers' house.

In 1849, a boost occurred with the arrival of George F. Bahnson of Pennsylvania, who served as a minister to Salem. He brought with him a business-like supervision with the hope of organizing the funds better and more efficiently. A committee was formed with businessmen Francis Fries, C.D. Kuhlin and Joshua Boner. This committee appointed teachers, set salaries and school fees, supervised enrollment and kept meticulous records while conducting semiannual examinations. After the separation of the church from political control in Salem in 1857, Bahnson and Fries, with the addition of businessmen E.A. Vogler and Lewis Belo, controlled the Boys' School Committee. This set the stage for the Academy for Girls and the Boys' School.

There were other Moravian educational ventures in the first half of the nineteenth century. The School for Negroes was abandoned soon after the North Carolina General Assembly of 1830 passed a law stating that teaching slaves to read was a crime punishable by fine or imprisonment. History shows that Salem continued to teach African Americans and to allow them to work in many fields that were unavailable to other African Americans in the country.

The first schoolhouse for African Americans in Salem was built in 1822. This was a state-of-the-art school compared to other schools across the country, since African Americans were, in most cases, not allowed to attend school at all. Earlier meetings had been held in West Salem at the Krueser farm to decide the methods for teaching African Americans. It was decided a structure was necessary so as to teach in a much more orderly fashion. Originally it was thought to have the school built in West Salem, since it was not entirely under the jurisdiction and rules of the congregational town. The elders decided to build the school closer to the town in order to oversee it better. The Schumann plantation, which was located to the east of the congregational town and became known as Liberia or Happy Hill, was the site of the first schoolhouse after the Civil War in 1867. The school was the first one built for blacks in Forsyth County after the war and it stood where children now play at Happy Hill Park off Waughtown. The first black church in Salem was St. Phillips Church.

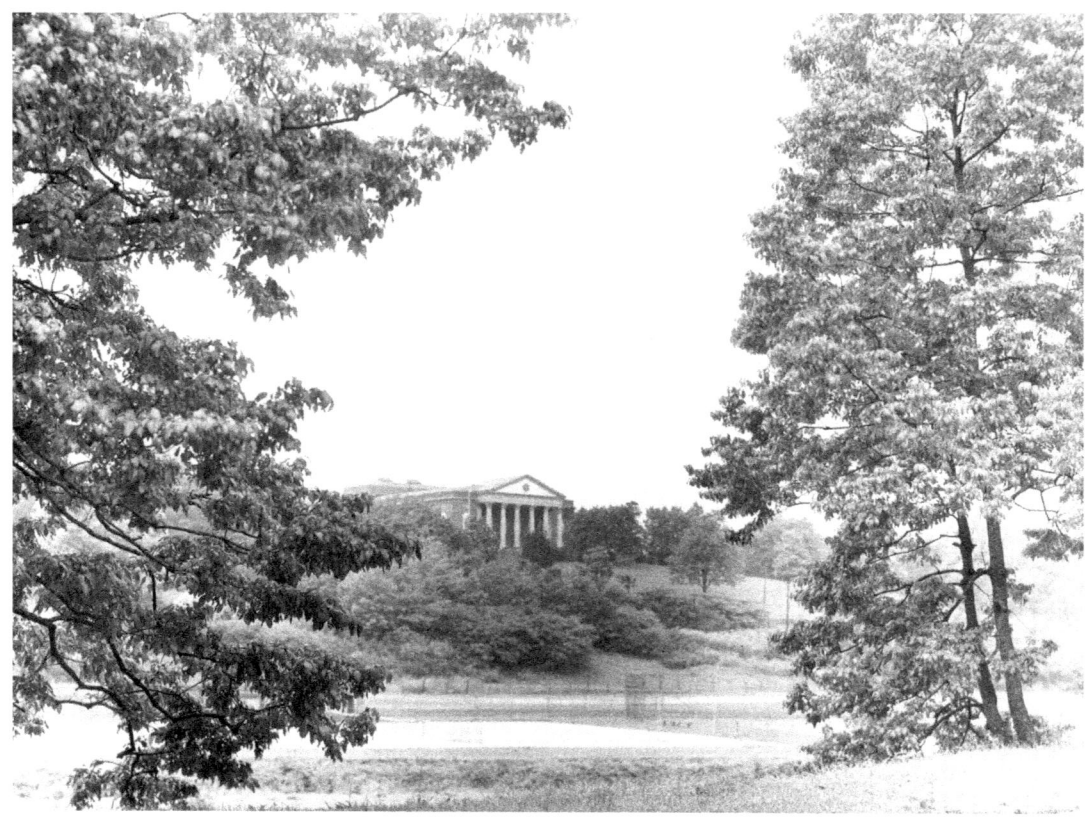
The majestic Reynolds Auditorium looms over Hanes Park in this 1960 photo.

The connection between the church and the school was intimate for the African American populace. Both black and white teachers taught at the school in 1867. Sunday school teachers from the African American church often taught at the school as well. The school was run by a man from Barbados, Alfred Lind. He was in charge from 1870 to 1871, when he moved from the settlement.

Education allowed the community to grow after the Civil War. Many of the African Americans left the surrounding farms and moved into town. The influx of the African Americans into the tobacco factories of the 1870s allowed better income and more control in certain areas. Some African Americans began to work as grocers and barbers, which at that time were considered middle-class occupations. Many people were choosing to live in Liberia, or Happy Hill, the first African American settlement in the area. Nearly two hundred people lived on the former Moravian plantation with small path roads leading to the church and the school. E.A. Vogler had helped to establish Liberia and was now the superintendent of the school. The school prospered and many in the African American community wanted to buy the land in the area, but as usual the church held tightly onto its land even into the twentieth century. The schoolhouse closed around 1893, and a new schoolhouse was built not far away in Happy Hill. Many of the stereotypes of that time often showed white Northerners setting up the schools for the African Americans, but this school was established by African Americans for African Americans.

After the Civil War the conservative government from 1865 to 1868 abolished the office of state superintendent of common schools and left public education to the local communities. The new constitution of 1868 re-created the position of superintendent and allowed for a system of free public schools for both whites and blacks to be created in 1869. At that time there were in Forsyth County twenty-two public schools and more than 1,100 pupils.

Teachers, as was usually the case, were poorly paid and overworked. In 1873, a protest was declared: "It is a fact well-known by teachers that parents pay for schooling their children more grudgingly than anything else. I would say give us free schools, in fact, as well as in name." Support arrived in 1874, which changed the public school systems and the way in which they were implemented. Calvin Wiley, who had been the state superintendent for common schools before the war, arrived in Salem. His energy and intellectual promise began the public system we know today. The first graded school to arrive under the new plan in North Carolina was the Winston Graded School in 1884. It resided on Fourth at Broad on the hill in the western part of Winston.

Winston continued an ambitious school program. Much of the curriculum that was taught was handed down from the Salem schools, which had existed before the Civil War. The prize library that was developed at the school later became the basis of the first library of Winston, the Carnegie Public Library of the twentieth century. The African American education expanded, with industrial training begun by Simon G. Atkins, who was principal at the Depot Graded School for African Americans in 1890. He brought education to new heights with his ambition and his gifted background. He had been both a slave himself and had attended St. Augustine College, as well as other schools. He enticed the Winston leaders, in 1892, to join together with the more affluent African Americans to found Slater Industrial School. The school started small, with a handful of students, and grew very rapidly. At the end of the nineteenth century, the Moravian schools in Salem and other private schools in Forsyth County were doing well. Public education for African Americans was doing just as well. The new century got off on the right foot with education for all.

In 1901, Salem College discontinued a time-honored and hallowed offering: the compulsory hour of plain needlework by all students was discontinued after 130 years of instruction. This was a minor event, but was an indication of the changing trends of a modern college. Salem College and Salem Academy flourished during the Depression years. The college library building was completed in 1937, bringing the total building count to eighteen on a 56½-acre campus. Between the 1910s and 1940s, the public schools of Winston and Winston-Salem saw a growing enrollment of students. The quality of schools also improved. The East Winston Graded School opened in 1901, and the City High School began operation in 1909. The African American community came together and built three new schools: Woodlawn Avenue (1910), Trade Street Grade School (1911) and Oak Street Grade School (1913).

In 1913, with the merging of the towns, Winston and Salem also consolidated their school systems. R.H. Latham became superintendent of schools. Latham brought a modern approach to the newly consolidated schools by understanding new school methods and teacher/student relationships, while also acknowledging the importance of student home

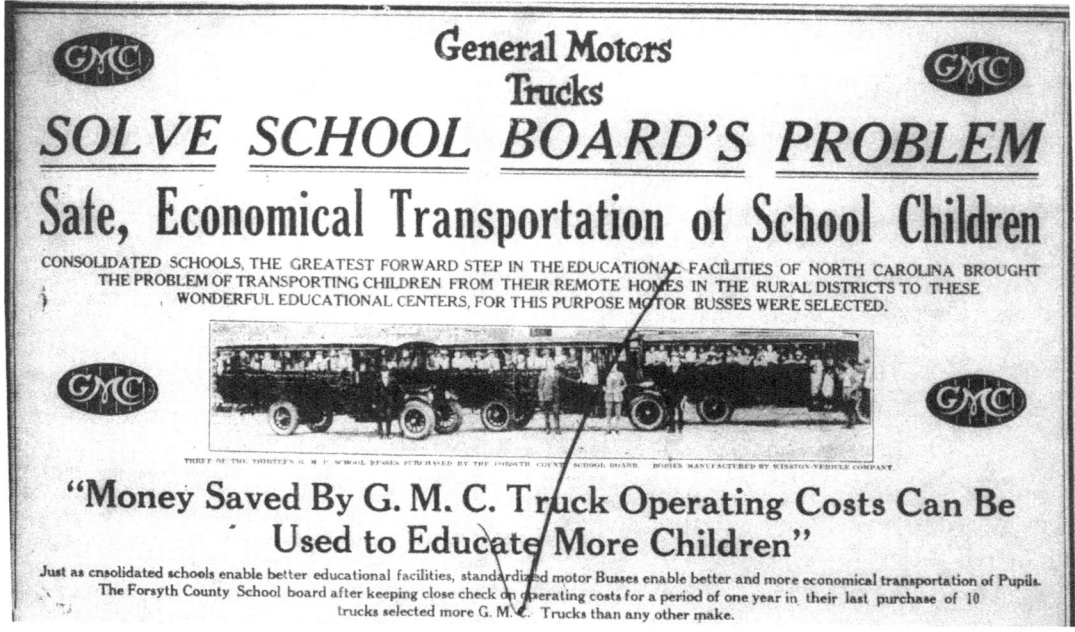

Early transportation is presented with the new school buses in this 1920s advertisement. Winston-Salem Journal.

environments and personal qualities. Edward Rondthaler of the Moravian Church had also been involved with the newly formed education system. He felt that, in their present state, "the Winston-Salem schools cannot begin to accommodate all children of school age, should they come to school." Even with the new schools being built, they still could not manage the growth of the number of young people in the town. Many of the students were gravely behind in their studies. This began an involvement of the Board of School Commissioners to enlist outside observers from the University of North Carolina at Chapel Hill to understand why the students were struggling. "A study of the Winston-Salem Schools" was the report that was accumulated and gave criticism and recommendations to the Twin City leaders. Much like the award of the title of a City of Industry of 1918, this study also opened the door for growth that had never been seen in Winston and Salem. Consideration was given to the overage of students, grade repeaters and dropouts. Tables comparing the school system with others in America of comparable size led to the conclusion that the local schools had a remarkable proportion of backward pupils, poor attendance, inadequate expenditures for the teachers and substandard school maintenance. Recommendations were made for a health officer, attendance officer, a business manager and additional clerical help for the superintendent.

The report was circulated extensively throughout Winston-Salem to the public and to businesses. The improvements that were suggested in response to the report were implemented in 1918. A school bond was begun by the citizens, which appropriated nearly $1 million for the 1919 budget. This was approved overwhelmingly and the restructuring

The Three Rs

of the schools began. The Winston-Salem High School burned in 1923, but its replacement—Richard J. Reynolds High School—had already been built overlooking the forty-acre P.H. Hanes Park. By 1930, accomplishments were had in several other schools. North Junior High School opened at Twenty-eighth and White Streets in the northeastern part of Winston. South Junior High School opened at 1900 Chapel Street, south of the old Waughtown Road. Also opened was Atkins High School for African Americans on North Cameron Avenue. Within a few years, Winston-Salem schools had improved so that they ranked at the top of the eight largest school systems in North Carolina. Despite the Depression that was underway, the public schools continued to progress. The city grew as well as it was able to acquire quality teachers. By the beginning of World War II, the public school system was at the top of all the schools of North Carolina. In 1940, the school system employed 23 superintendents, principals and supervisors, along with 430 teachers and an enrollment of nearly 18,000 students.

As the schools progressed into the 1950s, a new teaching facility was on the horizon—Wake Forest College. Bowman Gray, the president of R.J. Reynolds Tobacco Company, passed away in 1935, and the Bowman Gray Fund helped to establish the Winston-Salem Foundation. The foundation's first venture was focused on an improvement of the city's educational and cultural life. Their plan was to create a school of medicine and the opportunity was offered by Wake Forest College with the introduction of a two-year school. An endowment was set up and an affiliation was made with the North Carolina Baptist Hospital. The Bowman Gray School of Medicine was completed next to the Baptist Hospital at Queen and Hawthorne Road. The success of this medical school was found in the philanthropy of the Babcocks, Bagleys and Reynoldses. An idea arose to bring Wake Forest College to Winston-Salem. Wake Forest had existed continually in Wake Forest, North Carolina, since 1834. Many of the old supporters of the Wake Forest campus were hesitant about coming to a new larger town. In 1947, Wake Forest began to transfer larger educational institutes to the city. At the time Salem College was celebrating its 175th anniversary, the plans were underway for the new Wake Forest College.

By the 1960s, an emphasis was being put on the arts throughout the nation and especially locally. The philanthropy of the arts had been evident since the 1950s with the creation of Old Salem and several museums. The North Carolina General Assembly created the North Carolina School of the Arts in 1963, and Winston-Salem was chosen as the best location for the school. The former James A. Gray High School of the Salem area provided the building. The school prospered and became known nationally for its students as well as its teachers.

By the fall of 1965, Wake Forest had more than 3,000 students, including students in graduate and postgraduate programs. The Governor School had been formed earlier and was admitting no more than 400 students for its three six-week summer terms. The North Carolina School of the Arts had assembled a faculty of famous artists headed by Vittorio Giannini, a former professor at the Julliard School and Manhattan School of Music. The Forsyth Technical Institute was instructing students in the 1960s in trades and technologies. Two religious colleges were showing success: the Piedmont Bible College, with 250 students, and the Winston-Salem Bible College, with 35 African American students. There were also five Catholic schools: Bishop McGuinness Memorial High School, St. Leo's, St. Benedict's, Our Lady of Mercy Convent and St. Ann's Convent. The private institution of the Summit

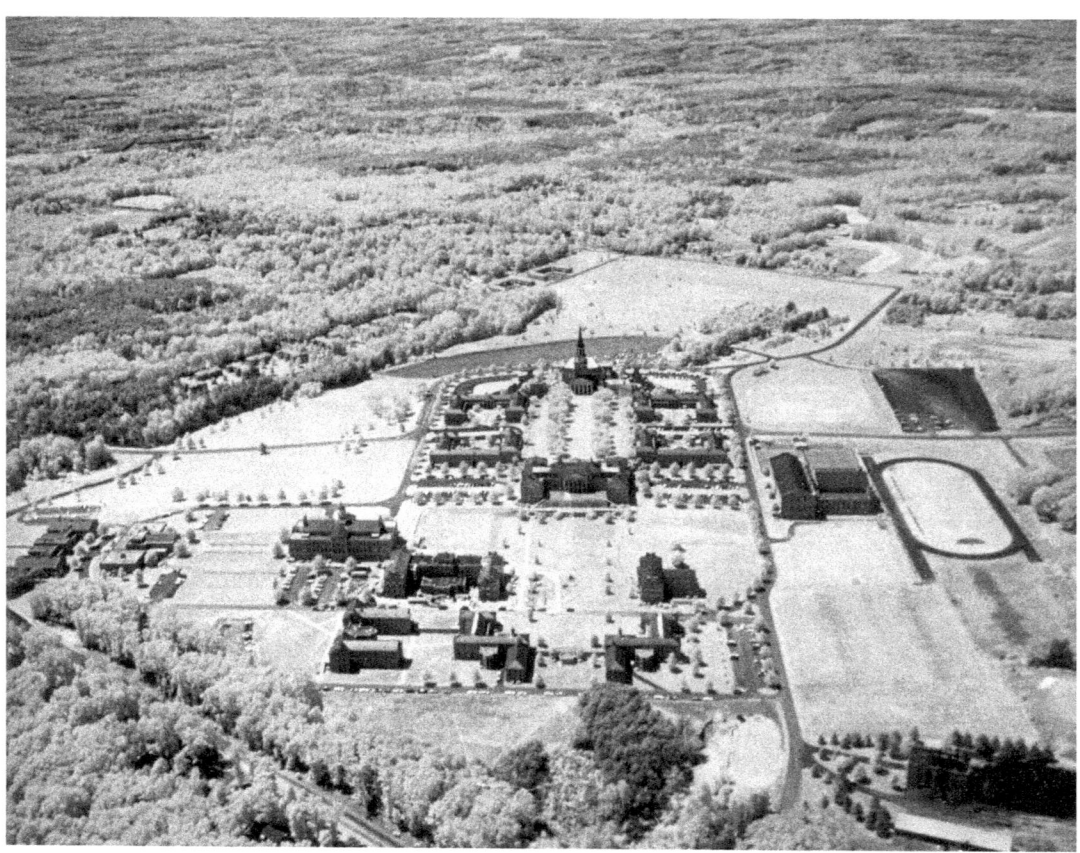

Wake Forest University in its early years is presented in this aerial shot from 1960.

School (1933) was teaching children from kindergarten through eighth grade. Several business colleges and beauty schools were also present.

Several stories originated over the years about the school system and education in the Twin City. A few of these, looking back, took us to the eighteenth and nineteenth centuries and to the time of the Depression. The first school was called the Free School House of West Salem (1847). The Free School House was a concept that began on a national and state level in the early 1800s. The government's hope was to bring schools and education to all citizens, rich and poor. The industries and farms of Winston and Salem had created working-class people who had been requesting a proper school from the Moravians for years. With the establishment of the Salem Cotton Mill and Fries Woolen Mill, along with funding from the state, the Moravians gave in and extended a road to the north of the Fries Woolen Mill. The schoolhouse was erected on Salt Street (later Liberty Street). This school helped to set the groundwork for the regular folks who needed education as well as their wealthier neighbors.

The Free School House was used later as the First School House of Winston (1849). The mystery of the school and what happened to it is an educational story in itself. The original structure of the school was moved from its site to make way for the Brown & Williamson

The Three Rs

Tobacco Factories in the 1890s. Many thought the school had just been destroyed. The school's new location was only discovered in the early 1980s. A clearing of older homes on Green at First Street in the West Salem neighborhood revealed a log structure enclosed in one of the small houses. This was an example of the recycling and reuse that was common among the Moravians from their early beginnings. This log house was saved and identified as the former Free School House of Winston. It was taken down, moved to the Dixie Classic Fairgrounds and reassembled. The schoolhouse is now a permanent fixture of the yesteryear village of the Dixie Classic Fair.

A bit of educational history can now be experienced as you walk this restored village. The other instance takes place in the 1930s. The *Black and Gold Annual* of Richard J. Reynolds High School's class of 1933 depicts the heart of the Depression. This poem designates it well:

> *"Depression"*
> *Four years ago old man Depression knocked loudly at our door,*
> *then we were buying like millionaires, when he leaves us, we'll all be poor.*
> *"We can end this depression," cry G.O.P.s and Democrats;*
> *we are offered budget balancers and these strange Technocrats.*
> *But alas, alack, all remedies fail, old man depression still remains;*
> *he holds us in his terrible grip and snatches all our gains.*
> *To remember these years in the future as queer as it may seem,*
> *with hopes of good times soon to come, we use "Depression" as our theme.*

Education in the Twin City had its good times and its bad times. Throughout it all, success was achieved and the old Moravian ideal of staying with something until you see it through was accomplished.

Medicine was one of the leading builders of our educational system in both the early years and the university years of the nationally known Wake Forest University and medical facilities. The early medical involvement of the Moravians was very basic. Bishop August G. Spangenberg's expedition led to the inclusion of a physician with the original party from Bethlehem, Pennsylvania, to North Carolina. Brother Hans Martin Kalberlahn was one of the most adventurous of the fifteen settlers who attempted the Moravian mission to North Carolina. Brother Kalberlahn was not called a doctor. He felt he was better educated than the majority of medical practitioners in the United States. At that time, most physicians were only trained by serving in an apprenticeship with an older doctor. Brother Kalberlahn had completed his medical education in a European setting, which was the dream of most colonial doctors. He was born in Norway in 1722 and grew up in the Lutheran faith. He studied in Copenhagen and, while there, met several Moravians. He was accepted into the brotherhood and moved to Germany. He traveled by Holland to London and arrived in Pennsylvania after a three-month sea voyage.

Brother Kalberlahn was chosen to make the long trip south, as his adventurous nature allowed him to do so. His route to the Wachovia tract forced him to practice his medicine by bleeding a servant. The doctor arrived in Bethabara and began his treatments right away. He was treating an "Irish man" and unfortunately in part of the procedure he scalded part

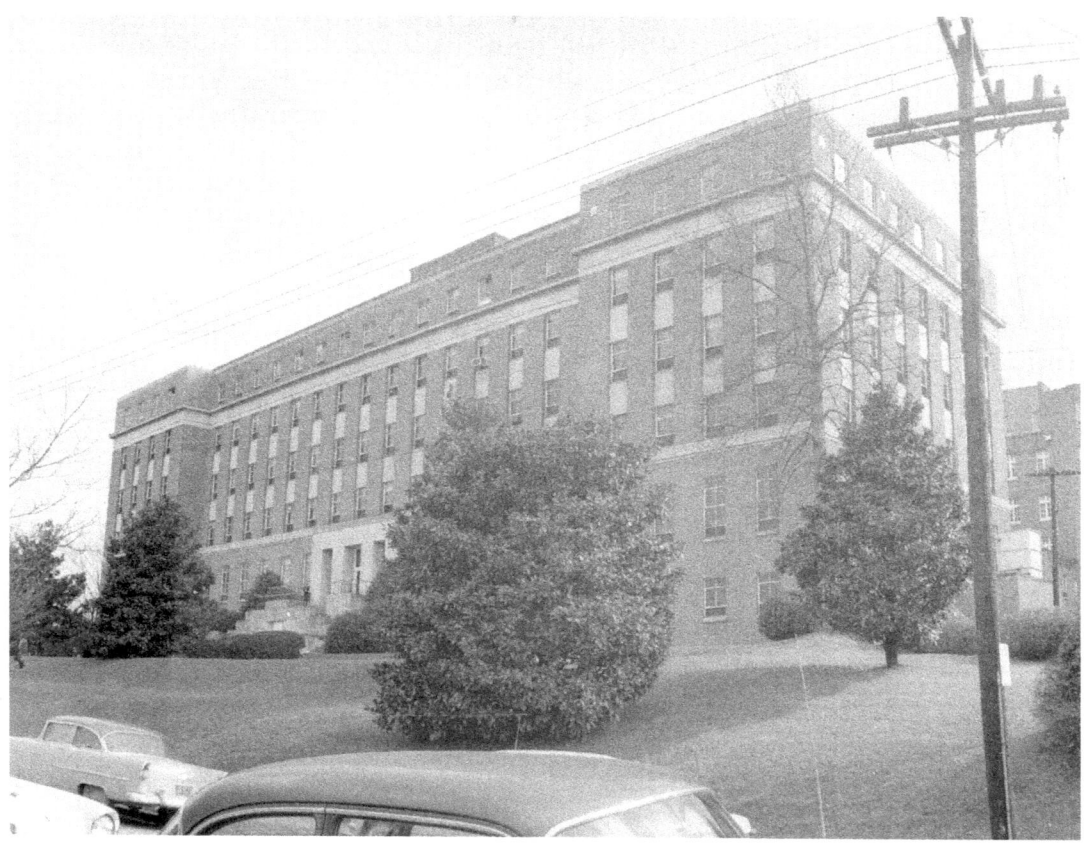

North Carolina Baptist Hospital, founded in the 1920s, on Hawthorne Road, 1960.

of his own foot badly. That did not stop him from practicing medicine. He bled several fellow colonists who had been hit on the head by a falling tree. Obviously bleeding is a very rare form of treatment today, but in the eighteenth century it was the major treatment for what ailed you.

His practice became very successful and he began to travel throughout the frontier of the Wachovia tract. In 1756, he laid out a medicinal garden. The location is not known today, and many of the plants that he used are no longer in use today. He also arranged for a laboratory to be built. The living quarters in Bethabara were not large, so a sick room was established in the Single Brothers' house in 1756. With this sick room it became the first hospital of the state. Brother Kalberlahn joined a Bethabara colony that was returning to Pennsylvania in search of wives. He taught two of the brothers to "let blood" in his absence. Brother Kalberlahn found a wife in Bethlehem, and they returned to Bethabara in 1759. On his arrival he discovered an Indian war was in progress and Bethabara had become a stockade town. Many in the surrounding area fled to Bethabara for protection during this war and unfortunately brought disease with them. A typhus fever created an epidemic in the Bethabara colony and in Virginia. Brother Kalberlahn treated all that he could from sunup to sundown. After four days of treatment, he developed typhus as well and died not long after in July 1759.

Two physicians took over Brother Kalberlahn's work, Brother Jacob Bonn and Dr. August Schubert. The two lasted until 1765, when they left the colony. Brother Bonn returned in 1766 and moved into the first house of Salem in 1772 with his wife and child. The first house is designated as the apothecary shop in the restored village of Old Salem. Brother Bonn also functioned as the sheriff and justice of the peace in addition to serving as the physician. He began one of the most controversial medical feats at the time: he was one of the first to begin the inoculation for smallpox, one of the most dreaded epidemic diseases of that time. The procedure was not the same as the vaccinations applied today. His procedure was performed by taking dried material from the sores of the skin and pressing it into the lacerated skin of someone who had not had the disease for the purpose of causing a mild attack of smallpox, which did not carry the threat of death and disfigurement, as in a full-blown infection. By 1781, the inoculation had begun and had an apparent benefit; however, the story may have been different since an anonymous letter was sent to the Moravian hierarchy stating that if they continued this practice, the village was to be burned to the ground. The procedure worked and the village stood.

The most well-known physician who is trumpeted in the restored town today was Dr. Benjamin Vierling. Dr. Vierling had studied medicine in Berlin, Germany, and began a twenty-seven-year career in Salem in 1790. Dr. Vierling often had problems with housing sick people who were brought to him, so he often boarded them in his own house. The brethren also trusted him with the tradition and requirement that the doctor examine any supposedly dead person before placing the body in the corpse house on the square. This was a system that had been born earlier in Europe as a protection against being buried alive.

In 1802, a new type of smallpox-preventive "cowpox" vaccination arrived in Salem. It had been developed only four years earlier in England. The vaccine was brought from Raleigh and the Salem residents were vaccinated. The doctor did not accept payment from the people, only charging for the vaccine. Dr. Vierling set a precedence that continued for several hundred years after his life as Winston-Salem physicians carried out mass immunizations against polio in 1964 and rubella in 1970. Dr. Vierling's policy of charging only for the cost of the immunization was adopted by these subsequent Winston-Salem physicians.

Dr. Vierling was also one of the first physicians to attempt rehabilitation of his clients. An example was an eighty-year-old patient with cataracts who had become a hypochondriac. Dr. Vierling suggested an occupational therapy in the form of sawing wood to forget his troubles, and it worked. Another early accomplishment of Dr. Vierling was in the health field. He helped to establish the first market where fresh meat could be bought. Salem had become like most towns and the effects of these changes were found in its medical practices. The Zevely family had, along with the Schober family, established a niche in Salem history. The offspring of the Zevelys settled in Winston. Dr. Augustus Zevely, physician, was born in Salem in 1816. After finishing the Boys' School he headed to Pennsylvania for his training as a doctor. He returned in 1836 and was asked to run the Salem's Sadderly, but his energy and his background forced him to pursue his interest in medicine. Dr. Zevely also expanded on Dr. Schuman's medical practice by opening a store that sold drugs and sundries—

an early pharmacy. Dr. Kuhln was also practicing in Salem at that time and continued to practice until his death in 1872.

The links between Moravians and their German heritage grew weaker during the second half of the nineteenth century. The medical field there fortunately became stronger. Dr. John F. Shaffner, from an old family of Salem, had joined the Confederate army during the Civil War and had studied at Jefferson Medical College. His experience at the college and, even more, his surgical experience during the war allowed him good training in the immediate effects of injury and disability. He returned after the war and had a long career as a physician and businessman. By 1868, he was on the State Board of Medical Examiners and served as president of the State Medical Society in 1880. Like his predecessor before him, Dr. Zevely, Dr. Shaffner also ran a drugstore. He expanded his interest as president of the Salem Water Supply Company. He was also vice-president of the Winston-Salem Building and Loan Association, as well as operating a cotton gin. With all these commitments, he still had time to serve as mayor of Salem! By spreading himself so thin, he concentrated more on the business ventures than his practice.

Another local homegrown doctor, who arrived in Salem and took over the esteemed practice of Dr. Shaffner, was Dr. Henry T. Bahnson. He was born in 1843 in Pennsylvania and came to Salem as a child. He too followed in the footsteps of Dr. Shaffner and served on the State Board of Medical Examiners and also the newly formed State Board of Health. He served in the Civil War. Upon the end of the war he returned to the University of Pennsylvania to acquire his medical education. Dr. Bahnson was a fixture in Twin City history for many years. One of his crowning achievements was his leadership in establishing the first hospitals in Winston for both whites and African Americans. He served the community into the first part of the twentieth century. Many more important doctors practiced in the Twin City in the twentieth century and also functioned in other civic duties. This list includes Dr. Fries, Dr. Singleton, Dr. Belt, Dr. J.B. Britton, Dr. J.R. Gray, Dr. King, Dr. Westmoreland, Dr. Motsinger, Dr. Preston Roan, Dr. R.F. Gray, Dr. S.J. Montague, Dr. A.L. Mock, Dr. D.N. Dalton, Dr. H.S. Lott and Dr. J.G. Ector.

In 1889, Winston's first African American physician, Dr. Harvey H. Hall, arrived from Salisbury. His practice took him through forty-six years of the city's history. He had also attended the Leonard Medical College of Shaw University, which was for many years the only school that trained African Americans. Dr. Hall was also instrumental in encouraging future African American doctors in the area. He established his own drugstore on Church Street, and with his involvement and with the help of the drugstore he helped to set up the staffing for the city's first African American hospital. He set up the Twin City Medical Society, which was the African American counterpart of the white Forsyth County Medical Society.

Hospitals of a permanent nature were a late development in the county. What began as a sick room at Bethabara in the eighteenth century expanded over the years, although much more slowly than in the North. By 1658, hospitals existed in New York, and in 1751 they found their way to Philadelphia. The history of the hospitals and the need for them was set up for one main reason—scientific medicine was needed to take care of people whose living quarters were not adequate to allow them to be helped at home. The earlier days had meant that injured people were taken care of by family members, with an occasional visit by the doctor paying a house call.

The Three Rs

The hospital idea entered Winston in 1887, when the Episcopal rector suggested that local women should be involved with a charity project. In June 1887, thirty-one women met with Dr. Bahnson at his home in Salem and begin to write the charter of the first local hospital. From this the Ladies Twin City Hospital Association was formed, with Mrs. James A. Gray Sr. as president. The Martin-Grogan home at 236 North Liberty housed the first Twin City Hospital and admitted its first patient. In order to help the new hospital, pharmacists and other doctors donated drugs and clothing. In 1891, the facility closed after the death of Grogan. The women did not stop, but secured an established home and facilities on Brookstown Avenue at the present intersection of Brookstown and Second Avenues.

In 1895, the second Twin City Hospital opened here and the first treated patient was admitted four days later for gallstones. The establishment could accommodate nineteen patients. The first licensed nurse was Mollie Spach. The hospital functioned for several years in the first quarter of the twentieth century. The hospital had its last entry of admissions in 1914. The last patient was number 3,344 of those treated over the years. A new city hospital was on the horizon in east Winston and was a huge and intricate building throughout the twentieth century. The Slater Hospital arrived in 1899 to serve the African American community.

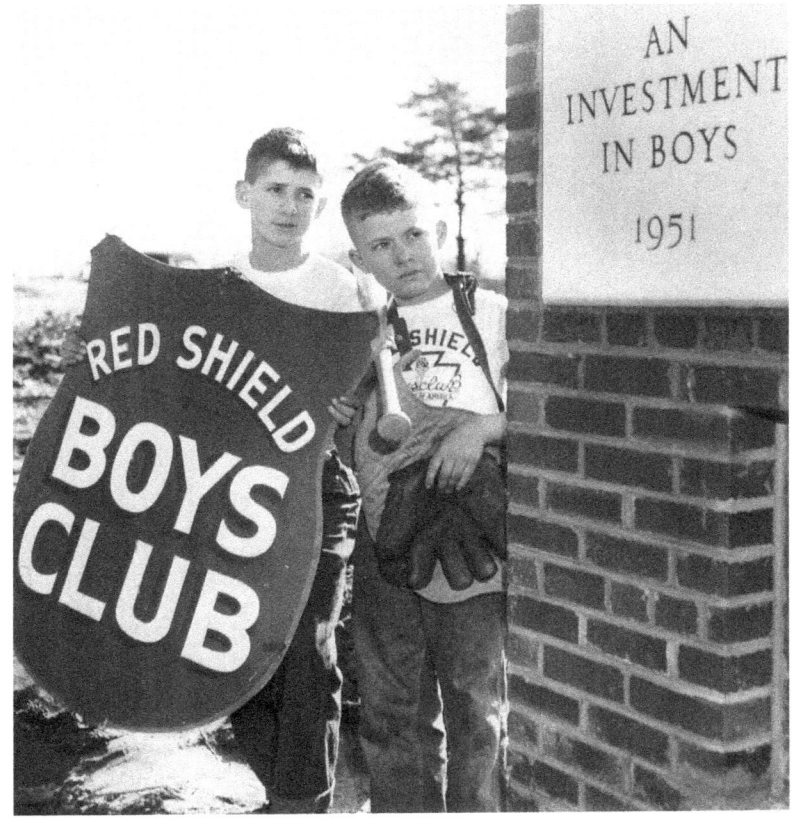

The Boys Clubs were an excellent investment in the youth of the Twin City. This establishment was built on Stadium Drive; circa 1960 photo.

Many more hospitals graced the landscape of the Twin City. Tuberculosis hospitals arrived in the county to serve this horrible affliction. The isolation for these patients was required in the early twentieth-century medical practices. A county hospital was run from the late 1930s until the 1960s near the established tuberculosis hospital. It served as a detention facility for psychiatric patients and was known as an "old folks" home. Parts of this building were used for the Sciworks of today. The Spencer Sanitarium was a thirty-five-bed private hospital beginning around 1912 and served until the beginning of World War I. In order to strengthen these hospitals and those that came later, the Twin City decided to create hospital bonds.

At the beginning of World War II, there was a need to consolidate the medical facilities into much larger, better trained and more modern facilities. The hospitals that followed began with the City Memorial Hospital in 1914. The land that was given by R.J. Reynolds had previously been his old racetrack property in east Winston on East Fourth Street. The Twin City Hospital on Brookstown closed and all the patients were transferred to City Memorial Hospital. The African American populace also saw growth in hospitals with Ray's Hospital (1910s) and the Williamson's Hospital near Vargrave Street and Stadium Drive. A larger and more complete hospital arrived in the 1930s with the Kate Bidding Reynolds Memorial Hospital, set up by the Reynolds family.

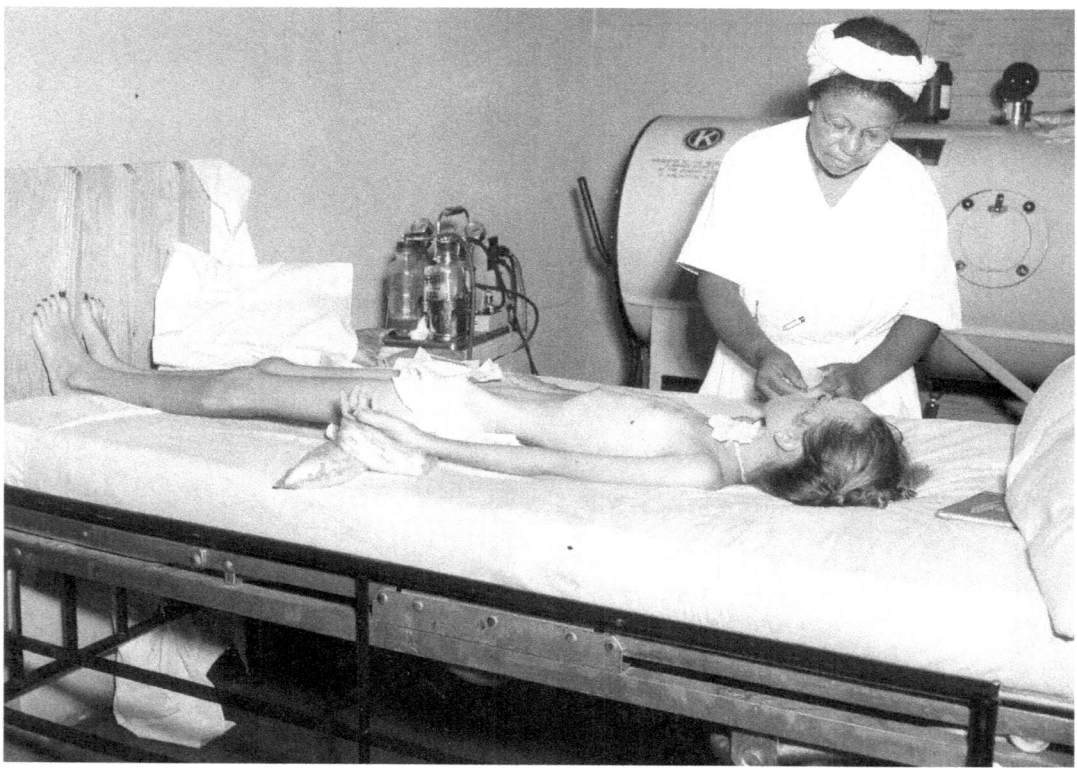

This photo from the 1950s depicts why the growth of medical facilities was important in the cases of our sick adults and children.

The Three Rs

The Bowman Gray School of Medicine originated from the arrival of Wake Forest medical facilities in the 1920s and expanded into one of the top medical facilities in the United States. The North Carolina Baptist Hospital and Forsyth Memorial Hospital arose from the roots of the Bowman Gray School of Medicine and City Memorial Hospital. The modern-day Wake Forest University of Physicians, North Carolina Baptist Hospital and Forsyth Medical Center compose a large area of the Ardmore neighborhood. From its early beginnings, the medical field in Winston-Salem has expanded greatly and has been very successful in creating hospitals and research facilities that rival any facilities in the world.

The last part of our journey into the three Rs is found in journalism, the place where history is kept. Three major newspapers were the main source of information for the Twin City from 1828 to the present day. These three were the *Weekly Gleaner*, the *People's Press* and the *Journal & Sentinel* periodicals. Before 1828, both the publishing of information and readers were limited. From the settlement of Bethabara in 1753, communications had been established first through Pennsylvania and later through the port cities of Norfolk, Virginia, and Charleston, South Carolina. Later the communication would follow cross creek (Fayetteville and Wilmington) in North Carolina. Up until the end of the 1700s, the

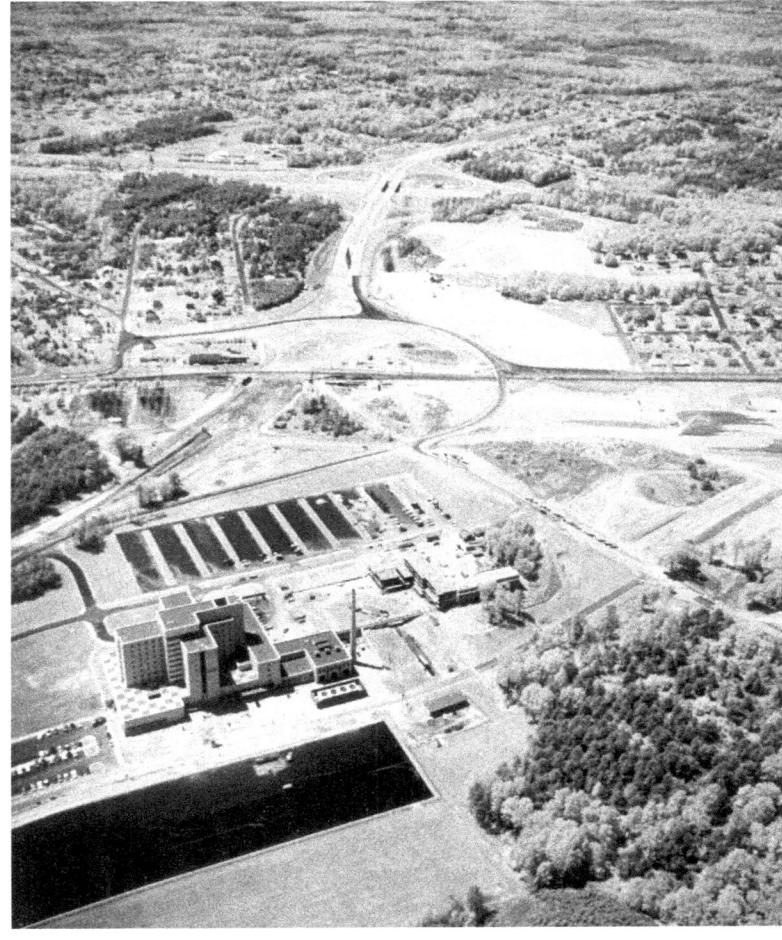

The western leg of Interstate 40 and Silas Creek Parkway are shown in their infancy as a backdrop to the new Forsyth Memorial Hospital at Hawthorne Road, circa 1960.

Moravians obtained nearly all of their news from oral transmission from the many travelers and settlers who passed through, as Wachovia was an isolated wilderness settlement. Many complaints were received from the congregation because of the slowness of the oral transmissions and the slowness of the newspapers that arrived from Pennsylvania. Without this news of a current material, many advertisements and obituaries were slow to arrive and affected the town in several different ways.

Before 1792, most of the items that were written about the town and in the town were done by hand. Manuscripts and records of the Moravians were finding it difficult in the bookbinding procedure. Brother Frederick Marshall wrote to Germany, "We would be glad to have a bookbinder, but at present he would not find work enough unless he had some other trade or was willing to work at anything needed." With the opening of Gottlieb Schober's paper mill in 1791, he hired an outsider to bind blank books for the populace to write its expressions. Brother George Biewighausen knew bookbinding skills and was invited to come to Salem, although he had to supplement his income by working at the pottery shop and the tobacco shop. David Clewell, in 1824, attempted to become Salem's first full-time binder and was granted permission from the congregation. He trained in Raleigh for six months, returned to Salem and opened a bindery under the guardianship of Brother Christian Blum. He remained the bookbinder until 1850. The paper mill had become more and more successful and began printing cloth paper. David Clewell sent those under him around the town to hawk for their old rags in order to make the paper. He found much shortage around the town for these rags and sent out requests in the *Fayetteville Gazette* to Hillsboro, Salisbury and Morgan districts for help in finding more rags. His ad went something like this: "Without rags, paper cannot be made. The economical housewife who supplies the paper mill with rags serves the country in her sphere as well as a soldier who fights for it does in his."

The mill and its operation became a favorite site for the scrutiny of visitors. The mill taught the paper makers that

> *the chief materials used were cotton and linen rags, old paper and straw. The processes were cleaning, boiling, washing, bleaching and reducing to pulp. The rags received at the mill were sorted carefully, the colored ones from the white ones and then dusted and chopped into pieces. They would then be boiled in a solution of lyme for the purpose of taking out fats, colors and other impurities were then added. Next came the washing process, a bleaching process followed, the pulp is then pressed into sheets, rolled, dried and cut.*

This mill marked the beginning of the bookbinding business, and thus the arrival of newspapers and periodicals. Brother John C. Blum of Salem began the *Weekly Gleaner* in November 1828. This was the first newspaper to be sent to print in Wachovia. The beginnings were small, with nearly only one sheet that was issued on Tuesdays. The information gathered for the Tuesday periodical was received by Monday's Northern mail. The *Gleaner* earned much of its income from advertising. It was not just restricted to Salem and Wachovia, but was also circulated in Germanton, Huntsville, Hamptonville, Rockford, Wilkesboro and Lexington. The *Gleaner* was the first of more than eighty newspapers and periodicals that appeared in Salem, Winston and the Twin City into the twentieth century.

The Three Rs

Most only lasted a few years here and there. A few enjoyed longevity. Three of the oldest ones were the *Union Republican* (seventy-five years), the *Western Sentinel* (seventy years), the *People's Press* (forty-one years) and the *Twin City Sentinel* (eighty-one years).

The Blum family led the *Weekly Gleaner* into the 1830s. At that particular time, Blum announced he had purchased the Schober Paper Mill. He managed the mill until 1842, when his health failed him. He sold the Salem Mill Company to Brother Fries, and Brother Fries sold it to his son-in-law, Rufus Patterson, in 1853. The *Weekly Gleaner* ended its operation by the mid-nineteenth century. Blum continued with a weekly publication, the *Farmer's Reporter*, which was not as successful as the *Weekly Gleaner*.

The weeklies during the Civil War and after, from 1851 to 1881, gave rise to another weekly publication of Blum & Son in Salem that made its first appearance in February 1851. The press had a political flair to it, with emphasis on the Whig Party and the Democratic Party of the new South. The press attempted to remain independent politically and announced it would support the newly formed American or "The Know Nothing Party and the old line Whigs." Francis Eugene Boner, who became the poet of national distinction from Salem, worked as an apprentice with Blum and helped to establish the *Western Sentinel* in Winston. The *People's Press*, in its earliest issues of 1851, gave indications of the town and its offspring Winston in their accomplishment. Here is an example from the *People's Press* of 1851:

> OUR VILLAGE
>
> *For the gratification of our distant readers, may we be permitted to say, that a considerable "change has come over the spirit of the dream" of quiet Salem and its vicinity, within the last few years. A new impulse has been given to business generally, and improvement, in various ways, is still "the order of the day."*
>
> *Our merchants are doing a large business; our mechanics are honest, industrious and, as a natural consequence, thriving; the Bank fully sustains its business character; the cotton and wool factories are in full time of successful operation; the Hotels are at all times prepared to entertain with the "best the market affords." And last, though not least, the "Salem Female Academy" is in a very flourishing condition, and bound to stand, in all time to come, upon an unshaken foundation.*
>
> *In short, the march of Salem is decidedly onward. May blessings attend the efforts of our enterprising citizens!*
>
> *Our young neighbor-town, WINSTON, can boast of the Hall of Justice, which stands out in bold relief, an ornament to the county, and surpassed by few, if any, buildings of the kind in the State. There let Justice reign supreme! Then comes the "Prison House," not yet completed: rather a gloomy looking place that!—May the mere sight of its grated windows prove a terror to evil doers, and its cells ever remain tenantless!*
>
> *Several dwellings, store-houses, hotels, and a church, (Protestant Methodist) have been erected, and in part, occupied. Other buildings are in progress.*

The *Weekly Gleaner* and *People's Press* were joined by a few other weeklies. Their demise arrived with the building boom and Industrial Revolution of the 1880s. Up to 1880, Winston-Salem had fifteen different newspapers, each appearing only once a week. Seven of these were printed by the Blums. Between 1882 and 1900, twenty-five entirely new papers began publication. The birth of the dailies began and changed the horizon of journalism. The major difference was from the politically oriented and controversy-laden weeklies to the more news-focused dailies. The *Twin City Daily* began in 1885 and provided the two towns with a permanent daily paper. The *Twin City Daily* changed hands many times until establishing itself at the turn of the twentieth century. One newspaper arrived on the scene and began the domination of journalism in the Twin City. The *Sentinel* arrived in 1897, and in 1901, the *Journal* purchased it. The *Journal & Sentinel* began its reign, and between 1901 and 1927 it expanded into a large publication. With the backing of the Gray family and the old elite of the city, the newspaper entered the new mediums of radio and television with **WSJS AM** (1930) and **WSJS** (1953). The *Winston-Salem Journal* became the parent company after the demise of the *Evening Sentinel*. The *Journal* boosted the city to a prominence not only in news, but in history as well. The newspaper has served as one of the major sources of research on the Twin City.

The Carnegie Public Library of the Twin City had an interesting beginning. The *Winston-Salem Journal* reported, "The building's story began in 1903, when J.C. Buxton, the chairman of the city school board, started a drive to get a public library for the town of Winston. Steel magnate Andrew Carnegie was helping towns nationwide get their first libraries through the Carnegie Foundation. The foundation gave the city $15,000 toward the construction of the building, which was named the Carnegie Public Library." On February 14, 1906, the library's first book was checked out. The library was located at the corner of Third and Cherry. The Twin City outgrew the small library and began a movement to build a new one. The land was purchased from the former estate of R.J. Reynolds and the building was constructed in 1952. The main library, which still exists today, holds a collection of the local history of Winston. The microfilm collection of the *People's Press, Winston-Salem Journal & Sentinel* and several other publications allows residents to step into a "time machine" and return to old days of Winston and Salem. This establishment is getting worn and is crying out for a larger and more modern facility. A downtown Winston museum is also called for. With these accomplishments, the next phase of the twenty-first century could be brought forward, revolutionizing the development of the downtown area.

CHAPTER 7.

The Neighborhoods

Winston-Salem's population grew at its largest rate ever between 1910 and 1920, with a 113 percent increase. This followed a national trend of suburban development in the United States. Suburbia first began after the Civil War and the boom of the 1880s in Winston-Salem. Before 1865, Winston and Salem only comprised three defining parts: East Salem, West Salem and Winston. All surrounding area was the country or other communities. By the 1890s, the only added neighborhoods within the city limits were the West End neighborhood of Winston followed by Southside, or Washington Park neighborhood, as it is known today.

Prior to the formation of these two neighborhoods, the land of which they were formed was considered West Salem. In 1891, the eastern part of Southside was incorporated as the town of Waughtown. The Waughtown Historic District of the twenty-first century had its founding in 1800, as Baggetown. By 1911, the Southbound Railroad had arrived to the Salem limits, cutting a divide between Waughtown and the 1890 development of Sunnyside, another Southside development. During the 113 percent growth period, neighborhoods began to sprout like weeds. Ardmore, the first automobile neighborhood, began in 1910 and became one of the largest. This was followed by the formation of the Granville Park suburb (1915), Reynolda Village with the development of Reynolda estate (1915), Crafton Heights and Melrose sections shortly thereafter, West Highland (1919) and Buena Vista (1920). By 1927, the neighborhoods to the west included Westover, Westview, Reynolda Park and Country Club Estates. To the north were Mountview (1920), Forest Hills and Whiteview. Bon Air arrived in 1923. The southern part of the city founded Anderleigh (1928) and Konnoak Hills (1929). The restricted neighborhood of African Americans (1920) was noted as the first restricted black suburb in the South.

Five examples of historic neighborhoods having the national distinction and representation of the National Register of Historic Places are presented here. The extensive excerpts from this organization's valuable research papers give us a view of the past in these stately neighborhoods.

Approximately three miles southwest of downtown Winston-Salem is located the Ardmore Historic District, roughly bounded by Queen and Cloverdale Avenue on the

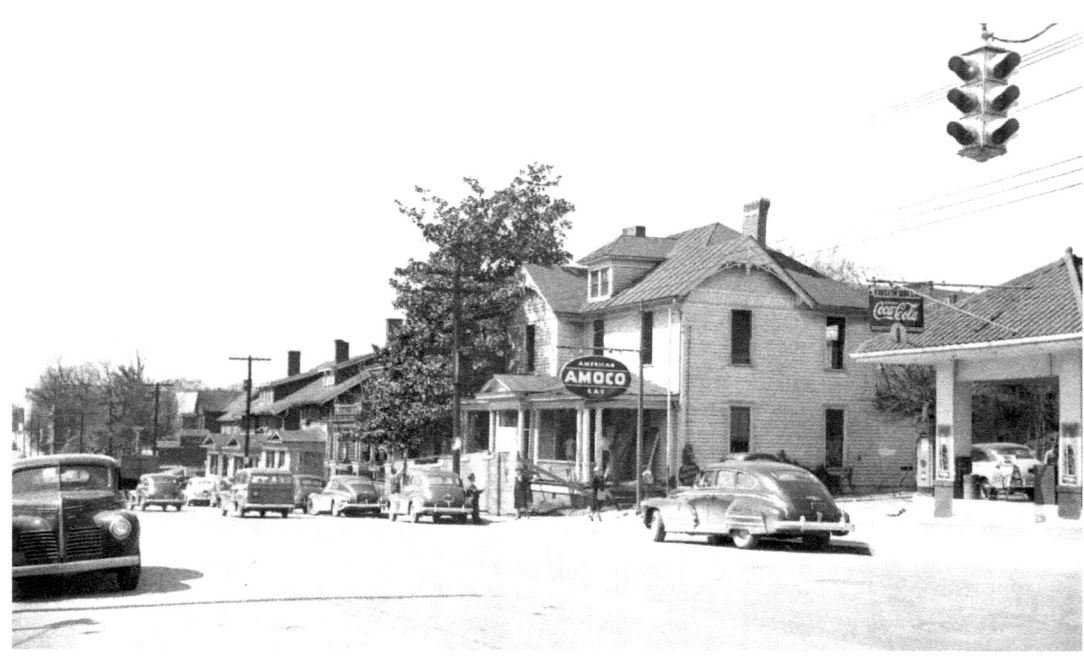

This view looking west on Fourth Street near the intersection of Spruce Street shows a different landscape than in today's businesses and buildings. This was originally an early neighborhood of the downtown area. Photo circa 1950s, before these homes would be razed.

north, Duke and Sunset Drive on the east, Ardsley Street and Walker Avenue on the south and Knollwood Street on the west. The district is quite large, consisting of more than 2,200 properties and extending approximately thirteen blocks in length and about ten blocks in depth. The area is overwhelmingly residential and consists of at least ten platted residential developments that were built from 1910 to 1924, as well as three large apartment complexes from 1947 to 1951. In addition to single- and multifamily housing, the district also contains a collection of historic commercial and institutional buildings, including several churches, two schools and one building from the large regional hospital located at the district's edge. The district also contains two historic parks.

The earliest homes in the district are found in Crafton Heights and date from around 1910. Probably two of the oldest houses are 402 Sunset Drive and 245 Corona Street. By late 1910, however, the early development in Ardmore had come to be dominated by the bungalow and Craftsman-style houses. The variety of bungalows is unequaled by any other architectural style in the neighborhood. In fact, bungalows account for approximately one-quarter of the housing stock in Ardmore and there are more than three hundred Craftsman-style examples.

After bungalows, Colonial Revival–style houses were the most frequent houses built in Ardmore before World War II, numbering about 125 examples. There are nearly 100 examples of the American Foursquare built throughout the neighborhood, particularly in the Ardmore plats, the area between Academy and Ardsley Streets and in the Westfield

The Neighborhoods

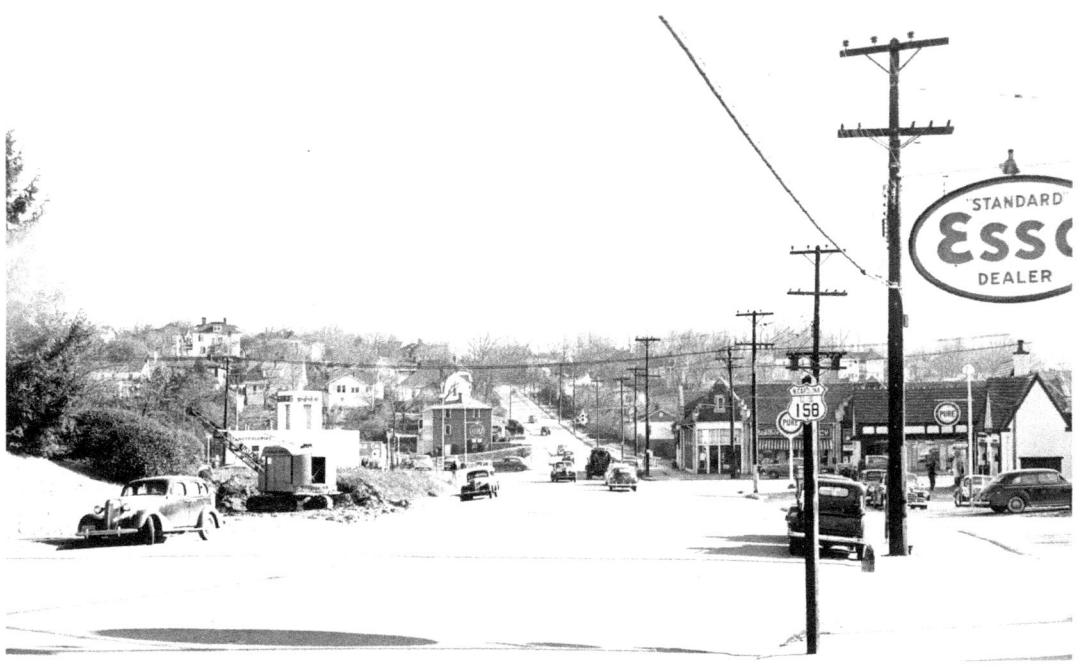

This scene at the corner of Hawthorne Road and First Street became a busy business area for Ardmore and West End neighborhoods.

development. Completing the pre-Depression architectural palette in Ardmore is the Tudor Revival style and its simpler variation, the English cottage. By the end of the Great Depression, bungalows had fallen out of favor, although period cottages and Colonial Revival–style houses continued to be built.

While Ardmore was marketed as a single-family neighborhood, duplexes and small-scale apartment buildings played a distinctive role in the neighborhood's development during the late 1920s through the mid-1950s. Several excellent examples remain as rental property (fueled in part by North Carolina Baptist Hospital students and staff) and are primarily located in the areas platted by the Ardmore Company (developers) north of Academy and in the Irving/Fenimore Streets area. An excellent quadraplex exists at 720 Hawthorne Road. In addition to these early multifamily units are the Ardmore Terrace and Cloverdale Apartments built around 1949. They are located in the 2300 blocks of Queen and Cloverdale Avenue. The important role of the automobile in Ardmore is reflected in the numerous garages in the neighborhood. About 22 percent of the pre-1953 houses in the district have historic garages.

In addition to residential properties, the Ardmore Historic District also has a number of institutional buildings, including five pre-1945 churches and the North Carolina Baptist Hospital Nurses' Home. The Nurses' Home is the only historic building on the hospital campus to maintain its integrity. Colonial Revival is the dominant style for Ardmore's institutional buildings, reflecting the national trends during the early twentieth century.

The earliest church in the neighborhood is Ardmore Methodist Church, located at 630 Hawthorne Road and built in 1925. This Colonial Revival–style church is brick with a classical portico, three-tier spire, arched, stained-glass windows and triple-arched, double-leaf entries.

Two important institutional buildings in Ardmore are Ardmore School, completed in 1929, and Moore School, built in 1951. Ardmore School is located at 1046 Miller Street. It is a two-story, brick and cast stone building that features art deco bas-relief designs. Moore School is located at 451 Knollwood Street. There are very few commercial buildings in the Ardmore Historic District. The Ardmore Historic District embodies the character of early twentieth-century suburban life in Winston-Salem.

The Holly Avenue Historic District is composed of fifty-nine acres in an approximately twelve-block area. One of the most important factors in the history of the neighborhood has been the landscape. At the heart of the district are springs that were used by the eighteenth-century Moravian settlers as a water source for the town of Salem, south of the district. Both the steep topography and the town of Salem's desire to protect the springs as a water source made the district less desirable for commercial or residential development. In 1903, with fairly dense development nearly surrounding it and no need to continue protecting the springs as a water source, the Moravian congregation subdivided the property around the springs. This tract, known as the Reservation, was bounded by Holly Avenue and Poplar, Spring and First Streets. Homes are one and two stories in height, while three- and four-story apartment buildings are found throughout the district. The Holly Avenue Historic District developed on the rolling, and sometimes steep, hills between downtown and the 1891 West End subdivision. The origins of this name remain unclear, though the neighborhood association took the name when it was formed more than twenty years ago. Queen Anne and early Colonial Revival homes were constructed through the early 1900s. From the 1910s through the 1930s, bungalows with Craftsman and Colonial Revival details became the common styles. After World War II, Minimal Traditional, with stripped-down Colonial Revival detailing, became the standard and was most commonly applied to the district's postwar apartment buildings. The three oldest homes are the 1885 Henry Case House on South Poplar Street, the 1889 James Jessup House at 134 Spring Street and the 1890 house at 127 Broad Street.

There are numerous outbuildings throughout the neighborhood, most of which are garages. The most stylish outbuilding in the district is the Kapp Carriage House, located at 642 Holly Avenue. The Kapp House has been demolished, but the 1904 carriage house remains. A nonresidential building is the Green Front Grocer (1937). It is a small, gabled, brick, Colonial Revival store at the corner of First and Broad.

Throughout much of the early twentieth century, many of Winston-Salem's citizens with the means to do so were moving to bourgeoning suburbs, yet the Holly Avenue Historic District, located downtown, experienced much of its new construction as well as reinvestment as smaller, older houses were torn down for new dwellings. The neighborhood historically was occupied by residents who represented a broad range of incomes and socioeconomic levels, from physicians and company presidents to factory workers, sawmill employees and store clerks. Within the Holly Avenue neighborhood prior to 1908, both white and black workers occupied the small homes on South Poplar Street in West Salem.

The Neighborhoods

These residents worked for the railroad and local factories and lived in hall and parlor and saddlebag houses with little or no regard for race. By 1908, the African American residents had been pushed out, and all the cottages were replaced in the 1910s and 1920s with modest bungalows and duplexes whose residents were white. The African Americans who left South Poplar Street apparently moved to nearby streets, such as Shallowford Road (Brookstown Avenue). Homes were eventually built on all the Reservation's lots subdivided in 1903, while older homes south of First Street were torn down to make way for bungalows and somewhat larger houses.

During the first half of the twentieth century, Holly Avenue residents maintained gardens and orchards and kept goats, sheep and chickens. Residents hunted and trapped rabbits and squirrels in a wooded area west of Brookstown Avenue. Children played in the numerous creeks that are now hidden by culverts and attended West End Graded School, Wiley School and Reynolds High School. Today, peach trees and other domestic plants occasionally gain a foothold on the interstate embankment between Poplar and Brookstown Avenue. By the middle of the twentieth century, property owners began leaving, either selling or renting their homes. This created a neighborhood with a transient population, absentee landlords and a crime problem. The historic nomination has helped to attract better clientele to the area.

The Washington Park neighborhood was designed by Jacob Lott Ludlow in 1891 and developed largely after 1900. Today it is one of North Carolina's finest examples of an early twentieth-century streetcar suburb. In 1791, George Washington visited Salem, traveling north from Salisbury through what became over a century later a planned suburb and a dedicated green space aptly named Washington Park. It is generally accepted that Washington Park was named in honor of George Washington, who passed through the area on his way to Salem on May 31, 1791. It is significant in the history of Winston-Salem as one of the early residential suburbs developed as a result of the streetcar, reflecting the city's development from a small business center to one of the leading manufacturing centers of the South. The residences of some of Winston and Salem's most prominent leaders of the period can be found here.

One of the most fashionable of the residential areas to emerge in the early decades of Winston's boom period, Washington Park was a planned development. The designer of Washington Park, Jacob Lott Ludlow, also drew the West End plat. Ludlow's plan for Washington Park, although believed to have been designed after his plan for West End, contained the more customary grid pattern in the center moving west into curvilinear streets, which heeded the topography of the ridge overlooking the flood plain of Salem Creek. Many alleys remain today; several still connect streets. Most believe the park itself has always been called Washington Park, but Ludlow's plan shows the name "Sunny Side Park" in the ravine. Adelaide Fries notes in her history of the county that the name Sunnyside was derived from a plantation owned by E.A. Vogler. City directories use "Southside" or "S'Side" to identify the location of streets in Washington Park, Sunnyside and elsewhere in the city's southern sector.

The streetcar's location on Cascade Avenue was the reason for that avenue's large showy houses, as well as for the hundreds of less elegant dwellings that make up the neighborhood that formed around it. Most of the earliest houses in the district are traditional vernacular frame buildings, generally one story in height, either gable-sided or L-shaped in plan, with ornamentation found only in the turned posts and sawn brackets of the front porch, and perhaps in a shingled gable. Larger, two-story I-houses were also built, as well as similar-sized houses in the Queen Anne style. However, the Craftsman style of architecture is perhaps the most well-represented style in this district.

The streetcar was essential to the development of the Washington Park neighborhood and others. It is no coincidence that the streetcar system was established only months before major development companies incorporated. The streetcars were painted yellow, and there were summer and winter cars. Summer cars were open on both sides with seats that spanned the cars. The winter cars had a different seating arrangement, with closed sides and a central aisle. Long seats at each end housed an electric heater as well as a sandbox with a mechanism to release sand on the icy tracks when needed. (Boys in the neighborhood would soap the tracks at the top of Main, which caused the conductor to use a foot control to drop sand onto the tracks.) The streetcar lines ran south on Main to Cascade, where a branch turned to the west on Cascade Avenue and traveled all the way to the park. As development continued past the end of the line, bus service was added to bring passengers to the streetcar lines for a transfer. Although a few wealthy individuals had cars earlier, the automobile did not appear in any sizable number until around 1915.

The developers of Washington Park were among the countless entrepreneurs who became wealthy during this period. Much of the wealth garnered by the city's successful industrialists was poured into large and grand houses. Indeed, Winston-Salem has had three areas known as Millionaire's Row. The first was on Fifth Street in Winston, in the 1880s and 1890s. The second was in West End, Winston's first streetcar suburb whose development immediately preceded Washington Park's. Ultimately the title passed in the 1910s and 1920s to Cascade Avenue, a residential boulevard lined with elegant houses of several prominent industrialists running through the center of Washington Park. Among the wealthy residents of Washington Park was Henry E. Fries (104 Cascade Avenue), head of the gas company, president of the Winston-Salem Southbound Railway and mayor of Salem.

The development of Washington Park was aimed at a white, middle- to upper-middle-class clientele. Only Rawson Street and the 100 block of Acadia appear to have been home to African Americans. The houses in these areas are working-class dwellings that housed tobacco and furniture workers as well as those who worked as maids, cooks, chauffeurs and gardeners for wealthy families.

The first church in the neighborhood was organized in 1914, and a lot was purchased at the corner of Banner and Hollyrood for $1,700. The Sunday school was organized a year later on the second floor of C.D. Couch's two-story frame grocery store at the corner of Acadia Avenue and Hollyrood Street, and in the fall construction began on Schlatter Memorial Reformed Church. The handsome brick Gothic Revival church was completed in 1920 at a cost of $20,000.

The neighborhood's commercial buildings are concentrated along Acadia Avenue near the intersection of South Broad, South Main and Hollyrood Streets. They include buildings housing drug and hardware companies, specialty retail establishments and automobile body shops. Several historic commercial buildings remain, though most are noncontributing due to alterations. Only two remain intact on Acadia Avenue: the 1929 Swaim's Fair Price Food

The Neighborhoods

Store, a brick-veneered corner grocery store at 232 Acadia; and Renigar's Hardware at 317 Acadia.

West End is one of the most fully realized and intact examples of a turn-of-the-century streetcar suburb in North Carolina, retaining to a remarkable degree the integrity of its primary period of significance, 1887–1930. The late nineteenth- and early twentieth-century urban neighborhood is defined by its picturesque landscape features, including a system of curvilinear streets, terraced lawns with stone retaining walls and steps and parks that take full advantage of the dramatic hilly topography of the site. It is also known for its rich and varied collection of architecture reflective of the West End's period of development. In the West End, the lush landscape establishes a complementary environment for the architecture that it surrounds. Steep lots with terraced front lawns and flights of steps provide impressive settings for similarly impressive houses. The crescent-shaped district is bounded roughly by West End Boulevard to the northeast and north, Peters Creek through Hanes Park to the northwest and west, Sunset Drive along the west and southwest, West End Boulevard

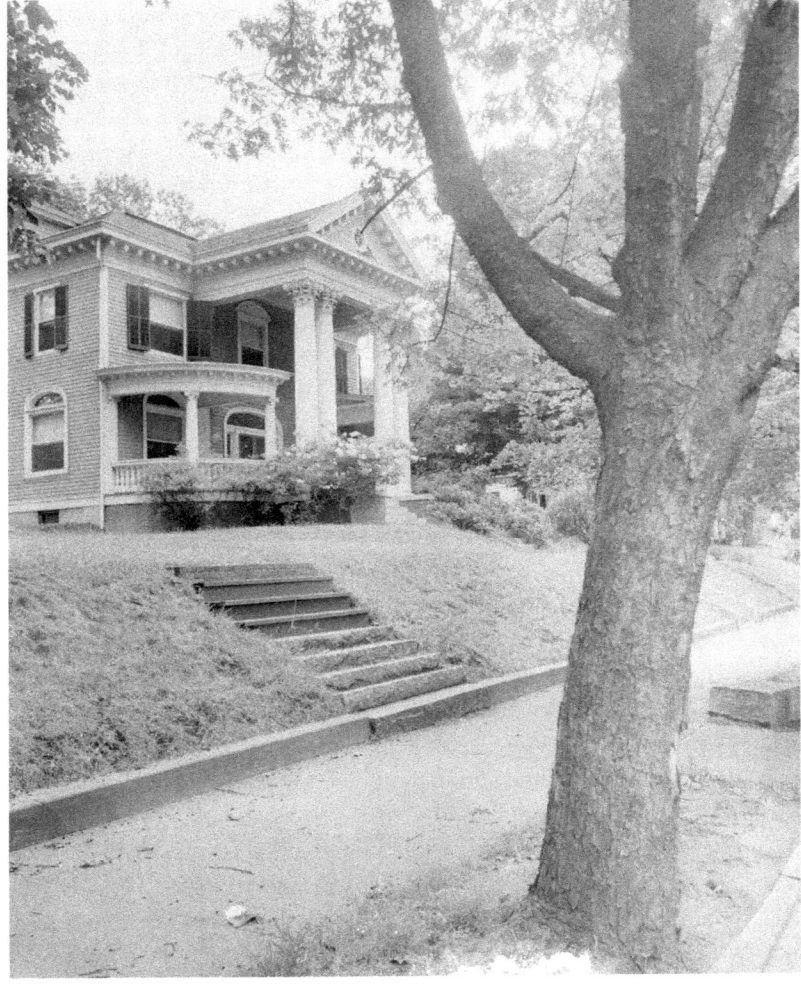

Rosenbacher mansion is shown on Fifth Street in this 1960 photo. It later was turned into a restaurant, Michael's, in the 1980s.

and Interstate 40 along the south and West Fourth Street along the southeast and east, meandering in a northeastward direction back to Fifth, Broad, Sixth and to the junction of West End Boulevard, Chatham Road and Buxton Street in the northeast corner. While all was originally known as the West End, the area today includes what is commonly called the West End, West End South (south of First Street) and Crystal Towers (east of Broad Street).

Of central importance to the character of the West End is its landscape plan as designed by Jacob Lott Ludlow, Winston's first city engineer. Influenced by the picturesque concept of suburban planning as promoted on the national level by Frederick Law Olmsted, the West End plan, which remains largely intact today, takes advantage of the dramatic topography of the area. Curving streets, with West End Boulevard a prime example, meander through the neighborhood along with some straight streets, creating an assortment of irregularly shaped blocks. The West End is a neighborhood of porches, with most of the houses built during the primary period of development having front porches and sometimes rear porches. These provide today, as they did originally, an easy transition from public (exterior) to private (interior) living spaces. They, like the sleeping porches found on the rear second story of many of the houses, also provide places for taking advantage of the cooling breezes often present in the hilly West End (as touted in an 1892 advertisement for the Zinzendorf Hotel). At the center of the district is Grace Court, a bowl-shaped park bounded by Fourth, Fifth and Glade Streets and an alley. Ludlow's plan also delineated Springs Park, which remains intact as a quiet wooded ravine retreat. Ludlow indicated a stretch of land along Peters Creek that he labeled simply "lawn." In 1919, P.H. Hanes donated this land to the city for a park to be called Hanes Park, with its impressive stone entrance at the foot of Clover Street, its avenue of maples and its footbridges over Peters Creek.

Building activity has occurred throughout the history of West End, but it has been most heavily concentrated between 1900 and 1929. While the surviving pre-1900 buildings are congregated along North Spring, Fifth, Summit and Fourth, structures representative of the subsequent building periods are mixed throughout the district. When the Depression hit in 1929, the West End witnessed a continuum of mainstream stylistic expressions, including examples of the late Victorian Queen Anne, the Neoclassical Revival, the Colonial Revival, the Craftsman and a variety of other styles that made brief appearances, among which were the Tudor Revival, the Spanish Mission and the Gothic Revival styles. The oldest houses in the West End are products of the late Victorian period and reflect to a large degree the visual variety associated with the Queen Anne style. Jacob Lott Ludlow's own house, poised at the prominent intersection of Summit and Fifth, is representative of the style. Erected in 1887 by Fogle Brothers builders, the house features a decorative wraparound porch and center bay balcony, sawnwork gable ornamentation and stained-glass windows.

The Poindexter House boasts a projecting corner tower. The nearby Tise House is one of the largest in West End. It is a massive two-and-a-half-story brick structure with a granite foundation ornamented with segmental arches filled with ironwork grills. Like the Rosenbacher House, the Tise House is dominated by a two-story central Corinthian portico.

One of the two most widely represented architectural styles in the West End is the Colonial Revival. At the top end of the spectrum are the 1902 John E. Coleman House and the 1920 Charles M. Thomas House. Both are large, two-story brick dwellings. The West End possesses a wealth of 1910s and 1920 bungalows in a wide range of types. Many are classic

The Neighborhoods

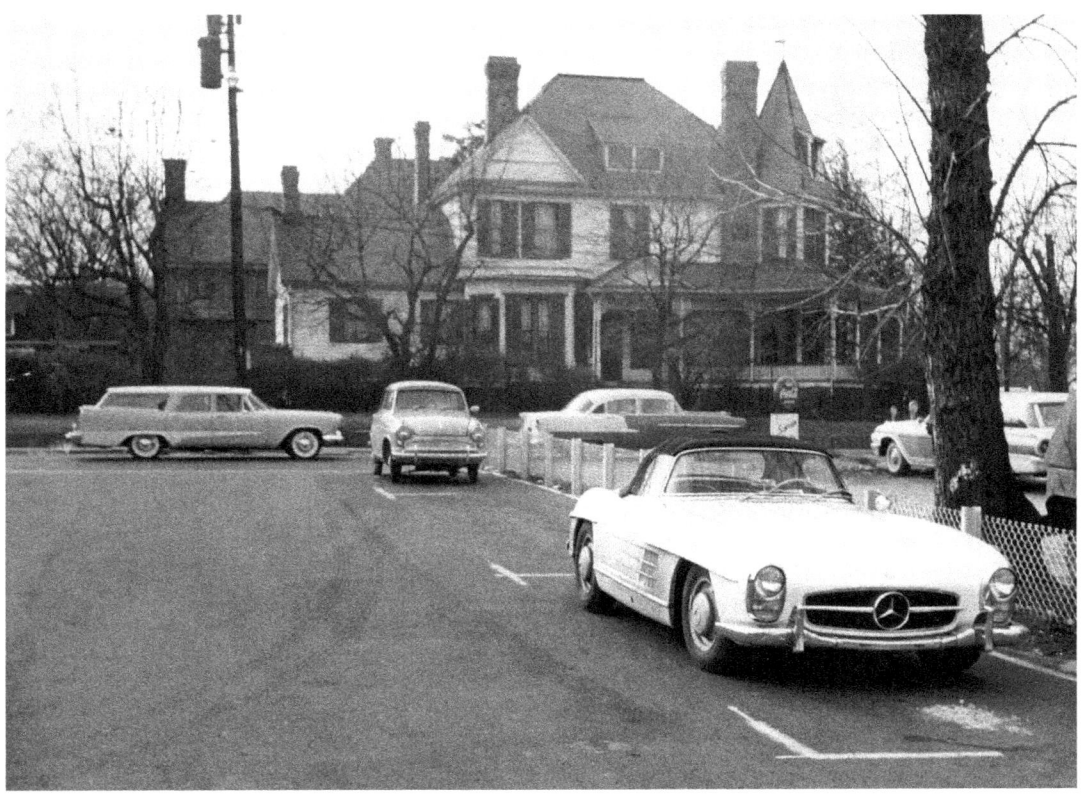

The last remaining mansion on Fifth Street was the Poindexter House. The Poindexter sisters lived here until their passing. The house was moved in the 1970s to make way for a business expansion. The house rests now in the West End neighborhood.

examples of the Craftsman style. Other buildings were designed in the Colonial Revival style. Prime examples are the 1927 Friends Meeting House and the 1924 First Church of Christ, Scientist. Apartment buildings erected in the 1920s also exhibit a simple version of the style, as exemplified by the Summit Apartments. This handsome, three-story brick building has a classical entrance, a balcony with round-arched sash window, other windows with keystone lintels and parapet cornice.

Two monumental Gothic Revival churches in the West End add significantly to the dignified character of the neighborhood. The grandest of these is St. Paul's Episcopal Church, one of the most outstanding Gothic Revival structures in the region. Magnificently sited on one of the highest elevations in the city, it was designed by the distinguished ecclesiastical architect Ralph Adams Cram of Boston.

Joyner's West End Grocery, one of the oldest buildings in the district, is a two-story brick, flat-iron shaped structure with a parapet roofline and a heavy bracketed cornice along the Fourth Street façade. Across Burke from Joyner's is the well-preserved 1915 drugstore attached to the west end of the row of four brick townhouses of the same date. At the northwest edge of the West End, the 1928 Summit Street Pharmacy is one of the most architecturally unusual buildings in the district. The two-story structure of vaguely Mediterranean-style influence is characterized by a rough stucco façade with applied slate blocks, an arcaded first story and an engaged porch across the second-story façade with a red and yellow tile roof.

The West Salem Historic District is located southwest of Winston-Salem's city center and immediately west of the museum village of Old Salem. The historic district is roughly bounded by Interstate 40 to the north; Beaumont, Granville Drive and Hutton Street to the west; Poplar Street to the east; and Salem Avenue, Walnut and Shober Street to the south. The neighborhood of West Salem is within the suburban development and the westward progression of the town of Salem. West Salem, unlike most of Winston-Salem's neighborhoods, has a very long history that is closely related to the late eighteenth- and nineteenth-century history of Salem. West Salem also played a noteworthy role in the early twentieth-century development of the newly created city of Winston-Salem. This dual role, within the growth of the town of Salem and later the Twin City, distinguishes the West Salem Historic District from other residential areas in the city.

The development of the neighborhood is complex, but began with eighteenth- and early nineteenth-century farmsteads on Salem's outlots. With the pronounced growth in the textile industry in Salem during the late nineteenth century, modestly scaled workers' housing was built in the Apple, Albert and Wachovia Streets area. Within the West Salem Historic District are examples of mid-nineteenth-century vernacular buildings illustrating the influences of the Greek Revival and Picturesque movements, but much more common are I-houses; side-gable, single-pile cottages; gable ell cottages; Queen Anne cottages; and pyramidal cottages that housed industrial workers and other low- to middle-income residents. The earliest resource in the district is the 1782 Stockburger Farmhouse. Its current appearance reflects significant 1900 alterations. After 1843, development was primarily on Poplar until the main wave of construction began around 1865, with the significant additions made to the 1854 Tesh-Butner-Bryant House and the 1870 construction of the Pfohl House. The district has more than one hundred structures dating to the nineteenth century. As part of the initial planning of Salem, outlots were designated to the west of the village.

The 1805 map of Salem shows two roads leading from Salem's center into the area immediately west of the village. The first was Papermill Road (now Bank Street), which led to Gottlieb Schober's paper mill. This mill was established on Peters Creek in 1791 at the western edge of the Salem town lot. The residential growth in the western section of Salem during the late eighteenth and early nineteenth centuries was accompanied by similar expansion in the northern and southern areas.

The residential construction in the West Salem area was far more diverse than a mill village, however, housing businessmen, tradesmen and industrial workers alike. Streets such as Walnut, Broad and Academy exhibit curves and slight bends that are the remnants of their eighteenth-century associations. Walnut, for example, began as Tavern Lane, a small path that led from Salem Tavern to the Stockburger Farm in the Salem outlots.

One other important design feature in the neighborhood is the Granville Place development, which was platted in 1914. In this plat, which originally included most of the southwestern quadrant of the district, the southern end of Granville Drive curves with the

The Neighborhoods

topography as it makes the rounded southwestern corner of Granville Park and turns into Walnut. The park, which is located on the block bounded by Granville Drive, Washington, Green and West, was heavily wooded during its early history and retains a good amount of wooded land. Indera Mill, for example, is an early twentieth-century textile mill located adjacent to the district's northeast corner. Within the district there is a historic Coca-Cola Bottling Plant and a freight terminal near the southeastern corner. Altogether, about one-third of the housing stock in the West Salem Historic District dates from the 1880 to 1915 period, while nearly 40 percent was built between 1915 and 1935. These later houses are overwhelmingly Craftsman bungalows, with 150 examples.

Because of its early period of development, there are a number of outbuildings in West Salem that are seldom seen elsewhere in the city. One of the best examples is the one-and-a-half-story, front-gable, 1900 outbuilding at 1010 South Poplar. The building has a single entry, four-light window, weather board siding and exposed purlins. The original use of the resource is unknown, but it may have served as agricultural storage. The extant agricultural buildings in West Salem indicate that small numbers of livestock were kept and a modest quantity of produce was grown during the neighborhood's earliest period.

The district includes houses, industrial and commercial buildings, as well as three important neighborhood churches. The impressive Christ Moravian Church, in the gothic Revival style, is the earliest, dating from 1895. It is a rare instance of a Moravian church not using the eighteenth-century Home Moravian Church as its model. Nearby is the Green Street Methodist Church, a Neoclassical Revival–style building built in 1921; it features a classical portico and central dome. The third church, Salem Baptist, no longer remains in its historic sanctuary, but the 1917 Education Building still stands.

No one can speak of any early twentieth-century neighborhoods without mentioning the influence of the neighborhood grocery store. The 1916 Winston-Salem City Directory

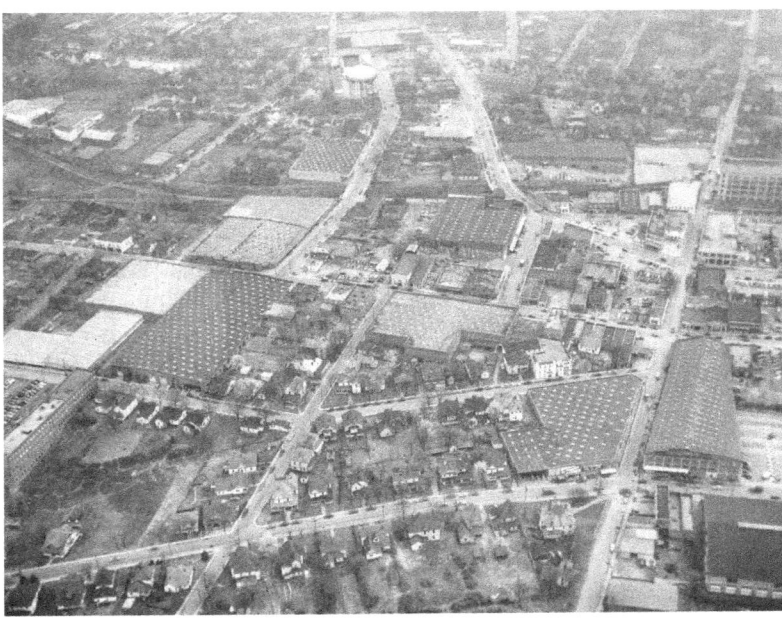

This photo shows the Cherry Street area near the Brown's Warehouse and the neighborhood between the Chatham Manufacturing Company and the downtown area of Liberty Street and Main Street.

shows that in the older neighborhoods profiled here there were more than 150 grocery stores within a couple-mile radius of the city. From the early 1900s to the 1970s, Winston-Salem has been blessed with many stores. A forty-year timeframe from 1915 to 1955 marked the heyday of old-fashioned neighborhood grocery stores. The large grocery store chains overtook the local mom and pop stores by the 1950s, undercutting prices and driving out smaller businesses.

An emphasis was put on historical preservation with the founding of the Old Salem Historic District in 1950. This was the first such district in the United States. The nation's bicentennial in 1976 helped more preservation to arise with the beginning of the next historic district of West End. Washington Park and West Salem would follow. The National Register of Historic Places is a historic tool and honor that ranks as the number one protector of history in the United States. The neighborhoods of the Twin City are so honored as Old Salem has been listed since 1950. For the first time the stories from the National Register, as presented above, were gathered from the North Carolina Archives of Raleigh. All contain current twenty-first-century research as well. Other neighborhoods that have recently attained historical status and those involved in the process are the following: Waughtown, Bellview, Reynoldstown, Hanes Town, Happy Hill and Konnoak. With the backing of the National Register of Historic Places and the involvement of historic groups, developers and the City of Winston-Salem, a complete historic midsize town could be presented. With Old Salem leading the way, all neighborhoods and their diverse history could finally be presented and the tourism business could grow immensely.

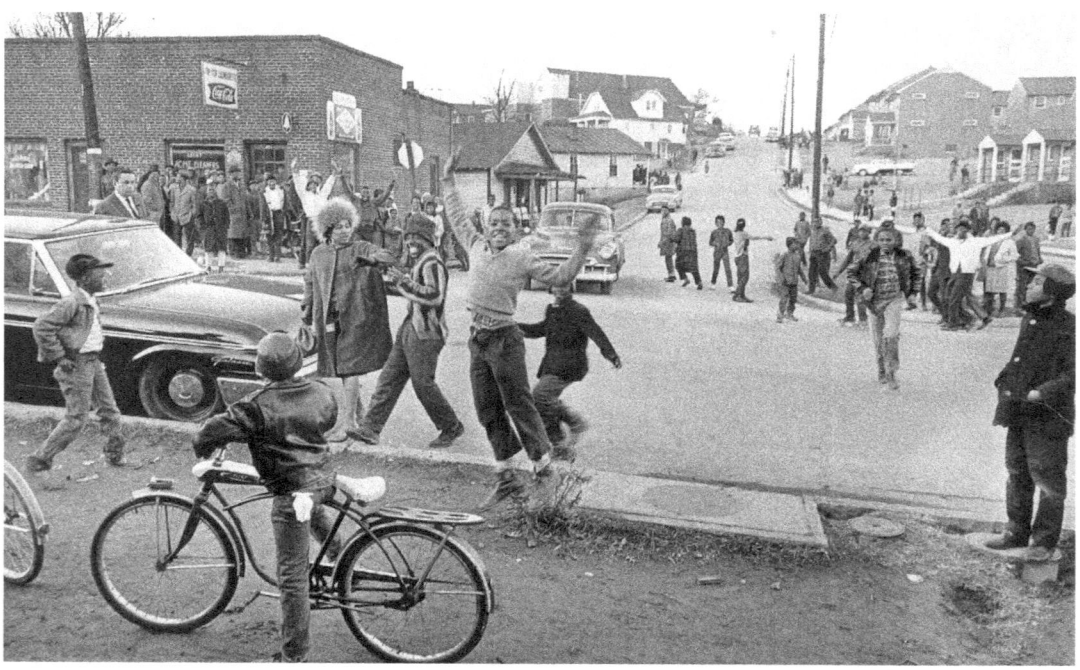

Block parties and festivities could be found throughout the Twin City in the 1960s. .

CHAPTER 8.

What Have We Learned?

In beginning to answer this chapter's question, permit me to return to the beginning, or at least the place where our Twin City began: Main Street in Old Salem. During the summer of 2006, my family and I were touring and exploring the recreated village of Old Salem. My wife and I believe the study of our roots as well as the city or place in which we reside deserves a review now and again. As my family strolled the major streets around the central district, another family was doing the same, with one difference—a grandmother assisted in this family's journey through the Moravian village and her insight was heard by all within a block radius. The lady had been a resident of Winston-Salem for more than seventy years and her tour was a tad different than the normal tours of Salem. As our fellow family members noted the architecture and beauty of the village, the grandmother replied "poppycock." She informed us that all the houses and surrounding landscape had been nothing more than an eyesore when she resided there in the 1940s and 1950s. She remembered how much time and money the founding families, not to mention the city and its taxpayers, had to invest in this rambling project over the years. Her remembrances of the 1940s and 1950s were of an old town needing the revitalization of a wrecking ball. Salem was spoken of in this way by the old-timers of my youth as well. They would ask, "Why save these decrepit buildings and houses? We, residents of Salem, need a grocery store and more modern businesses, like Winston and the downtown area." We, as current town residents, are grateful for the insight and determination to save the Moravian history; however, the point is at what cost. Many old-timers thought modernization and destroying the old was much more practical. Today we find ourselves in the same dilemma as our upset old-timers.

Forsyth County is losing historic properties at such a rate that many historic pieces throughout the city will soon be gone. These are irreplaceable parts of us and our ancestors that can never be duplicated. Forsyth County has lost 33 percent of what are known as "significant historic properties," about five hundred since 1980, according to figures from the State Historic Preservation Office. There are many more historic structures that have been lost before they had been even recognized. Three historic eighteenth-century Moravian settlements have nearly been lost to development alone, according to LeeAnn Pegram of the Historic Resources Commission of Forsyth County.

Winston-Salem

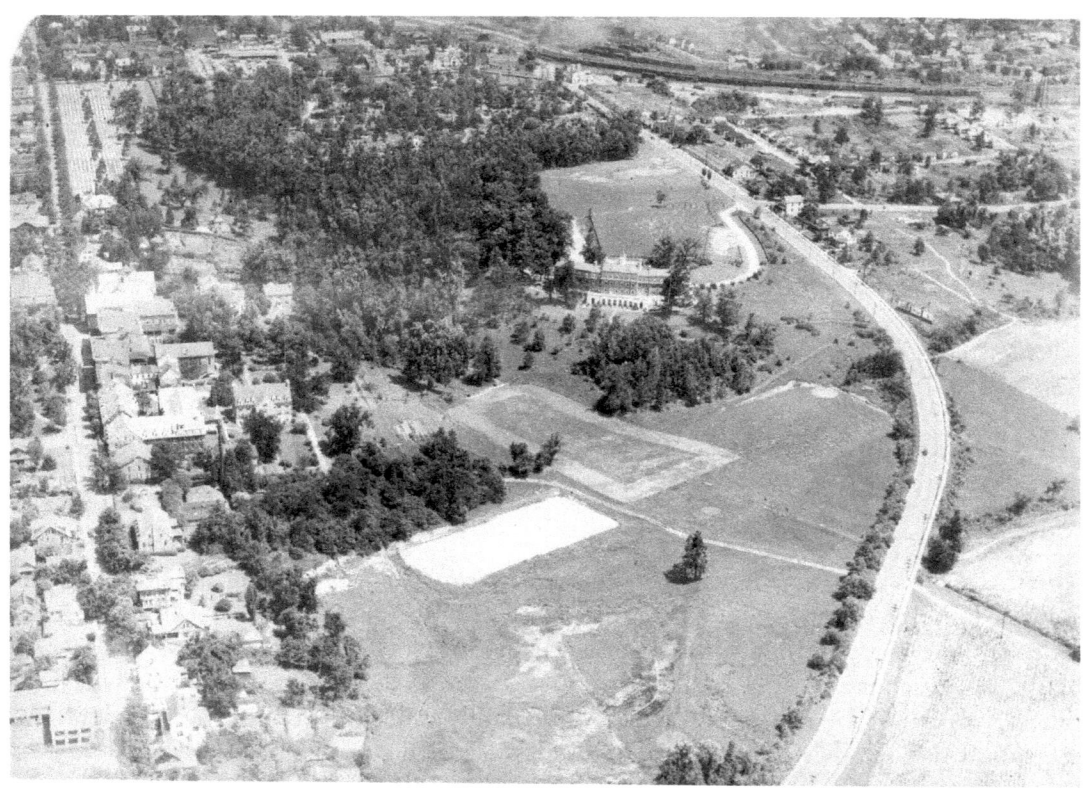

Salem College in Old Salem is shown in this 1950s photo. To the left of the university are the many homes that existed here before the restoration of Old Salem Inc. The landscape was changed extensively as these nineteenth- and early twentieth-century homes were razed to showcase the eighteenth-century Salem.

A *Winston-Salem Journal* article from December 2007, by Mary Giunca, a reporter who covers local history, sums up our search of losses of properties to date. Her article, "Vanishing Before Our Eyes," documents lost treasures of historic buildings. The list is a who's who of diverse structures from our Twin City past. Here are a few examples from a recent survey in Forsyth County to update a 1978–80 report by the State Historic Preservation Office.

1. Crawford Building, 1893
   110–112 West Fourth, demolished in 2000 after collapse
2. McDonald's, early 1960s
   Silas Creek Parkway, west of Main, sold in 1983 and then demolished
3. Modern Chevrolet, 1947
   800 West Fourth Street, demolished in 2005 for condominiums
4. Reynolds #256, 1895
   North Chestnut, destroyed in 1998 by fire
5. Alspaugh-Atwood Barn, 1920s
   Atwood Road near the 2800 block, now a subdivision

What Have We Learned?

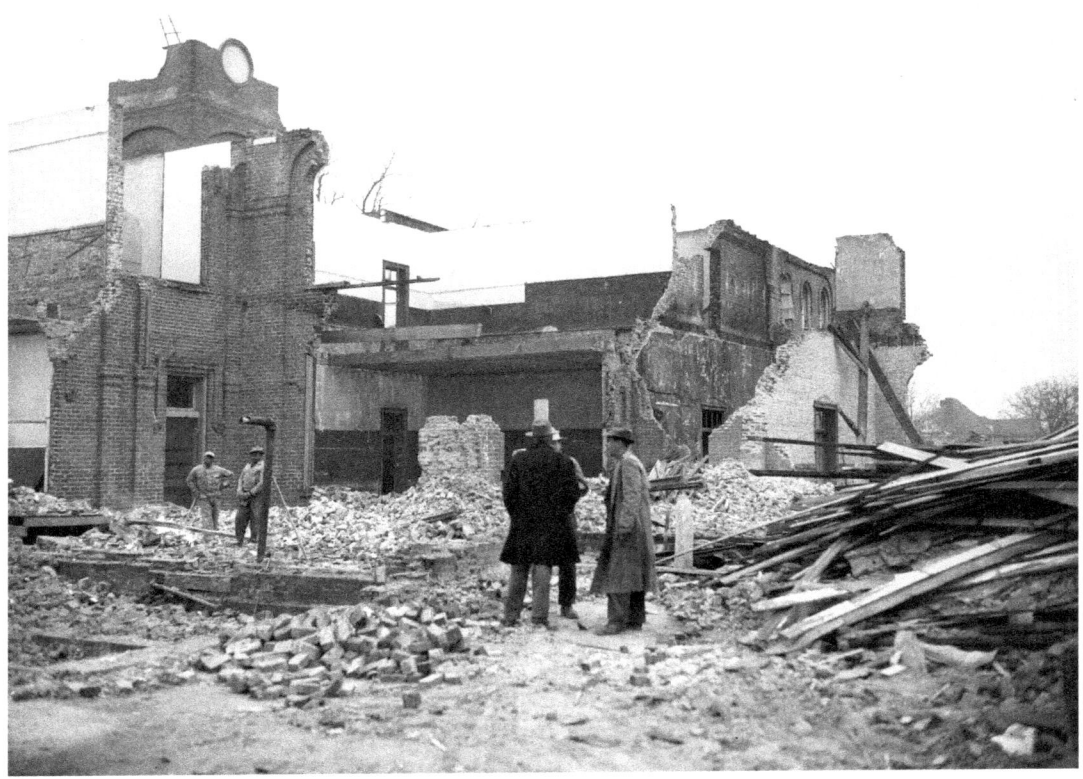

The razing of the West End School, originally the Winston Graded School of 1882, is shown. Once razed, the area would be occupied by the new Sears & Roebuck establishment, circa 1946.

    6. Phelps-Brewer House, mid-nineteenth century
       4288 Hampton Road, now an open field
    7. Crystal Ice and Coal Co., 1900
       411 South Marshall Street, demolished in 1985 for redevelopment
    8. Lemuel B. Mendenhall House, mid-nineteenth century
       3025 Greenhouse Road, now a vacant lot
    9. Kyles Heights, 1900
       1612 East Fourteenth, demolished 1992

Unfortunately, one of the largest losses of property and structure to date occurred in late 2007, in a cutoff section of the West Salem neighborhood district of 1782. The northern section of the historic neighborhood became the Watkins Street neighborhood because of the invasion of Interstate 40 in the 1950s. Nearly everyone in the Twin City and surrounding counties knows this land today as the site of the new minor league baseball stadium developed by the City of Winston-Salem and Brookstown Development Partners, LLC. However, few know of the history of this area. The lost housing stock around this neglected neighborhood, which borders Green, First, Peters Creek Parkway

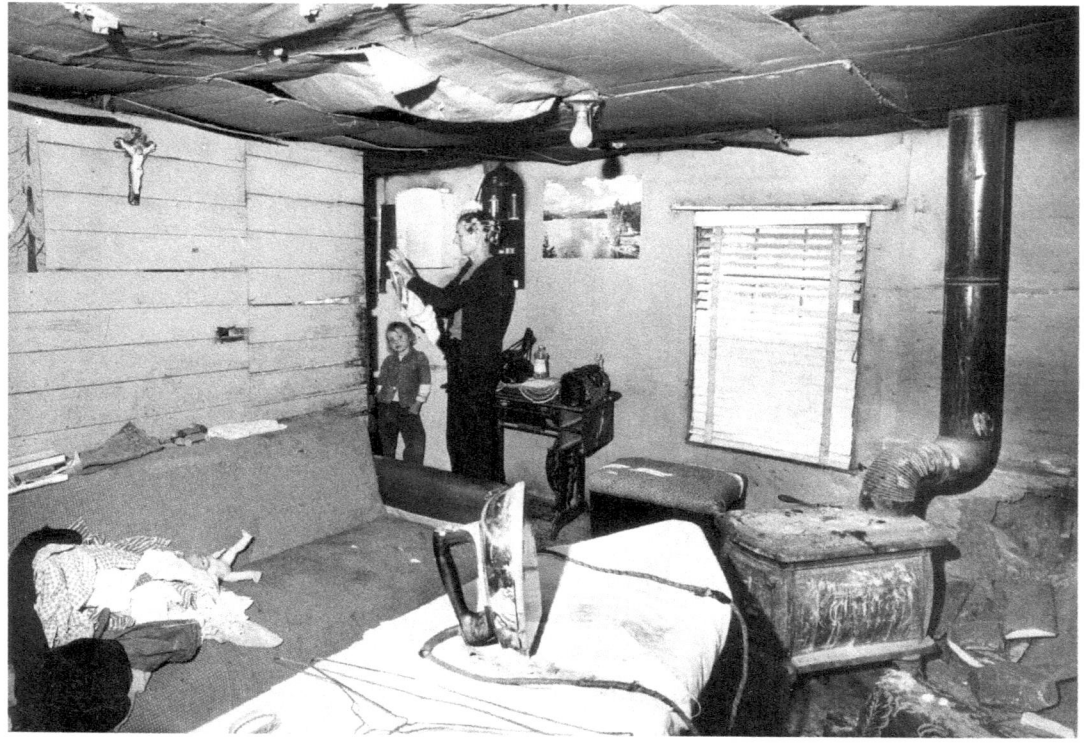

Urban renewal arrived in the mid- to late 1960s. It would change the landscape and would allow for better facilities to be rebuilt. This was one that desperately needed it. Photo 1960s.

and Interstate 40, was rich in diverse history. African Americans had called this land home since the late 1700s, when the area was part of the Paper Mill Settlement in 1790. Between 1890 and 1905, Watkins at South Green, south to Granville Drive included an enclave of African American and white workers who called the street home. The building of the proposed baseball stadium destroyed four houses that dated to the late nineteenth century at South Green and Watkins alone. Also lost to the proposed complex will be the Park Circle pocket neighborhood across Peters Creek Parkway. These homes and their histories, as well as the Watkins Street community, were not reviewed or considered for preservation. The Park Circle homes dated from 1918 to 1927.

The following is a list of the Winston Salem streets that were changed by the construction of Interstate 40. Documentation presented is from 1918–1950s street directories.

Street	House Numbers Destroyed by Interstate 40
Broad (South)	202, 203, 209, 210, 213, 214, 215, 216, 217, 219, 221
	Total Lost: 11 homes
Cherry (South)	130, 131, 134, 135, 140, 146, 147
	Total Lost: 7 homes

What Have We Learned?

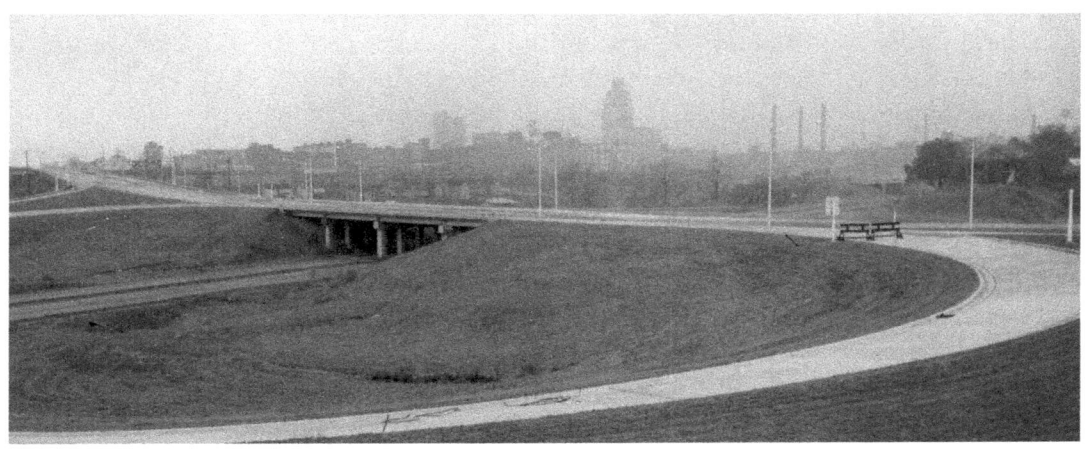

An early ramp to Interstate 40 shows the city from the southeastern side in this 1960 photo.

Granville Drive	114, 115, 117, 118, 119, 120, 123, 124, 128, 132, 207
	Total Lost: 11 homes (all homes belonged to African Americans)
Gray from Watkins	928, 932, 939, 940
	Total Lost: 4 homes (all homes belonged to African Americans)
Hickory (Carter)	I-40's path was along Hickory, totally destroying the street
	Three house numbers were changed when the Hickory name was adopted
Liberty (South)	108, 109, 113, 116, 117, 118, 124
	Total Lost: 7 homes
Marshal (South)	112, 114
	Total Lost: 2 homes
Peachtree Alley (West from 112 Granville Drive)	
	204, 210, 224, 216, 320, 324, 326, 328, 729, 913–929
	Total Lost: 19 houses. These homes may have originated from the Paper Mill Settlement around Peters Creek and Bank Street (Papermill Road)
Pond (South Poplar)	
	Total Lost: 1 home
Watkins	104, 105, 217, 301, 302, 306, 308, 309, 310, 312, 314, 318, 321, 335, 339, 401, 405, 409, 413, 415, 419, 422, 426, 914, 109
	Watkins extended westward and southwest toward the Paper Mill Settlement. It was called "Watkins Row."
	Total Lost: 25 homes

Total houses lost: 92

With these losses, we appear not to have learned anything about preservation. This is a shame, as a *New York Times* article by Martha Stevensen Olson in 2003 reports, "Traveling back into history is increasing." Americans' interest in the past and heritage tourism is gaining momentum. After the slowdown in air movement after the 9/11 Twin Towers disaster, people began to travel again, but for most part restricted their travel to within the United States. The Travel Industry Association of America and the *Smithsonian* magazine conducted a joint study that shows from 1993 to 2003, 118 million people seeking history and culture hit the roads. This was a 13 percent increase over the period. Interest in African American history, the civil rights movement, the women's rights movement and the Civil and Revolutionary Wars were the main historical reasons for travel. Our city has all that and more. The Watkins neighborhood had it as well, but was not preserved or even studied.

As Old Salem archaeological studies have shown the city over the years, what is underground is just as important as what is above. The first water system of the eighteenth-century Moravians in the present Holly Avenue Historic District is a good example. All history, not just the history of a few, needs to be preserved and presented. Historic tourism speaks well of this in our present economy, which cries out for good investments. Where tourism can be expanded on in the Twin City addresses the question, "What have we learned?" In another way, we have connected the histories of our older neighborhoods with the revitalization of downtown and the success of Old Salem. A good example of connecting the dots of Twin City history is in the presentation of the original town of Salem as a complete entity. East Salem and Old Salem of 1766 meets West Salem and the West Salem Historic District of 1782 to present the full story of a town told through two distinct parts. Parallels between East and West Salem can be drawn throughout both neighborhoods' existence. One important parallel found while researching the articles of West Salem churches and schools was rather uncanny. The Moravian congregational church of Salem helped to build the oldest girls' school in the United States, Salem College. In West Salem, Salem Baptist Church helped create the Salem Baptist Christian School. At the time of its creation, the Christian school was the largest school of its type in the United States. Also, Piedmont Baptist College, another creation of Salem Baptist Church, would gain the reputation of one of the top Bible colleges in the United States. Four national treasures— Salem College, Salem Academy, Piedmont Baptist College and Salem Baptist Christian School—were all in our Twin City's backyard. If the town of Salem could be presented as one, who knows the goals our neighborhood could achieve and the tourism that could be had. Now that is something to think about.

One may ask, as the old-timers have, is local history really that important? The answer begins with the "Legacy Vision" of Forsyth County. This major advisory plan was adopted several years ago and is the building block of the Twin City to the completion of the plan in 2015. The Legacy Vision focus groups have envisioned in their report, "Forsyth County Tomorrow," more livable neighborhoods in our urban areas, suburbs and small towns. New neighborhoods and revitalized older neighborhoods contain a diversity of housing types and people, and better access to neighborhood shopping and services, recreational facilities and educational opportunities. A united effort to address social issues such as crime, quality of education and homelessness has helped to strengthen the relationship between our neighborhoods. With careful planning, appropriate design standards and citizen empowerment, neighborhoods have become the building blocks of our community.

What Have We Learned?

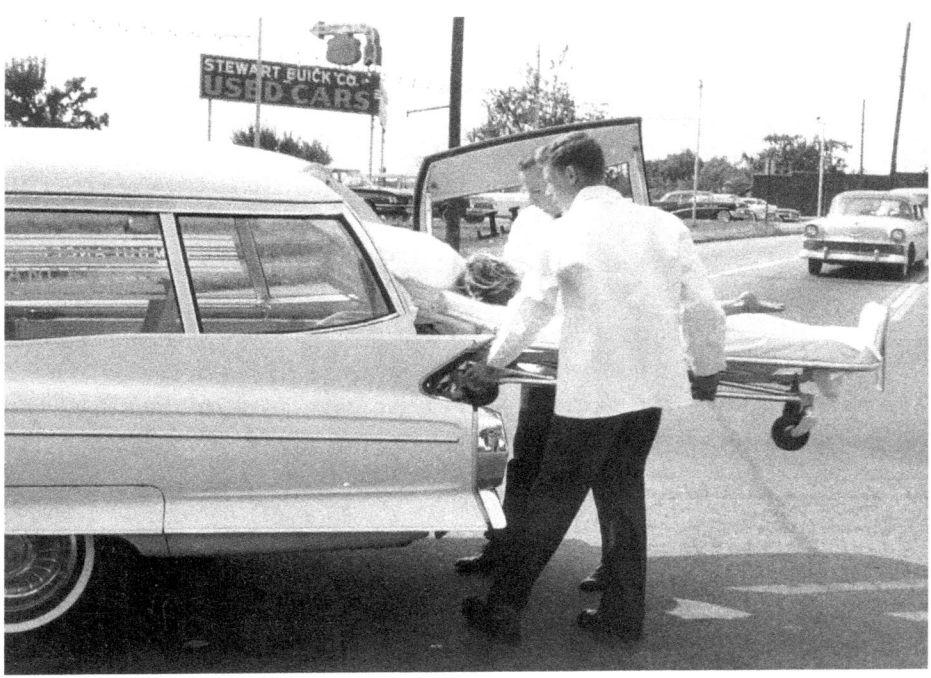

An accident had just occurred at the intersection at West First Street and Broad Street in this 1962 photo.

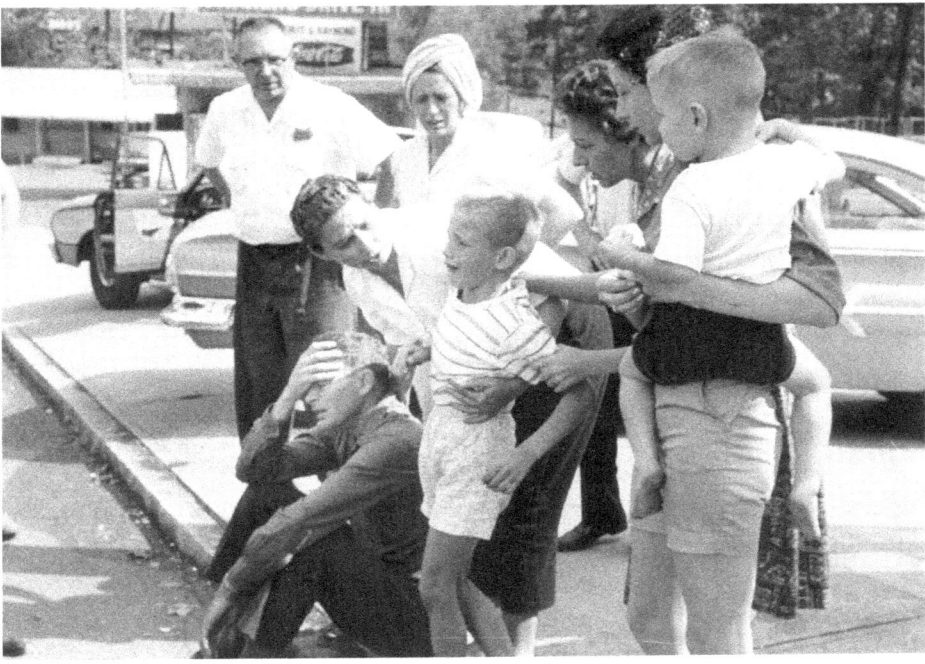

The little child is somewhat distraught, as is the gentleman kneeling beside him. The little girl had been struck by an automobile. The child shown standing is the victim's brother. Luckily, the child only sustained a minor injury.

The historic preservation recommendation of the South Central Area Plan of Legacy is the best example of historical preservation of all diverse people and their legacies. The plan covers history's strength in the Twin City: the older neighborhoods. A few direct quotes from the South Central Area Plan and its recommendations are:

> *Legacy promotes historic preservation as a priority for Urban Neighborhoods due to its contribution to the aesthetic, social, historical, cultural, and environmental quality of neighborhoods as well as to the economic development of the community. In the area plan process, neighborhoods can be identified for potential National Register, Historic, Historic Overlay, or Neighborhood Conservation Overlay Districts.*
>
> *Work with Washington Park and Holly Avenue residents to determine support for and establishment of Local Historic Overlay (HOWEVER) District Designation and the adoption of Design Review Guidelines. Such work should be performed in conjunction with the Historic Resources Commission; other HOWEVER District representatives; and, through a public involvement process.*
>
> *Work with Old Salem, Inc. and West Salem Neighborhood Associations to nominate the Salem Town Lot area for expansion of the National Landmark District for Old Salem. Such work should be in conjunction with the Historic Resources Commission, City-County Planning Board (CCPB), the NC State Historic Preservation Office, and the National Park Service, and through a series of public meetings.*
>
> *Work with the Historic Resources Commission to expand the number of Local Landmark Property expansions in the area. Potential designations include the archeological resource for the Salem Reservoir (Second) in Holly Avenue; the Butner-Bryant (622 Poplar) and Ackerman-Reich (608 Poplar) Houses in West Salem; the H.D. Poindexter House (130 West End Boulevard) in West End; Hillcrest (450 Sprague) in Sunnyside; the Frederick F. Bahnson (28 Cascade Avenue), Christian R. Fogle (29 Cascade Avenue), and A.H. Eller (129 Cascade Avenue) Houses in Washington Park.*

The landmark and local historical overlay of the plan is more solid assurance that historic preservation will exist long after 2015, for our grandchildren and beyond. Donald M. Neilsen, former chairman of Forsyth County Resources Commission, states it this way:

> *Landmarks do not cost the city money, they are an economic benefit. The State legislation* [that] *authorizes local landmarks explicitly recognizes that the preservation of landmarks stabilizes and increases property values and strengthens the overall economy of the state. One purpose of our local preservation unified development ordinances, passed by this very same city council not very long ago, is to stabilize and improve these property values by local historic landmarks. The city council should be encouraged to help preserve Winston-Salem's history, not just because it is the right thing to do, but for the economic benefits that come from preserving quality and character.*

If this is not enough to convince our readers by what we have learned, permit the introduction of the town of Salem survey, 1999, by Michael and Martha Hartley, the Old Salem archaeologists. This Old Salem document that contains years of research at a cost

What Have We Learned?

of thousands of dollars to produce, courtesy of the North Carolina Division of Archives and History, includes details of extending the Old Salem landmark district into West Salem. Based on the findings of this survey, it is recommended that expansion to the National Historic Landmark District is considered, which would reflect a broader geographical area of Salem as well as an increased temporal period of significance. Many elements remain in the area beyond the present landmark boundaries that contribute to this increased recognition. A number of these, such as the Arista Mill or the mansions of industrial leaders of the period, are already on the National Register of Historic Places, reflecting recognition of individual elements. A landmark expansion that gathered these into a coherent context would heighten awareness of the meaning of Salem as an important developer of industrial and commercial power in the nineteenth and early twentieth centuries. There are also resources in the survey area that relate to Salem within the congregation town period of interpretation and require inclusion in a landmark expansion. Factory Row (New Street) and its houses could easily be attached to the present landmark. They are contributing elements in the mid-century evolution toward secular Salem. Other important contributing resources are the Stockburger farm of the eighteenth century, archaeological sites and several houses and the graveyards in north Salem. These resources should be explicitly included in a landmark expansion.

FORSYTH COUNTY LOCAL HISTORIC LANDMARKS (CHRONOLOGICAL ORDER)
*All listings located in Winston-Salem unless otherwise noted.

1766	First House, 446 South Main
1767	Third House, 440 South Main
1768	Fifth House, 434 South Main; reconstruction, 1976
1768	Fourth House, 438 South Main
1769	Single Brothers' House, 600 South Main
1770	Hauser-Reich-Butner House, 5575 Main, Bethania
1771	Miksch Tobacco Shop, 532 South Main
1772	Anna Catharina House, 8 West
1772	Community Store, 626 South Main
1772	Johann Christian Loesch House, 5576 Main, Bethania
1782	Bethabara Dyer's & Potter's House, Historic Bethabara Park
1784	Salem Tavern, 800 South Main
1787	Lick-Boner House, 512 Salt
1787	Traugott Bagge House, 10 West
1788	Bethabara Gemeinhaus, Historic Bethabara Park
1793	Ebert-Reich House, 731 South Main
1794	Boys' School, 3 Academy
1797	Christoph Vogler House, 710 South Main
1800	Winkler Baker, 527 South Main
1802	Vierling House, 463 South Church
1803	Bethabara Distiller's House, Historic Bethabara Park
1804	River John Conrad House, 1606 Conrad Road, Pfafftown
1805	Schroeter House, 520 South Main

Winston-Salem

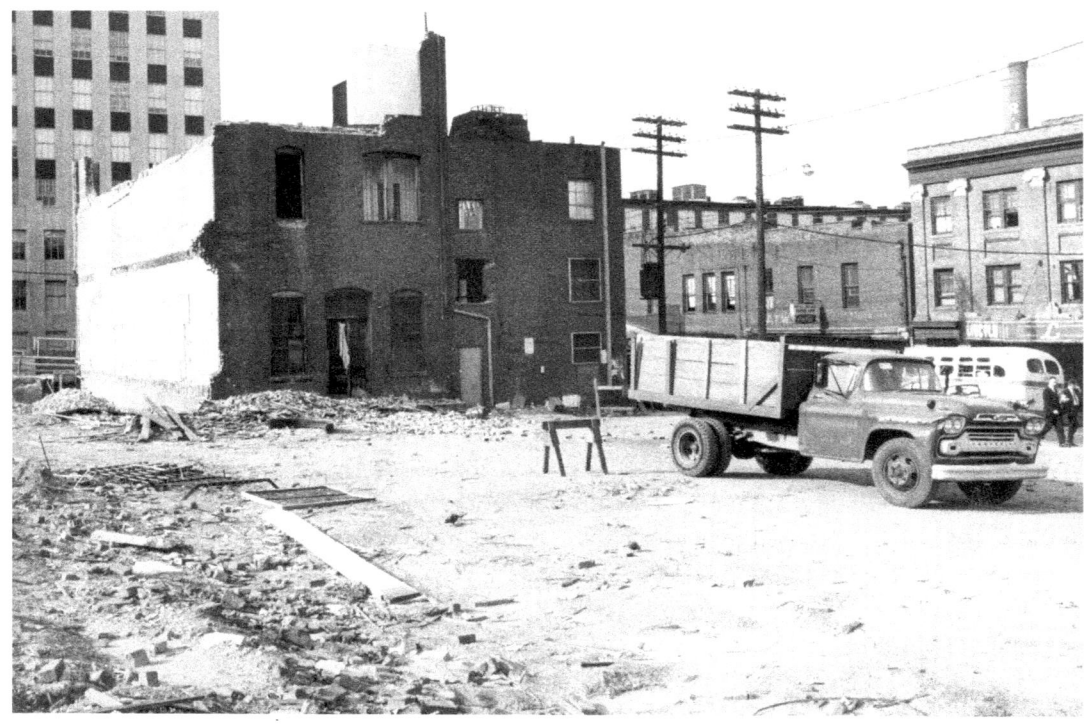

This scene shows an end to the African American business interests of the early twentieth century. This photo from 1960 shows the beginning of the razing of several buildings. By the 1970s, the last remaining buildings, the LaFayette and Lincoln Theater, would be torn down.

1805	Shore-Lehman House, 5524 Main, Bethania
1809	Schroeter Wash-Bake House (portion of historic Salem lot 57), 520 South Main
1810	Butner House, 5531 Main, Bethania
1815	Bethabara Log House, Historic Bethabara Park
1815	Blum House, 724 South Main
1815	Zevely House, 901 West Fourth
1816	Hagen House, 520 Salt
1816	Salem Tavern Dining Room, 736 South Main
1816, 1879	John and Matthew Clayton Farm, 5809 Stanleyville Drive, Rural Hall
1816	Volz House (portion of historic Salem lot 96), 916 South Main
1819	John Vogler House, 700 South Main
1819	Shultz House, 714 South Main
1820	Levering House (portion of historic Salem lot 56), 516 South Main; reconstruction, 1972
1821	Herbst House, 511 South Main
1822	John Ackerman House, 500 Factory Row; reconstruction, 1985
1822	Leinbach Granary and Stable, 508 South Main; reconstruction, 1971

What Have We Learned?

1822	Leinbach House (portion of historic Salem lot 55), 508 South Main
1822	Solomon Lick House, 524 Salt
1824	Philip Reich House, 813 South Church
1824	Traugott Leinbach House, 807 South Main; reconstruction, 1974
1825	Butner Hat Shop, 521 South Main; reconstruction, 1965
1825	Jacob Christmas House, 500 Salt
1825	Thomas Christian Shultz House, 3960 Walnut Hills Drive
1827	Anna Johanna Vogler House, 823 South Church
1827	Hall House, 421 South Main
1827	Leinbach Wash-Bake House, 807 South Main; reconstruction, 1974
1827	Shultz Shop, 712 South Main
1829	Butner House, 517 South Main
1829, 1930	Middleton House, 2721 Robinhood Road
1830	John Jacob Schaub House, 5622 Balsom Road, Pfafftown
1831	Kuehln House, 901 South Main
1831	Timothy Vogler Shop, 913 South Main
1832	Denke House, 498 Salt
1832	Eberhardt House, 921 South Main
1832	Philip Reich Shop, 817 South Church
1832	Timothy Vogler House, 909 South Main
1834	Charles A. Cooper Shop, 419 South Main; reconstruction, 1979
1834	Eberhardt Shop, 919 South Main; reconstruction, 1967
1836, 1880	Brookstown Mill, 200 Brookstown Avenue
1839	Christian F. Sussdorff House, 448 Factory Row
1840	Theophilus Vierling House, 327 South Main
1841	Beitel-Van Vleck House, 427 South Main; reconstruction, 1976
1842	Siewers Shop, 15 Walnut
1844	John Siewers House, 832 South Main
1844	Zevely Inn, 803 South Main
1845	Jacob Siewers House, 823 South Main
1847	Bank of Cape Fear (portion of historic Salem lot 54), 500 South Main
1847	Jones House, 5836 Bethania Road, Bethania
1850, 1929	Burton Craige House, 134 Cascade Avenue
1852	(Former) Bethania Moravian Church Parsonage, Grabs Drive, Bethania
1852	Samuel B. Stauber Farm, 6085 Bethania-Tobaccoville Road, Bethania
1856	Edwin Theophilus Ackerman House, 440 Factory Row
1857	Nathaniel M. Kerner House, 312 South Main, Kernersville
1867	Kernersville Moravian Church, 504 South Main, Kernersville
1870	Rephelius Byron Kerner House, 225 South Main, Kernersville
1873	Dr. John Francis Shaffner House, 428 South Main
1875	Isaac Harrison McKaughan House, 510 Salisbury, Kernersville
1875	Livingston N. Clinard House, 512 Factory Row
1875	Nathaniel Schober Siewers House, 715 South Main
1880	Korner's Folly, South Main, Kernersville

Winston-Salem

1884	Conrad-Starbuck House, 118 South Cherry
1884	Hylehurst, 224 South Cherry
1885	Rogers House, 102 South Cherry
1886	St. Paul United Methodist Church, 401 Church, Kernersville
1888	Rural Hall Depot, Railroad, Rural Hall
1890	W.F. Smith & Sons Leaf House, 406 East Fourth
1891	Thomas A. Crews House, 4997 Main, Walkertown
1892	Henry C. Korner House, 303 South Main, Kernersville
1893	David Reid House, 1820 South Main, Kernersville
1894	Lloyd Presbyterian Church, 748 North Chestnut
1895	Brown Brothers Tobacco Prizery, 401 East Fourth
1901	Colonel William Allen Blair House, 210 South Cherry
1902	Peter Blum House, 111 North Poplar
1905	John Henry Pfaff House, 4798 Pfaff Lane, Pfafftown
1906	Rosenbacher House, 848 West Fifth
1907	Brickenstein-Leinbach House, 426 Old Salem Road
1910	Conrad-Starbuck Carriage House, 119 South Marshall
1910	Oak Grove School, 2637 Oak Grove Circle
1911	Cicero Francis Lowe House, 204 Cascade Avenue
1911	Odd Fellows Cemetery, south of West Thirtieth, west of Millbrook Drive, north of West Twenty-eighth and east of Shorefair Drive
1911	(Former) Wachovia Bank & Trust Company Building, 8 West Third
1912	Salem Town Hall, 301 South Liberty
1913	Winston-Salem Southbound Railway Freight Warehouse and Office, 300 South Liberty
1915	Fourth Street Row Houses, 840–848 West Fourth and 807–809 Burke
1915	Main Post Office Building, 101 West Fifth
1917	Charles R. Fogle House, 29 Cascade Avenue
1922	John Wesley Snyder House, 2715 Old Salisbury Road
1924	Henry L. Mickey House, 1162 Waughtown
1925	Gilmer Building, 416–424 West Fourth
1925	William Milton Scott House, 1941 Georgia Avenue
1926	Former Union Station, 300 Martin Luther King Jr. Boulevard
1926	Nissen Building, 310–314 West Fourth
1926	Winston-Salem City Hall, 101 North Main
1927	(Former) Spruce Street YMCA, 315 North Spruce
1928–30	Mamie Gray Galloway House, 1040 Arbor Road
1929	Sosnik's/Morris-Early Commercial Block, 500 West Fourth
1930	Joseph Franklin Bland House, 1809 Virginia Road
1930	Shell Service Station, 1111 Sprague
1932	Graylyn, 1900 Reynolda Road
1940	P.H. Hanes Knitting Company—Warehouse and Shipping Building, 600 North Chestnut
1966	Wachovia Building, 301 North Main

What Have We Learned?

If we have learned anything from our search, let it be the hope that historic preservation will become like a virus and spread to all our citizens. Take up the torch of history; research your own family's history. Surf not only the worldwide web, but also your public facilities, libraries, schools, retirement homes and attics for those histories. A local celebrity journalist and staff reporter of the *Winston-Salem Journal*, Roy Thompson, says it best in his poem of a learning experience from a building that holds precious memories for many Twin Citians.

"And Still It Waits—But For What?"
A too familiar story…
Old now…and looking it
On a shelf. No apparent use. Filed away.
All but forgotten. Gathering dust, cobwebs and memories.
Brooding in the night.
Guarded only by pigeons that rustle and grump in the dark when a car clatters
Down the street below and stirs them from their sleep.
The old YMCA on Spruce Street.
No one would suspect…looking at it now…what a grand place it was in its youth.
The cornerstone tells the story. It says that Jesus is the chief cornerstone.
People up in the country used to let their sons come to town on condition
That they would stay at the YMCA.
Less temptation there.
The men were separated from the boys by separate entrances.
Girls didn't go there much except for basketball games.
Anybody suggesting that a girl be allowed to join would have been put away.
When the place was closed down it still served a purpose.
Men with no homes, jobs, assets or religious leanings found ways into the place,
And they slept there to get in from the cold and wet.
Then someone found out, and the place was sealed so they no longer had their sanctuary.
It's quiet now.
Only the pigeons know ways to get in, and they don't make much noise.
It used to be a very noisy place.
Crowds yelling at basketball games.
The "click…click…clickclick" of checkers.
The "click…click…" of chess. The "clickclick-click" of caroms.
The sharp pop of a wet towel on a skinny little bottom…
Closely followed by a loud wail of pain and indignation.
The soft whishing of magazine pages being turned in the lobbies.
The always unexpected ringing of a telephone.
The hubbub of the gatherings of throngs of boys at their appointed times…
The clamor of their leaving.
The soft sobbing of a homesick boy in his room at night.
There came a time when its people left the old Y and moved into a new and grander
building

*It was used a time or two as a Halloween house…which explains the sign in the gym about
"The Devil's Children."
Now it just looms over Spruce Street and waits.
Another tombstone in the downtown graveyard for people who think downtown is dead…
Or another opportunity for almost anything.
Old.
But, as is said of so many things, "They don't make 'em like that anymore."
Waiting.
Guarded only by pigeons.*

Thompson was a card and a regular with the old-timers at the Green Front Cash Store. The historic YMCA did have a happy ending with historic preservation. Hopefully more success stories will be had with our help in the "Search for Winston-Salem."

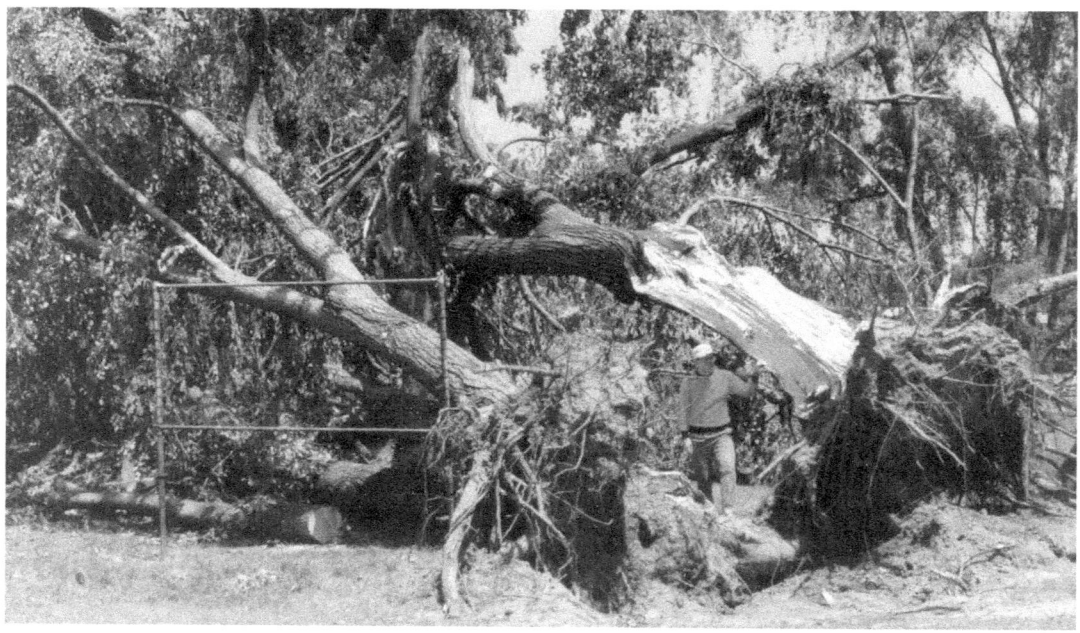

The destruction caused by the 1989 tornadoes and storm is evident in this picture in Hanes Park in the West End neighborhood. The author is shown with some of the devastation.

Bibliography

Black and Gold Staff. *The 1933 Black and Gold Annual.* R.J. Reynolds High School, 1933.

Bradley, Betsy Hunter. *The Works: The Industrial Architecture of the United States.* Oxford University Press, 1999.

Bricker, Michael. *Historic West Salem—Images of America Series.* Charleston, SC: Arcadia Press, 2006.

Brownlee, Fambrough. *Winston-Salem, A Pictorial History.* Norfolk, VA: Donning Co., 1977.

Church, William Hal. Interview by Michael Bricker, November 2002.

Cranford, Reverend William A. *Christ Moravian Church: The First One Hundred Years.* Centennial Committee, 1997.

Davis, Chest. "Vogler Service: 1858—A Century of Service in the Mortuary Field." *Winston-Salem Journal*, October 16, 1963. Reprinted from *Winston-Salem Journal and Sentinel*, March 16, 1958.

Dudley, William. *American Slavery—"Turning Points in World History" Series.* Farmington Hills, MI: Greenhaven Press, 2000.

Elliott, J. Eric. *Winston-Salem's Historic West End—Images of America Series.* Charleston, SC: Arcadia Press, 2004.

Forsyth County Historic Properties Commission, Information Forms.

Bibliography

Fries, Adelaide L. *Forsyth: A County on the March*. Chapel Hill: University of North Carolina Press, 1976.

———. *Historical Sketch of Salem Female Academy*. Salem, NC: Crist and Keehin Printers, 1902.

Fries, Adelaide L., ed., et al. *Records of the Moravians in North Carolina*. Vols. 1–6. Raleigh: North Carolina Historical Commission, 1922–43. Vols. 7–11. Raleigh: State Department of Archives and History, 1947–69.

Hartley, Michael, and Martha Boxley. "Salem Survey." North Carolina Division of Archives and History. Raleigh, 1997.

James, Hunter. *Old Salem Official Guidebook*. Edited by Frances Griffin. Old Salem, Inc., 1994.

Larson, John C. "A Mill for Salem." *Three Forks of Muddy Creek* 9. Frances Griffin, ed., 1983.

Lee, Bryant W. Interview by Michael Bricker, March 2003.

Lefer, Hugh Talmage. *A Guide to the Study and Reading of North Carolina History*. Chapel Hill: University of North Carolina Press, 1969.

Mayer, Barbara. *Reynolda: A History of an American Country House*. Winston-Salem: John F. Blair, 1997.

Moravian Church. "A History of Christ Moravian Church." Thesis presented to the faculty of Moravian Theological Seminary, 1949.

National Register of Historic Places. "The South Trade Street Houses," 1978.

Neilson, Robert W., ed. *History of Government, City of Winston-Salem, North Carolina*. Winston-Salem: Community Government Committee, 1966.

Oppermann, Langdon Edmonds. "Winston-Salem's African-American Neighborhoods: 1870–1950." Preliminary Planning report, 1993.

People's Press, 1830–1870.

Prichard, Robert W., MD. *"Medicine" Winston Salem in History*. Vol. 11. 1977.

Rawls, Molly Grogan. *Winston-Salem in Vintage Postcards—Postcard History Series*. Charleston, SC: Arcadia Press, 2004.

Rondthaler, Reverend Edward. *The Memorabilia of Fifty Years, 1887 to 1927*. Raleigh: Edwards & Broughton Company, 1928.

Bibliography

Ruger & Stoner. *Bird's Eye View of Winston-Salem*. 1891.

Salem Academy and College Library Archives. Salem Academy and College. Winston-Salem.

Sanborn Insurance Company. Map Series: 1885, 1890, 1895, 1900, 1907, 1912, 1917, 1949.

Sensbach, Jon. *African-Americans in Salem: Brother Abraham and Peter Oliver*. Old Salem, Inc.

———. *A Separate Canaan*. Chapel Hill: University of North Carolina Press, 1998.

Smith, James Howell. "Industry and Commerce 1896–1975." *Winston-Salem in History*. Vol. 8. Winston-Salem: Historic Winston, 1977.

Taylor, Gwynne Stephens. *From Frontier to Factory*. North Carolina Department of Cultural Resources, Division of Archives and History, and the Winston Salem/Forsyth County Historic Properties Commission, City-County Planning Board of Forsyth County and Winston-Salem. Winston-Salem, 1981.

Tise, Larry Edward. "The Churches." *Winston-Salem in History*. Vol. 10. Winston-Salem: Historic Winston, 1976.

———. "Government." *Winston-Salem in History*. Vol. 6. Winston-Salem: Historic Winston, 1977.

———. "Industry and Commerce 1766–1896." *Winston-Salem in History*. Vol. 7. Winston-Salem: Historic Winston, 1977.

Tursi, Frank. *Winston-Salem: A History*. Winston-Salem: John F. Blair, 1994.

Vogler, E.A. *Map of Winston and Salem*. 1876, revised 1884.

von Redeken, Ludwig Gottfried. *A View of Salem in North Carolina*. Watercolor, 1787. Reprint by Wachovia Historical Society.

Wellman, Manley Wade. "Transportation and Communication." *Winston-Salem in History*. Vol. 4. Winston-Salem: Historic Winston, 1977.

Wellman, Manley Wade, and Larry Edward Tise. "A City Culture." *Winston-Salem in History*. Vol. 5. Winston-Salem: Historic Winston, 1977.

———. "Education." *Winston-Salem in History*. Vol. 3. Winston-Salem: Historic Winston, 1977.

Bibliography

West Salem Historic District of Historic Places. Interview by Mary Guinca, March 2003.

Winston-Salem City Directories, 1880–1950. North Carolina Room, Forsyth County Library.

Winston-Salem city maps, various.

Winston-Salem Journal & Sentinel, 1870–1950. North Carolina Room, Forsyth County Library. Microfiche Library Section.

Winston-Salem Journal & Sentinel, 1960–2007. Author's personal collection.

Woodard, Sarah. "Report on the History of Five Bridges in Salem." Old Salem Inc., 1996.

Yafa, Stephen. *Big Cotton*. New York: Penguin Group, 2005.

www.ingramcontent.com/pod-product-compliance
Lightning Source LLC
Chambersburg PA
CBHW060748300425
25937CB00006BA/41